Contents

NUMBER 35 AUTUMN 1998

The Ethics of Violence

NEW FORMATIONS

New Formations is
published three times
a year by
Lawrence & Wishart
99a Wallis Road
London E9 5LN
Tel: 0181-533 2506
Fax: 0181-533 7369

SUBSCRIPTIONS:
For 1998, subscription rates to Lawrence & Wishart
are, for 3 issues
UK: Institutions £70, Individuals £35.
Rest of world: Institutions £75; Individuals £38.
Single copies: £14.99

CONTRIBUTIONS AND CORRESPONDENCE:
Send to:
The Editor, *New Formations*
Dept. of English, University of Southampton
Highfield, Southampton SO17 1BJ

BOOKS FOR REVIEW:
Send to:
Alasdair Pettinger
Scottish Music Information Centre
1 Bowmont Gardens
Glasgow, Scotland G12 9LR

Prospective writers are encouraged to contact the editors to discuss their ideas and to obtain a copy of our style sheet.
Manuscripts should be sent in triplicate; experts in the relevant field will referee them anonymously. The manuscripts will not be returned unless a stamped, self-addressed envelope is enclosed. Contributors should note that the editorial board cannot take responsibility for any manuscript submitted to *New Formations*.

ISSN 0 950 2376
ISBN 085315

Text design and setting by Art Services, Norwich
Printed in Great Britain at the University Press, Cambridge.

Notes on contributors

Renata Salecl is a researcher at the Institute of Criminology, University of Ljubljana and is currently a fellow at the Institute for Advanced Study, Berlin. She is the author of *The Spoils of Freedom* (Routledge 1994), *(Per)versions of Love and Hate*, (forthcoming Verso), 1998 and co-editor with Slavoj Zizec of *Gaze and Voice as Love Objects*, (Duke UP, 1996).

Étienne Balibar is Professor of Moral and Political Philosophy at the University of Paris-X Nanterre. He is the co-author with Immanuel Wallerstein of *Race, Nation, Class*, (Verso, 1991) and the author of *Masses, Classes, Ideas*,(Routledge, 1994), *The Philosophy of Marx*, (Verso, 1995) and *Extreme Violence and the Problem of Civility* (forthcoming from Columbia UP).

Henrietta Moore is Professor of Social Anthropology and Director of the Gender Institute at the London School of Economics. Her recent books include *A Passion for Difference*, (Polity, 1994), *Space, Text and Gender*, (Guilford, 1996) and *The Subject of Anthropology: Essays on Lacan and Levi-Strauss* (forthcoming from Polity Press).

Juliet Flower MacCannell has taught at the University of California, Irvine and also at Berkeley, and she has also begun working as an artist with collaborative shows in San Francisco and Houston. She is the author of *The Time of the Sign* with Dean MacCannell, *Figuring Lacan* (1986), and *The Regime of the Brother* (1994). Her essay is part of her forthcoming book *Things To Come: An Hysteric's Guide to the Future Female Subject*.

Parveen Adams is the convenor of the MA in Psychoanalytic Studies at Brunel University on which she also teaches a module on 'The Image'. She recently published *The Emptiness of the Image*, (Routledge, 1996) and is currently working on death.

Alain Abelhauser is a psychoanalyst and associate professor of psychopathology at the University of Haute-Bretagne, Rennes and is a consultant at the Hôpital Bicetre, Paris. He is the author of numerous articles on psychoanalysis.

Mladen Dolar is associate professor of philosophy at the University of Ljubljana. His essays on psychoanalysis and German idealism have appeared in *new formations*, *October*, *Qui Parle* and the *American Journal of Semiotics*.

Slavoj Zizec is Senior Researcher at the Institute for Social Sciences, University of Ljubljana. His most recent books include *The Indivisible Remainder*, (Verso, 1996), *The Plague of Fantasies*, (Verso, 1997), and *The Ticklish Subject* (forthcoming from Verso, 1998).

Alenka Zupancic is a researcher at the Institute of Philosophy, Slovene Academy of Sciences. An English translation of her book *Die Ethics des Realen: Kant mit Lacan*, (Turia & Kant), 1995 is due to appear in 1999.

Cecilia Sjöholm teaches literature at the University of Stockholm and the University of Essex. She has published two recent books in Sweden: *Alone and Perverted*, (1995, with Sara Arrhenius) and *Representations of the Unconscious* (1996). Her current work is on psychoanalysis and tragedy.

Jane B. Malmo is a former criminal defence attorney and professor of law. She is now Assistant Professor of English at John Jay College, City University of New York. Her essay comes from a work in progress entitled 'Just Violence' on the troubled triangle of violence, law and subjectivity in late Renaissance literature.

Marinos Diamantides lectures in medical law and ethics at Birkbeck College, University of London. In 1995 his first publication won the Socio-Legal Studies Asssociation award for the best work by a new scholar. An essay on parenting will appear in Michael King (ed), *Moral Agendas for Children's Welfare*, (forthcoming from Routledge, 1998).

THE ETHICS OF VIOLENCE

Introduction

Why do subjects engage in violence? What are they trying to solve by using open aggression against their fellow beings? What are the modalities of violence witnessed today, from direct bodily (ethnic, sexual) violence, such as rapes and lynching, through more refined forms of symbolic violence, up to the violent aspects of the very endeavours to circumscribe and fight violence? How is violence not simply external to symbolic communication, but also based in it and legitimised by it? Doesn't the very shift from the body and its violent materiality to thought's ethereal ideal universality involve the gesture of an extremely violent abstraction and/or repression? Not only does Kant's ethics, perhaps the most sublime philosophical expression of the ethical attitude, rely on a core of violence; its apparent opposite, Sade's assertion of the unlimited right to the pleasure provided by torturing other people, is itself based in an ethical stance - that is why Lacan insisted that Kant and Sade have to be read together. Acts considered as fulfilments of the highest ethical duty are often perceived by the community in which they occur as extremely violent impositions - consider the violence discernible in Christ's statement: 'If anyone comes to me and does not hate his father and his mother, his wife and children, his brothers and sisters - yes even his own life - he cannot be my disciple'. (*Luke* 14:26) Doesn't the same hold for Antigone, this commonly accepted literary example of insisting on one's ethical duty? And how are perceptions of violence dependent on a specific cultural context, so that circumcision which, for a Western gaze is the utmost humiliation of a woman, is, in some cultures, perceived as an act that secures respect for women? And how do ritualised acts of violence in so-called 'primitive' societies differ from the 'neo-tribal' mutilations of the body (tattooing, piercing) in contemporary life-styles and artistic performances? In what way are today's 'irrational' modes of violence (like the juvenile delinquency acts in our suburbs) the product of the very tolerant multiculturalist 'open' society that more and more precludes any proper articulation of political antagonisms?

The present issue of *new formations* explores all these dimensions of the uncanny and ambiguous relations between ethics and violence. Étienne Balibar focuses on the intimate connection between ideality and cruelty, i.e. on the violence the very gesture of idealisation has to rely on. Following Henrietta Moore's psychoanalytic account of violent initiation rituals, Renata Salecl and Juliet Flower MacCannell deal with the rise of violent sadomasochistic practices in contemporary life and art, i.e. with the way these practices reinscribe and displace 'primitive' violent rituals. In her analysis of *Crash*, Parveen Adams interprets Cronenberg's film as a special case of today's sexualisation of violence. The next group of essays deals with the fundamentals of power: Alain Abelhauser approaches in a new way the old Freudian thesis of the murder of the father as the origin of legitimate power, while Mladen Dolar engages in a dialogue between the Foucauldian and the Lacanian accounts of power. Slavoj Zizek deals with the connection between Kant and Sade asserted by Lacan: is Sade really the hidden truth of the Kantian ethics? The two texts that follow, by Alenka Zupancic and by Cecilia Sjöholm, focus on what is perhaps the highest exercise of Lacan's ethical thought, his reading of the figure of Antigone, and locate it in the modern philosophical discussion from Kant to Heidegger. Jane Malmo adds another literary analysis (of the violence of ethics in Shakespeare's *Measure for Measure*), while the volume closes with Marinos Diamantides's account of the violence involved in today's medical ethics.

The focal point of all the articles is thus that violence is the real, the hard core of every ethical endeavour: it stains attempts to contain or erase it, so the only authentic choice is to assume full responsibility for it. While the fight against racist, sexist, economic and other forms of violence is more urgent that ever, one should bear in mind that nothing is more shattering in its violence than an authentic ethical act.

Violence, ideality, and cruelty[1]

Étienne Balibar

1. The French version was published as 'Violence, idéalité et cruauté' in E. Balibar, *La crainte des masses. Politique et philosophie avant et après Marx*, Editions Galilée, Paris 1997.

To put together *violence* and *ideality* (a generic term in which I include ideas, ideals, and idealisations) is to draw our attention towards a series of paradoxical questions. I want to examine two reciprocal propositions: *first*, that violence is, of necessity, part of what we might call 'the "economy" of ideality' (just as there is an economy of salvation), that's to say, violence is part of its conditions and effects; and *second*, that 'ideality' is also part of the economy of violence, although we must admit that it is never its only determining factor. If these propositions are true, then there must exist in each case a profound ambivalence in the relationship between violence and 'ideality'. As a consequence, there can be no *simple*, universal discourse on the question of violence. Something will remain irreducibly problematic or ambiguous, if not immutable. We all assume, more or less, that we have a desire or tendency to escape violence, in its many different forms, to reduce its incidence in our public and private lives, to 'civilise our customs' (*moeurs*) as Norbert Elias would put it; and we also assume that this cannot be achieved without resorting to ideals, 'idealising' and sublimating some of our own inclinations. But, if the propositions I advance here are true, any stance that is taken, any move that is made *against* violence (and this is certainly an essential part of politics) will have to come to terms with a backlash. It will not be able to offer a programme for the complete elimination of violence.

I said that we all assume a desire to escape violence, but I would like to begin by reminding you how ambivalent our attitude is. And I will take 'our' to refer to 'us' as *intellectuals*. Here are two brief examples.

Shortly after the end of the Second World War, in an essay entitled 'Utopia and Violence' (reprinted in *Conjectures and Refutations*), Sir Karl Popper expressed his fear that the victory over nazism might be followed, not by a reduction in the level of violence in the world and in world politics, but on the contrary, by new outbreaks of barbarism. He referred to the fact that the anti-nazi alliance, especially in the United States, had borrowed some of their weapons and methods from their enemies, and had themselves engaged in retaliation on a massive scale, terrorising and even exterminating entire civilian populations. He was explicitly thinking of the Hiroshima bombing. But what worried him even more was the prospect of a new wave of political and social utopias, of the 'Platonist' type, which would aim at transforming the world and human nature itself, de-constructing and re-constructing the whole fabric of society according to ideal principles of justice. He warned that, as always, this would not be done without the use of extremely violent means. Rather than espousing a simple conservatism, since he recognised that there was much that needed to be changed on this earth, Popper pleaded for a reformist policy, and advocated what he called a realistic 'piecemeal engineering' of society. This is indeed a classic version of the critique of idealism and its terroristic effects, one of the models of which, paradoxically enough, can be found in an author whom Popper did not appreciate very much – Hegel's description of the French Revolution and the *Terreur*. The reason why I am mentioning it, however, is that if you read Popper's text again, you may be struck by the fact that it is rhetorically organised around the repetition of such phrases as 'I hate violence', 'those who, like me, hate violence, will agree that ...' This produces an extraordinary collapse or short-circuiting in his discourse, in the argument of his essay, and in his own subjective position. In a sense Popper himself recognises this in the text, since he explains that his stand against violence cannot ultimately be justified by rational argument, but is best described as a bias in favour of humanity.

The difficulty which Popper faced can be highlighted by juxtaposing his essay with an excellent analysis by Phil Cohen which deals with the racist discourse of violent groups of so-called hooligans, whose favourite motto is simply 'We hate humans!'[2] Popper certainly does not write anything like: 'I hate violent people', or 'I hate those-who-hate-humans', but he says that he hates Violence, in other words he hates what is, precisely, an ideal term, or an 'ideality'. Now it is always necessary to make a distinction between ideas or principles and the individuals who profess them: to reject and suppress the former when they are pernicious either in themselves or in their consequences, but always to respect the latter as persons and, if possible, to release them from the beliefs they hold. It is vital that we retain this classic distinction since it has to do with the very conditions under which it is possible to speak of rights and of justice. However it is not always possible to *separate* people from their ideals - in other times we might have said: from their souls or their spirits - and above all, we may wonder whether there does not exist something which serves as an *intermediary* between ideas and individuals, sticking to both of them: namely, *groups* or *collective bodies* or *collectivities*.

2. Papers from the Centre for New Ethnicities Research, The University of East London.

As soon as we consider them - and how can we *not* consider them, especially in the social and political realm? - we are faced with a real dilemma. When we 'hate violence', in order to eliminate its causes and reverse those violent tendencies in society which suppress liberty and dignity, are we hating something which is merely an idea or an ideal, or are we also hating groups - institutions, forms of organisation, collectivities which *embody* violence, so to speak - and attempting to eliminate them? In other words, do we destroy those who would destroy us? What other options do we have? Is 'non-violence' a possibility? Leaving aside for the moment the question of its effectiveness, let me suggest that even a quick reading of Freud might teach us that our problems do not end here, since non-violence may be linked to a hatred of violence, or violent instincts, *within oneself*, and will therefore always border on self-destruction or the desire for one's own death, at least in symbolic terms. It is as if our only alternative lay between two forms of destruction: *counter-violence* and *self-destruction* or *self-annihilation*. This is perhaps the place to suggest that Popper is much more of a Platonist than he could ever have admitted, as anyone who idealises the law (or the free exchange of ideas or the human person) probably is, and who regards it as an absolute that offers an antidote to violence: in other words, anyone who thinks that violence can be fought by idealising its opposite(s), the various figures of non-violence such as Law, Justice, Love, Respect.

The second, and contrasting, example that I want to discuss briefly is that of Georges Bataille. Not all of his work, though much of it, is concerned with the question that we are dealing with here. I want to isolate one specific episode, because it has been frequently mentioned in debates surrounding the alleged fascination of intellectuals, or at least some intellectuals, with violence. Between 1933-34 Bataille wrote a famous essay called 'La structure psychologique du fascisme' in which he proposed an explanation or interpretation of fascism, and especially nazism, in terms of the opposition between two aspects of social life: one that he called the 'homogeneous', in short the *order* or system of norms within which social conflicts must be confined and organised if the structure of power and authority is to remain in place; the other he called the 'heterogeneous', referring to those irrational forces which are released as soon as antagonisms become irreconcilable, and which can express themselves only in the form of violence.[3] Although Bataille did not use the phrase 'surfascisme' in this text, there was a clear association between this theoretical analysis and the political motto that he and some of his friends would propose in *Contra-attaque*, the anti-fascist group of artists and intellectuals which he had created together with André Breton and other surrealists. Bataille explained that a political movement of those revolutionary intellectuals and workers who wanted to resist nazism should not properly be *anti-fascist*, but rather 'surfasciste', that is it should transcend fascism by 'learning' something from fascism itself, drawing upon the same violent 'heterogeneous' forces that fascism was unleashing and using them in order to destroy the capitalist order which the fascists were defending. This was one of the reasons which quickly led to a break between Bataille and André Breton, who together with his own friends - some of whom joined the Communist Party - were supporting the Popular Front strategy.

3. See G. Bataille, *Oeuvres complètes*, 1970, vol. I, p339-71.

Without entering into the controversial debates surrounding this story, I would simply like to recall two facts. *One*, contrary to some allegations, the majority of Sadeian-Nietzschean intellectuals in twentieth-century European history were *not fascists* (while some fascists believed that they were Nietzscheans, no fascists, to my knowledge, ever called themselves de Sadeians), though some of them came extremely close to the idea that there is some truth in fascism, or that fascism in some sense can be fought only 'from the inside'. *Second*, if something like a 'fascination of intellectuals for violence' exists, then it has indeed to do with a call for the transgression of some *interdit* or prohibition. But among the prohibitions that must be broken is not only that which in the name of 'Law and Order' outlaws rebellion and secures individuals under its yoke (remember Father Malebranche's fantastic formula: 'the supreme virtue is the Love of Order'), but also the prohibition that bans investigation and inquiry. I refer to *l'interdit de savoir* about violence in general and every particular instance of violence, as if there were some powerful vested interest in keeping violence *outside* the realm of the knowable and the thinkable or, more precisely, outside the realm of what is thinkable as a 'normal' factor in social relations and a cause of political, social and historical effects; as if there were some sort of thought-police whose work parallels that of the regular police who, on the street, warn good citizens to keep away from the place where crimes or riots are taking place. Of course the police do allow some 'experts' to study their cases, applying statistical, sociological and psychological methods in order to make this or that form of individual or social violence an *object* of investigation and, possibly, control. But is this not exactly the reason why some intellectuals, again, are tempted to break the prohibition, and also why some of them - possibly this temptation has occurred to all of us at one moment or another - imagine that *nothing* is to be thought, really, at least nothing decisive, *outside* violence, if thinking or writing does not become itself 'violent', or *mimetic* of some act of violence?

Let me now tackle the question from a more substantive angle. We can begin with the classic problem concerning the uses and ambiguous meaning of the German term *Gewalt*, which *we*, according to circumstances, would translate as *violence*, *power* or *force*, or would find untranslatable. Derrida has aptly commented on this in his recent book *Force de loi*, taking his cue from others such as Marx, Weber, Benjamin, and Raymond Aron. I too will take up this theme, but with two caveats. First, I consider that the equivocality of *Gewalt*, its oscillation between 'power' and 'violence', presents a problem that echoes (and is basically equivalent to) the question of the balance of forces that are inside and outside the institutions or apparatuses which have historically secured *hegemony*, in an extended Gramscian sense. Such institutions or apparatuses are *legitimate* by definition, even if they are not always capable of imposing their legitimacy everywhere. We may note in passing that the idea of a legitimate power or *Gewalt* that is absolutely recognised, and therefore automatically obeyed, is a contradiction in terms. Such apparatuses are of necessity dependent upon the existence of grand 'idealities', great transcendant *forms* in the Platonic sense, which, in turn, idealise them and idealise their functioning. Suffice it to name here God and the State, or God and the Nation, or the Law itself - as *Torah*, *Nomos*, *Chariah* or *the Constitution*. (Is it an advantage that English does not, unlike French, distinguish between *Loi* and *Droit*, or rather does not make the distinction between *Law* and *Right* in the same way?). This would allow me to reformulate Althusser's thesis that State institutions are 'Ideological State

Apparatuses'. But I am also very tempted, I must say, in identifying this *nexus* of power, violence, and 'ideality', to borrow Hegel's notion of the (objective) *Spirit* as it is used in his *Philosophy of History*, since many of the questions that we have to confront here are already included in the Hegelian theory of history and the emergence of the state, insofar as the latter is presented as a theory of the objective Spirit - provided we try to remain, so to speak, at the threshold of the contradictions which are designated by this term, which reflects the hegemonic functioning of the state (and also of religion).

My second caveat is that no reflection on social and historical violence can ever be circumscribed by or limited to questions of *power*, not even if one thinks of it as decentered and decentralised. This is precisely what the polysemy of the word *Gewalt* in German can help us to grasp, since it already goes beyond the limits of 'power'. The question of power really lies at the heart of what I earlier called the economy of violence: for there is a primary violence of power, and a counter-violence against this power, or an attempt at building a counter-power which takes the form of counter-violence. But there are forms, or layers, of violence, which do not gravitate around the alternative of power *v* counter-power, although they inevitably return to them and *infect them* (pathological metaphors are difficult to avoid here, since the very representation of power has to do with a certain concept of normality). This is, if you like, the most 'excessive', the most 'self-destructive' part of violence. There is a risk of tautology at this point: we designate a certain violence as *self-destructive* or *irrational* because we feel that it overtakes the logic of power and counter-power (I remember that these terms were used, together with other explanatory discourses, about the so-called 'extreme forms' taken by the 1993 riots in Los Angeles immediately after the first Rodney King trial). Sometimes we do that to frighten ourselves, sometimes also to idealise violence, for example, when we use the term *sacrifice*, to which I will return.

By way of clarification, I could say in criticism of Foucault (or in criticism of something that has been read into Foucault) that there does exist an apparatus of power which has a centre, however complex and multiple this 'centre' may be. Certainly power is never simple, nor is it stabilised and located for ever here or there, in these or other hands, in the form of such and such a 'monopoly'. But it is always *a reduced complexity*, as sociologists like Luhmann would say. And it can reduce this complexity, and *ipso facto* this diversity - already a fairly violent process, in some cases - not only because of the material force of power, which by itself would never suffice, but in virtue of its own imaginary transcendance: in other words, through the 'tautological power' and violence of its own *ideality*, as this is expressed in such formulas as *God is God*, *Law is Law*, phrases which try to encapsulate the Absolute.[4] But this *being said*, I shall parody Lacan and add: power cannot be everything, and so it is essentially 'not-everything' (*pas-tout*), it finds itself lacking, even if we include its opposite and adversary, counter-

4. On the ambivalent effects of such 'tautological' formulas, see Stanislas Breton, 'Dieu est Dieu: Essai sur la violence des propositions tautologiques', *Philosophie buissonnière*, Jérôme Millon, Grenoble 1989.

power, or if you prefer, revolution and rebellion, 'anti-systemic movements', etc. Especially if we do so.

At a more abstract level, let me suggest that, in order to cope with this insufficiency in the dialectics of power (or *Gewalt*, or *Spirit*, or domination), we need a third term. We cannot think in terms of simple antitheses like force and violence, or power and violence, but we need a *third* notion. Which notion? Any choice of terminology is partly conventional. I could have proposed *barbarism*, but I shall avoid it, because this term has very precise ethnocentric connotations which derive from its opposition to civility and civilisation. In fact one uses this term because one believes that there exist (or have existed) 'barbarians', who could return among us (*Ultimi Barbarorum*, Spinoza once wanted to post on the walls of his city). I prefer, again with some arbitrariness, to use the word *cruelty*. I shall say that a phenomenology of violence has to deal at one and the same time, with the intrinsic relationship of violence to power (expressed in the term *Gewalt*) and to cruelty, something very different. Or rather that the phenomenology of power includes a dialectics of power and counter-power, state and revolution, orthodoxy and heresy, which throughout its development is made up of violent deeds and relationships - what Hegel called the Spirit or the World-Spirit - yet it also includes, not beyond or apart from this dialectics, but permanently intertwined with it a manifestation of cruelty, a glimpse of another world, another reality. Although a major part of the question is to understand why power *per se* (and also counter-power) has to be not only violent or potent or brutal, but also cruel or savage or sadistic (i.e. why it has to generate a measure of 'enjoyment' or *jouissance*[5] for those who exercise it, whether via state power, or colonial rule, or male domination), it seems to me that the key issue is that, contrary to what happens in the dialectics of the Spirit, there is nothing like a *centre*, not even a decentred centre, in cruelty. I should say, borrowing Bataille's term, that this is a phenomenon that is intrinsically *heterogeneous*. Cruelty must have a quite different relationship to ideas and 'ideality' (and therefore to ideology) than to power - which is not to say that there is no relationship at all. Possibly we could suggest that the violence of power, the *Gewalt*, has an immediate relationship with ideality and idealities, because, while it serves some very precise public and private *interests*, it never ceases to materialise idealities, to implement them, to constitute itself as *the force* which crushes all resistance or ideal principles: God, the Nation, or the Market. Whereas the forms that cruelty takes have a relationship with materiality which is *not mediated* (especially not symbolically mediated). In this 'naked' relationship with materiality some terrible idealities *return*, so to speak, but they come to be deployed as *fetishes* or exhibited as *emblems*. And this could have to do with the fact that in every process through which the material forces of history come to be symbolised (which produces the very possibility of a representation of history - and the narratives of the state, of revolution, of commercial and colonial expansion, and technological

5. cf. Slavoj Zizek, *The Metastases of Enjoyment. Six Essays on Women and Causalities*, Verso, London 1994.

progress are highly symbolic in this respect), there always exists a *remainder*, a residue of materiality.[6] Now why this remainder emerges mainly in the form of cruelty, or why it has to emerge in the form of cruelty, is something extremely embarrassing, I admit it, for anybody who is not purely and simply ready to start a discourse on *evil*, among other reasons because he/she is not ready to start a discourse on *Good* and *Goodness*.

6. cf. Jean-Jacques Lecercle, *The Violence of Language*, Routledge, London and New York 1990.

Now there is of course no question of discussing in detail the dialectics of power and the residue of cruelty. What I would like to do in the space that is left to me, is simply the following. First, to enumerate a number of classical questions - or, if you prefer, moments - which I think should figure in any presentation of this dialectic. And second, to go back to the enigmas of cruelty and say a few things about the reasons why it seems to me that we are now considering them to be anything but marginal or secondary.

1. A dialectics of *Gewalt* should begin with the question of the *law*, including its two aspects: the violent force of the law and codified violence, or legitimate violence, or the right to exercise violence. On the one hand, the traditional antinomy which results from the fact that state power has a monopoly of violence and weapons (albeit not all of them, and not everywhere), in short from the fact that it *removes* violence and the means of violence from 'society' by taking them *for itself* and *upon itself*. Discussion of the meaning and the forms of this antinomy, of its theological and political mysteries, have ranged from Hobbes to Kant, from Weber to Derrida. But on the other hand, there is also the more ordinary and everyday aspect of the law, stemming from the codification of violence: the violence of repression, punishment, ancient and modern types of slavery, etc. Whenever we study concrete examples, such as the functioning of the prisons, we discover that it is extremely difficult to draw a clear line of demarcation *within* the realm of the law itself - I don't mean within a totalitarian juridical system, but within our 'normal' civilised and liberal system - between *justice* and *violence*. For basically I think that the so-called 'foundational violence' of state power can only exist (or appear as foundational), not only if it is idealised, or sanctified, which is clear enough, but also if it is *actually* performed and effectively materialised *at certain specific times and places*, in some visible spots or zones of the system. Hence the importance and difficulty of the problem of the death penalty, for instance. But here we realise that, in many cases, we are bordering on cruelty. And hopefully it is not a mere play on words if I say that we also come up against the question of *borders*: for social and territorial borderlines are privileged places for legitimate violence to border upon cruelty.

2. A dialectics of violence should continue to reflect upon the fact that the permanent confrontation between power(s) and counter-power(s) does not only imply the periodic unleashing of violence and counter-violence,

whose effectiveness on both sides depends upon the strength of their symbolic justifications or whether they contain a 'sublime' ideological element. For there is a supplementary twist. It seems to me - and the more I listen to discussions about violence among historians, philosophers, lawyers, and political theorists, the more I become convinced of this - that the fundamental, possibly the *only* logical and rhetorical scheme for the *legitimation* of violence is that of *preventive counter-violence*. Any violence in the sense of *Gewalt* that has to become legally or morally legitimate, must present itself, if not as retaliation, at least as the correction and repression of *violent forces*, be they rooted in human nature or in social conditions or in ideological beliefs, that have somehow disturbed or destroyed an originary or ideally peaceful, non-violent order, or that threaten it with destruction. And this schema can be applied either directly, in positivistic legal terms, at once combining description and prescription, or it can be referred to as some mythical or transcendental archetype which always tells the story of how order and disorder, justice and violence, have been eternally in conflict. Of course the state itself or divine authority can also appear or be portrayed as a violent disturbing force in this sense, perhaps even as the most violent and most disturbing of all. Hence the possibility of an infinite series of mirror-games between 'society' (or 'civil society') and 'the state' in which such terms as illegality, rebellion and revolution, will constantly occur.

The main point I would like to make here is this: if, at a fundamental institutional level, violence can only be justified as preventive counter-violence, then something called 'violence' or 'disorder' or 'violent behaviour' (whether in public or in private, individually or collectively) will only exist insofar as its violent repression has already been anticipated. In other words, what we call 'violence', and the lines of demarcation between what is supposed to be violent behaviour and what is not, will only exist retrospectively as the anticipated recurrence of counter-violence. And this has a direct effect upon the investigation of violence, upon the knowledge and conceptualisation of violence. A power which organises itself as preventive counter-violence *undoubtedly* needs a certain knowledge of violence, legal categories, sociological and psychological explanations and predictions, statistical records of its growth or decline - this is part of its policing and its politics. But there will always be a suspicion, at least among those who contribute professionally to this research, that a blind-spot, a basic element of *misrecognition* must exist in the midst of this continually expanding body of knowledge, which stems from the fact that it is a knowledge, not only associated with power - which all knowledge is - but produced under the auspices of preventive counter-violence, or the re-establishment of order. This is the point at which a careful discussion of Foucault's epistemological investigation into the productivity of power cannot be avoided.

3. Finally, I think that a dialectics of *Gewalt* has to include a discussion of the most idealistic, the most spiritual and apparently 'soft' forms of violence that are part of the history of power. In a recent text on the history of state institutions, Pierre Bourdieu quotes a terrible passage from one of Thomas Bernhardt's novels in which education is equated with violence, or more accurately with state violence.[7] Any rudimentary process of education is a way of integrating the individual into the structure of hegemony to which I referred earlier. It not only 'normalises' its subjects, but also *constructs* their individuality by making them the bearers of society's values and ideals. What is achieved - primarily by *intellectual* means - is not just mere *learning*, the acquisition of capacities, knowledge or ideas, which would be inscribed on a *tabula rasa*, as empiricism and classical liberalism so neatly imagined. Rather a deconstruction and a reconstruction of an already existing individual identity has to take place. I would even go so far as to say that there has to be a *dis-membering* in order for a *re-membering* to occur, that is a reshaping of the mind - a process which inevitably confers upon the mind a mode of existence which is akin to that of the body.

You could put that in religious terms: any education is a conversion. And a long story could be written here, full of breaks and continuities, beginning for instance with the *compelle intrare* in Saint Luke and Saint Augustine (we all know that, although it had military applications, its basic meaning was a spiritual one) and passing on to the crises of the modern school system, in its 'authoritarian' and as well as its 'libertarian' forms. Sometimes the libertarian forms are *the most violent*, because they put the burden of dismembering and remembering upon the child and therefore ask him or her to be his or her own surgeon and engineer and torturer. And it is here, again, that we have to investigate how the dialectics of *Gewalt*, violence and ideality, *borders on cruelty*, or floats knowingly or unknowingly over cruelty's abyss. And since I was citing Bourdieu, I might add that the very situation which he had described initially as the most favourable one in terms of educational success - namely that of the heirs (*héritiers*) of the bourgeoisie, those who through their families have already received the linguistic, literary and moral preconditions of everything that the school will require of them - might very well be the most ambiguous situation of all. Their position is no doubt socially rewarding, but it is not clear that they are well equipped to deal with their own ferocious *superegos*. Which might explain - if it is indeed the case - why kids from the working class, the popular classes, may either reject the school system (or be rejected by it) or improve their social status through schooling, but are seldom psychologically destroyed by it. Of course I am not forgetting that more obviously economic factors are also at work here.

7. The novel is *Ancient Masters*. See P. Bourdieu, 'L'Etat et la concentration du capital symbolique', in B. Théret et al., *L'Etat, la finance et le social*, Ed. la Découverte, Paris 1993, p73.

Let me now go back to cruelty, and finish with a few words on the reasons why the question is so especially relevant today. At the outset, I should confess that I am not at all certain that the phenomena I have in mind have any real unity. They are clearly heterogeneous, and we had better not try to impose some sort of common essence upon them - such as the notion of *evil* - which would be purely metaphysical. On the other hand, I suspect that this heterogeneity is intrinsic to the very way cruelty seems to appear in experience or in history. Let me mention two kinds of phenomena.

First, some typical aspects of what is often referred to as the 'new poverty', but which I would call the *internal exclusion of the poor* in our societies (the so-called 'affluent' societies), and the reasons why it is so desperate. I am perfectly aware that the element of cruelty, or something bordering on cruelty, was never absent from the exploitation of labour (and unemployment) in its classic form. This had to do with the fact, for which Marx provided a fairly convincing explanation, that the capitalist economy is not only based upon exploitation, but on an *excess of exploitation*, or overexploitation, a point we have sometimes tended to forget. I am also not forgetting that the most massive form of poverty in today's world is the one which occurs in the *under-developed* countries, where a combination of the destruction of traditional ways of life, the domination of foreign financial powers, the establishment of a so-called New World Order has created a situation - which of course nobody *wanted* or anticipated - in which millions of human beings have become *superfluous*. Nobody needs them, they are so to speak 'human garbage' to be thrown away (*l'homme jetable*), to borrow the extremely violent phrase which Bertrand Ogilvie proposed at a recent conference in Montevideo.[8]

8. cf. B. Ogilvie, 'Violence et représentation: la production de l'homme jetable', from the Conference *Violencia y traumatismos historicos*, Montevideo 1994, reprinted in *Lignes*, no. 26, Paris 1995.

These people are facing, and we too are once more facing, the prospect of extermination. The forms extermination takes are not only violent but also quite specifically *cruel* - I am thinking for example of the half-voluntary/half-involuntary, half-conscious/half-unconscious ways in which AIDS has been spreading throughout Africa right from the beginning. But even if 'the North' does not exactly experience this kind of situation, there is something extremely disturbing about the new poverty, which has to do with the fact that the contemporary 'underclass', particularly the second or third generation of young unemployed people, do not, by definition, *come before* the institutionalisation of the welfare state; instead, they *come after* its partial failure and dismantling. Hence a kind of 'post-historical' predicament, a double bind which Marx could not have anticipated, since he thought that unemployment was a cyclical phenomenon, a temporary phase used by capital to lower the level of wages as part of a process of continuous expansion. Now, temporary or not, the current situation is one in which 'human garbage' is being thrown out of work by the million, while at the same time they are being kept *within* the boundaries *of the market*, since the market is an absolute, possessing no *external limits*. The global market is exactly that: the whole world. When it excludes you, you cannot leave it, you cannot search for another America, a place from which to settle and start again.

A second form of cruelty which we face is warfare, and particularly those so-called 'ethnic' and 'religious' wars with their apparent irrationality, which have reintroduced the concept of genocide or extermination into the post-Cold War world, both North and South, under the name of 'ethnic cleansing'. It's still upsetting to recall that one of the future theoreticians of ethnic cleansing actually served as my respondent after a lecture I had given at Boston University some years ago. The very fact that ethnic cleansing is not only practiced, but also *theorised*, that again and again the violence of extermination appears as a kind of 'acting out' or *passage à l'acte*, the *realisation* of a theoretical script which is obviously fantasmatic (although deeply rooted in the imagined community of the nation state) could be considered, I think, as a sign of the current upsurge of cruelty. That is, it indicates a kind of violence which is not completely intelligible in terms of the logic of power or the economy of *Gewalt*.

I deliberately mentioned the indirect relationship between underdevelopment, so-called overpopulation, and the spread of AIDS in Africa. For although the connection may seem obscene, it allows us to point tentatively towards a frightful kind of symmetry. 'Human garbage' is certainly a social phenomenon, but it tends to appear almost as something 'natural' or as a manifestation of violence in which the limits between what is human and what is natural, or what is post-human and what is post-natural, tend to become blurred: what I would be tempted to call an *ultra-objective* form of violence, or *cruelty without a face*. Conversely, the practices and theories of ethnic cleansing confront us with what I would call the *ultra-subjective* forms of violence, or *cruelty with the face of a Medusa*. This of course has to do with the fact that they unleash 'in the Real' (at a collective level) processes which are not and cannot be completely symbolised, what in Freudian terms would be described as primary or pre-Oedipal processes. I am not necessarily taking on board all the theoretical baggage that goes along with these terms, but merely the general perspective they offer. For in these extreme situations - witness for example the collective rapes in Yugoslavia or in India - social violence becomes heavily sexualised. More precisely, what happens is that the sexual character of ordinary social practices in modern societies crosses a certain threshold, beyond which the distinction between the individual and the collective, the real and the imaginary, becomes confused. This was indeed already the case with nazism and perhaps with other totalitarian phenomena in history. Hence a careful comparative study of all these practices is necessary, including both those that are global and those that are local, the 'exceptional' and the 'mundane'. I am reminded of a terrible tale by the Spanish writer Rafael Sanchez

Ferlosio, which he wrote for the Fifth Centenary of the so-called 'Discovery of America', in which he depicted the way the Spanish *conquistadores* used their hunting dogs, for which they had invented noble names and genealogies, against the American Indians.[9] There is indeed little difference between this form of cruelty, and those rituals of cruelty employed by the nazis, particularly the SS. Yet it should be remembered that the *conquistadores* were acting within the framework of a widely accepted form of *hegemony*, that is to say, under the sway of an extremely powerful *ideality*: viz. the Catholic religion with its messianic faith and legal apparatus, which allowed them to place their practices of cruelty under the banner of civilisation, producing a spiritual and material violence which could be disciplined and idealised. We are faced here with the question of the boundary between 'pure' cruelty - if such a thing can be said to exist - and civilisation or culture. It is precisely this boundary which is so compelling, because it is so puzzling.

9. See the French translation, 'Lâchez les chiens! Prélude au 500e anniversaire de la découverte des Amériques', *Les Temps Modernes*, no.509, Décembre 1988.

Hence my conclusion, or rather my final remarks and questions, which are: (a) How can we imagine new institutions (whether they be state apparatuses, forms of revolutionary action or of counter-power) that will circumscribe or limit the spread of cruelty in today's world and that will continue the dialectics of *Gewalt* in the era of globalization? (b) If we accept - as I do - that the experience of cruelty always engenders a particularly pressing demand for some sort of *ideality*, either in the sense of *non-violent* ideals, or an ideal of *justice*, how are we to deal philosophically and practically with what I take to be an inescapable constraint that is simultaneously an obstacle to, but also a condition of, civilised life? For, on the one hand, there can be no freedom from violence, no resistance to its worst forms, and especially no *collective* resistance (since resistance that is not collective is hardly resistance) *without ideals*. Yet, on the other hand, there is no guarantee, and there can be no guarantee, concerning the 'good use' and the 'bad use' of ideals; or, if you prefer, while there are certainly *degrees* in the amount of violence which goes along with civilising ideals, there is nothing like a *zero* degree. In short, there is no non-violence. We should bear this in mind, I think, as we struggle against every form of violence.

Anthropology and initiation

Henrietta L. Moore

Anthropological and psychoanalytic explanations of initiation rituals have most usually supported a dominant line of argument relating to circumcision, arguing that its purpose is to manage a weak or ineffectual resolution of the Oedipus conflict. The castration anxiety invoked through male circumcision is held to buttress the prohibition of a renewal of desire for the mother, and is frequently accompanied by taboos against contact with senior women. Such taboos are themselves interpreted as a means to reinforce incest prohibitions. The rituals surrounding circumcision are seen as reworking the repressed conflicts of childhood, and by means of catharsis, somehow reconcile the young man to the authority of his father and to the cultural values he represents. The origins of these theories lie in the work of Freud, and derive most directly from *Totem and Taboo*, where Freud describes the relationship between totems and the prohibitions on incest, and suggests that totems represent the accession to the authority of the father and to culture.[1] However, Freud does not discuss initiation or circumcision explicitly in *Totem and Taboo*, and theories focusing on the reinforcement of the weakened oedipal resolution and on the reworking of the repressed conflicts of childhood which purport to explain circumcision are, in my view, problematic. Their problematic nature becomes even more evident when we consider their value for the explanation of the wider initiation rituals of which circumcision is a part. What follows is an example.

INITIATION IN TANZANIA

In the past, there were chiefdoms among the Chagga people of Tanzania who initiated their young men first by circumcision and then through a period of seclusion and instruction in the forest.[2] Children and young women were told that during their time in the forest, the newly circumcised youths would undergo a second operation to plug and stitch their anuses. Once the young men were in the forest, they were immediately taught that the story of anus stitching was a falsehood, but they were obliged to take a number of oaths never to tell children and young women that they defecated nor ever allow them to see them defecate or to find their faeces.[3] No doubt, 'the closed anus was an open secret as far as the women were concerned, but the question which concerns us is how to make sense of this story'.[4]

The form of Chagga initiation involving seclusion in the forest has not been practised for a long time, but it has been interpreted by anthropologists as connecting to broader ideas about the control of fertility, of reproductive

1. Freud, *Totem and Taboo*, 1950 [1913].

2. The Chagga are a group of people living on the slopes of Mount Kilimanjaro in Tanzania. A number of anthropological studies have been written on the Chagga, and this paper is based on a reinterpretation of the data offered in the following sources: C. Dundas, *Kilimanjaro and its People*, Witherby, London 1924; M. Emanatian, 'Everyday metaphors of lust and sex in Chagga', *Ethos* 24(2), 1996, pp195-236; B. Gutman, *Das Recht der Dschagga*, C H Beck, Munchen 1926; B. Gutman, *Die Stammeslehren der Dschagga*, Volume I, C H Beck, Munchen 1932; B. Gutman, *Die Stammeslehren der Dschagga*, Volume II, C H Beck, Munchen 1935; B. Gutman, *Die Stammeslehren der Dschagga*, Volume III, C H Beck, Munchen 1938; S. Moore, 'The secret of the men: a fiction of Chagga initiation and its relation to the logic of Chagga symbolism', *Africa* (46), 1976, pp357-370; O. Raum, *Chagga Childhood: A Description of Indigenous Education in an East African Tribe*, Oxford University Press, London 1940; O. Raum, 'Female initiation among the Chagga' *American Anthropologist* 41(4), 1939, pp554-565; P. Setel, 'AIDS as a paradox of manhood and development in Kilimanjaro, Tanzania' *Social Science And Medicine* 43 (8), 1996, pp1169-1178.

power, and of relations between women and men.[5] The organising idea behind the story of the stitched anus is that men should be closed, whilst women should be open. A woman is open; as open as the vagina into which the penis is inserted and out of which the child comes. A man has no vagina, he is closed and his closure connects to his fertility and to his control over procreative powers. An initiated man is a socially procreative one, one who can marry and have children. A woman is only closed when she is pregnant, at the time when she retains the blood inside her. During pregnancy, she is at the height of her procreative power and her fertility. Chagga women say that the original *ngoso*, the original plug, the secret of the masculine control over procreative power once belonged to them, before it was stolen from them by men.[6] 'Pregnancy they say is the female *ngoso*'.[7] The theft left women not only without a penis, but with an open body which can only be closed during pregnancy.

A man's faeces and a woman's menstrual blood make them vulnerable to sterility if these body substances are appropriated by or pass into the control of others. Sterility is connected straightforwardly to death and to the inability to have children and to perpetuate human society.[8] In Chagga thought openness and closedness are associated with human sexuality, with the inauguration of sexual difference, and with life and death. The point we should note is that the focus of male initiation is as much on the period of seclusion in the forest and the story of a bodily transformation which does not take place, as it is on that bodily change which is the specific result of initiation, the circumcision of the penis. If the purpose of the rite is to buttress a weak resolution of the oedipal conflict then presumably we should be approaching the story of the stitched anus from the point of view of the trauma and the threat of symbolic castration.

However, this line of thought seems to offer a rather impoverished interpretation of the Chagga material. To explain why involves a discussion of some details of the initiation ritual. Faeces played a particular part in the male initiation ceremony in the past. At the beginning of their seclusion, the young men dug two adjacent pits, one for faeces and one for urine. The initiates had to use these two pits during their training, and each morning they rubbed themselves with urine-wet mud from the urine pit, and this coating was the only covering they were allowed during their period of seclusion.[9] The faecal pit was consecrated before use, was very deep, and tales were told of previous initiates who had fallen in and been left to die.[10] Ritual or 'mock' hunts were part of the young men's training during seclusion, and the ritual of hunting was connected with the faecal pit. A piece of every animal killed was used to swear the binding oath of silence. The meat was dipped into the pit, and the young men then had to lick the meat and swear that they would keep the secrets of initiation from children and young women. On the last day of seclusion, the young men dipped locusts into the pit, licked the covered insects and swore never again to eat locusts. Locusts were a favourite food of women and children.[11] The initiation

3. Raum, 1939, *op. cit.*, pp554-555; 1940, *op. cit.*, pp314-336.

4. Moore, *op. cit.*, p357. Raum notes that the teacher of female initiates in the female initiation rites of the Chagga 'must have discovered the male secret. Then on one occasion observing a man defecate, she waits till he has gone, removes a small quantity of the faeces, and mixes it with ochre and water. On the day of the shiga, as the female initiation is called, this mixture is painted on the novice's head', *op. cit.*, p555.

5. It is not known when the last initiation camps for boys were held, but possibly around the 1890s or the turn of the century. There are obvious questions about the reliability of the anthropological data on the male initiation rituals which was all collected through recollection. However, the crucial role of faecal material in Chagga symbolism and ritual is well attested to by more recent data. Even if we assume that some of the accounts of the initiation rituals are fabrications, we should remember Freud's injunction that all lies contain some elements of the truth. The correctness of the data is therefore perhaps less important than the fact that the stories take the particular form they do.

instructor was reported as saying: 'This is the blood pact of the men! This is your secret. The strokes which you received in this camp prohibit you from eating locusts henceforth. For if you eat the blood pact of man, that is the locust which you licked, the curse of initiation will cut through your connection with the ancestors, and you will bear no offspring ... Liberate these creatures for they are our brothers with whom we have made a blood pact. We may not harm them'.[12]

Sally Falk Moore, one of the ethnographers of the Chagga has made an interpretation of the practice and symbolism of the initiation rite which does not focus on the prohibition against incest, nor directly on accession to the law of the father. When a youth passes through initiation, he acquires the right to beget children. Moore asks what the association is between the begetting of children and the fiction of the closed anus. Her response is that the explicit link for the Chagga is the prohibition of homosexual intercourse. If a man violates this prohibition, he may die. Once a man has passed through initiation, he is as fertile as any woman, he has assumed his socially reproductive powers. 'Once he can beget children, he runs the risk of becoming pregnant or of impregnating another man through anal intercourse. For a man to become pregnant in this way would mean death because, being closed, he has no birth canal out of which the child can pass. The anus of the initiate is not literally plugged and stitched, but is figuratively so. He is closed to other men'.[13] The idea is that in order to achieve fatherhood, to ensure social continuity, a man must have sexual relations with women and forswear those with men. Sally Falk Moore extends this analysis to explain the oath relating to locusts, where she suggests that the identification between men and locusts established in the rite means that when the young men swear not to eat the locusts their brothers, they are, in fact, swearing not to eat themselves. Since the analogy between eating and sex is a persistent theme in Chagga symbolism as elsewhere, the prohibition on eating locusts and eating faeces is an analogy for the prohibition on anal intercourse.[14]

HOMOSEXUALITY AND THE ORIGINS OF CULTURE

The association between a prohibition on homosexual sex and the origins of culture is one which has been made before in anthropology. Georges Devereux responded to Lévi-Strauss's discussion of the origins of human kinship in *The Elementary Structures of Kinship* by arguing that the circulation of women through marriage and the necessary prohibition on incestuous union with sisters could not possibly explain the origins of kinship and culture because it focused exclusively on sociological facts, at the expense of psychological ones. Devereux argued that the exchange of women at marriage revealed not just a system of exchange, but an obsessional desire for symmetry which should be understood as the expression of a latent male homosexuality.[15] Kinship, he suggested, is not rooted in heterosexual

6. Raum, *op. cit.*, p557.

7. Moore, *op. cit.*, p358.

8. *Ibid.*

9. *Ibid.*

10. Gutman, 1926, *op. cit.*, p323.

11. Moore, *op. cit.*, pp361-62.

12. Raum, 1940, *op. cit.*, p320.

13. Moore, *op. cit.*, p359.

14. Emanatian, 1996 *op. cit.*, Setel, 1996, *op cit.*

15. Devereux, 1978, *op. cit.*, p204.

drives, but in homosexual ones, and what marriage does, through the exchange of women, is to allow men to achieve their goal in symbolic form, through subterfuge, by disguising relations between men as heterosexual acts. 'Marriage is sacred, that is dangerous, precisely because it permits what is forbidden; it consecrates a sacrilege'.[16] Gayle Rubin argues in her influential essay, 'The Traffic in Women', which discusses Lévi-Strauss, that the incest taboo in fact presupposes 'a prior less articulate taboo on homosexuality', and suggests that this must logically be necessary for a regime of compulsory heterosexuality to be enforced.[17]

16. *Ibid.*, p211.

17. G. Rubin, 'The traffic in women: notes on the "political economy" of sex', in R. Reiter (ed), *Toward an Anthropology of Women*, Monthly Review Press, New York 1975.

Outside anthropology, Judith Butler has recently made an argument very similar to Rubin's. Her starting point is that Freud's theories of the acquisition of the masculine and feminine positions, which are laboriously established through prohibitions that demand the loss of certain sexual attachments, imply that heterosexuality is always tenuous. What is involved therefore is the pre-emption of the possibility of homosexual attachment, a foreclosure which makes homosexuality an unliveable passion and an ungrievable loss. 'The oedipal conflict presumes that heterosexual desire has already been accomplished, that the distinction between heterosexual and homosexual has been enforced (a distinction that, after all, has no necessity); in this sense, the prohibition on incest presupposes the prohibition on homosexuality, for it presumes the heterosexualisation of desire'.[18] In its simplest form, the argument assumes a certain psychoanalytic logic: if a girl is to transfer her love for her father to a substitute object, she must first renounce the love for her mother and do so in a way which forecloses its possibility.[19] Butler's argument is very close to Rubin's, but what is interesting about it is the link she implies between a prohibited homosexuality and the inauguration of gender difference. The underlying thesis contains two contradictory elements. On the one hand, there is the idea that what a man repudiates, in renouncing homosexual desire, is the feminine within: he refuses to be a woman. He will not identify with his feminine self and therefore he will not desire another man. On the other hand, there is the rather contrary notion that what the repudiation of homosexuality achieves is the stabilisation of gender difference through the disavowal of sameness. This is the supposition that underpins both Rubin's and Butler's assertion that heterosexual relations depend on a prior prohibition of homosexual relations. Such discussions, and the alternatives they propose, are fully contained within a psychoanalytic logic, a logic of exegesis, but they do not necessarily connect to the social and psychic experiences of lived symbolism, even allowing that a part of that symbolism is barred and cannot be lived properly speaking. However, the idea that initiation rituals might be linked to a lack of difference; that is, to the problem of a fundamental similarity between women and men does help to make some sense of the Chagga data, and indeed of ethnographic data from other parts of Africa.

18. J. Butler, 'Melancholy gender - refused identification' *Psychoanalytic Dialogues* 5(2), 1995, pp165-180.

19. *Ibid.*, p169.

Once a Chagga man had a circumcised child himself, a moment which was said to symbolise the end of his period of procreation and fertility, he could resume defecating. In the distant past, a man and his lineage mates would perform a ritual which involved slaughtering a goat and then they would tie pieces of goat meat to the man's thighs so that the blood ran down over his legs. The meat was removed and the man's wife called. She was told that he was bleeding because he had removed his *ngoso* for the sake of his sons, and that from then on her husband would defecate. Sally Falk Moore notes: 'whether this ritual was actually performed or not matters less than that the report of it was made, that Chagga talked about such an "ancient" custom'.[20]

20. Moore, *op. cit.*, p361.

The idea that women and men have to be different in order to be procreative, to produce children successfully, is a common theme in much ethnographic material. What the bleeding man resembles, once he removes his *ngoso* for the sake of his sons, is a menstruating woman, one who has let the blood go and is no longer pregnant. There is puzzlement and envy involved in the constructions of gender difference which initiation inaugurates. The puzzlement has to do with the secret of fertility, both human and natural; with how the power of procreation and fertility is to be controlled and captured. This is not an esoteric question in the context of a rural African society, where human control over the fertility, and therefore the reproduction, of humans, land and animals is frequently precarious. Both women and men are aware that they do not have the secret of life.[21] Women say that they once had the secret, but that the men stole it, and all they have left is pregnancy.[22] The men may have penises, but they do not have the capacity to get pregnant. These two capacities have to be combined for successful procreation.

21. *Ibid.*, p363.

22. *Ibid.*, p364.

It might be thought that this should be no problem, that women and men already have the naturally differentiated capacities whose combination is necessary for successful reproduction, but that is not necessarily how the Chagga see it. Chagga statements, rituals and symbolism would seem to suggest that they are preoccupied with sameness and difference between women and men, and with how it can be managed to ensure social continuity. The contrasting images of women as open, as defecators of faeces and menstruators of blood, and men as closed, as retainers and containers of blood and faeces are created in the course of the initiation rites, and emphasised through the procreative years of married life to produce and maintain the categories of gender difference. The question is why does this difference need to be made? There is a sense in which we could interpret this discourse on difference as somehow involving an act of repudiated identification. The blurred line between being male and female, or, more accurately, the duality and mutuality of gender identifications is revealed in the ritual of the removal of the *ngoso*. At that moment, the man resembles a menstruating woman and thus reveals that he has been pregnant all along, that his male procreative power has depended on what he has contained in his body, and that that is the purpose of the anal plug. Perhaps we should pursue this point further and ask exactly what it is that he contains.

FAECES, BABIES AND PENISES

Freud made a well-known equation - often regarded as preposterous - between faeces, babies and penises. Freud appeared to have derived this equation from children's fantasises about faecal pregnancies, and linked it also to his discussion of developmental sequences and the relationship of the anal-erotic impulses to the later emergence of genital organisation.[23] The interchangeability of faeces, baby and penis was seen by Freud as something occurring in the unconscious. The link between the penis and the baby connected to a woman's desire for a penis which was then replaced by her desire for a baby. Freud writes: 'It looks as if such women had understood (although this could not possibly have acted as a motive) that nature has given babies to women as a substitute for the penis that has been denied them'.[24] On the surface of it, this sounds rather like what Chagga women have to say. The only problem is that the process of analogy, of establishing equivalence, which Freud describes as part of the unconscious process, is part of ritual, myth and explicit statement for Chagga women.

In his discussion of this set of equivalences or analogies, Freud goes on to suggest that since a part of the eroticism of the pregenital phase becomes available for use in the phase of genital primacy, and since babies are often regarded, presumably only by children, as something which comes out of the body by way of the anus, then an identity between babies and faeces can be established. The idea that both babies and faeces are gifts in some way, and that the baby is gifted through the mediation of the penis somehow binds all three elements in a chain of associations.[25] This argument is perhaps less convincing, to my mind, than a subsequent suggestion made by Freud. He goes on to propose, on the basis of case material, that some individuals make a direct analogy between the faecal mass and the penis, and that the mass inside the rectum represents the first penis, and the rectum thus becomes associated with the vagina. The result is that in fantasy the penis and the vagina come to be represented by the faecal stick and the rectum. One cause of this fantasy may be related to the moment when the boy discovers that women do not have a penis, and this leads him to conclude that the penis must be a detachable part of the body, like faeces.[26]

I am not concerned here with whether Freud's conclusions, interpretations, and somewhat dubious assumptions are true, and I certainly have no interest in asserting that they are valid cross-culturally, and/or are connected to universal developmental sequences. My purpose in discussing Freud's views is to show how psychoanalysis works over a set of themes which it claims are part of the unconscious process, whilst Chagga myth, ritual and social practice works over the same themes from a point well within consciousness. However, a possible further reason for using Freud's analysis emerges when we consider it as 'something good to think with'. When we ask ourselves the question, 'what does the body of the closed Chagga man contain?', we might want to respond that not only was he

23. Freud, 1977 [1917], pp296-302.

24. *Ibid.*, p297.

25. *Ibid.*, pp298-299.

26. *Ibid.*, pp301-302.

pregnant with a foetus, as the Chagga themselves suggest, but that he also contained a penis inside himself. A penis representing the homosexual identification which the story of the suturing of the anus was supposed to prevent. In short, Chagga men are multiply sexed, but the secret is that they remain so even after the initiation rite which is supposed to render them categorical males. This multiply sexed male is one who contains that duality inside him, whatever evidence the external penis might represent. The fact that he retains this duality inside him accounts, in part, for his procreative powers, since he contains both the elements necessary for social reproduction and continuity to take place.

What is interesting about the Chagga material is that it suggests that an interpretation which sees circumcision as simply reinforcing a resolution of the oedipal conflict and as buttressing the prohibition on the renewal of the desire for the mother is likely to be a very impoverished one. This is particularly the case when circumcision, as an act, is removed not only from the context of the larger initiation rite, but from the ongoing social context in which it becomes relevant. However, there might be a sense in which we would still want to approach the story of anal stitching from the point of view of a form of symbolic castration; but to demonstrate why this might be so, I need to turn to the other side of the world, to Melanesia.

MARRIAGE IN MELANESIA

Gillian Gillison argues in her analysis of Gimi symbolism and ritual that the unconscious meaning of marriage in Gimi society is of a fruitful homosexual alliance between father and son-in-law. She takes her inspiration here from Georges Devereux.[27] Much of Gillison's analysis rests on an analogy that the Gimi make between the secret flutes belonging to men and the male penis. These flutes, which signal control over reproductive power, were once owned by women before they were stolen by men. During male initiation, which ideally takes place for boys at the same time as their sisters are being married, the adult men play the secret flutes and sing of how men are born of women. At one point in the rite, the flautists reveal themselves to the initiates, and at that moment the mother's brothers of the boys hold stone axes to the boys' throats and tell them that if they reveal the secret that it is men who play the flutes then their throats will be cut. A flute is placed across the thighs of each initiate and a piece of salted pork is put in his mouth. This, the big men tell the boys, is the faeces of the flute: 'we give you this food to make you grow quickly'.[28] During the initiation ritual, men repeat various versions of the flute myth and recount for the boys how it was women who first owned the flutes and had the powers and prerogatives men now own.

In the male myth, the flute was stolen by a boy from his sister, and this theft caused her to menstruate or, as the Gimi say, 'to be killed by the moon for the first time'.[29] The woman's first husband is thus both the boy

27. G. Gillison, 'Symbolic homosexuality and Cultural Theory: the unconscious meaning of sisters exchange among the Gimi of Highland New Guinea', S. Heald (ed), 1994, p213. See also A. Deluz, *Anthropology and Psychoanalysis*, Routledge, London 1994.

28. G. Gillison, 'The Flute myth and the law of equivalence: origins of a principle of exchange', *Big Men and Great Men*, M. Godelier and M. Strathens (eds), Cambridge University Press, Cambridge 1991, pp177-178.

29. *Ibid.*, pp180-182.

who stole the flute, and caused the woman to bleed by severing her from her penis, and the father of the moon whose penis had resided inside the woman, making her complete. Her completeness was itself symbolised by her ownership of the original flute. Women's myths tell the story of the first man, whose penis awoke in the night and went out by itself to search for woman. The penis found her asleep, but could not penetrate her because the vagina was closed. The penis ate an opening to gain entry and the woman awoke and cut off the enormous thing that had invaded her: the blood of the moon or first man was the blood of menstruation, which was also the blood of a severed penis.[30] What is interesting here is that in both versions of this story, the original woman has a penis inside her.

30. Gillilson, *op. cit.*, p217.

However, the penis inside women turns out to be a problem when it comes to marriage. When a man gives his daughter in marriage, he sends with her a pair of flutes decorated with a design which is also tattooed around her mouth before marriage. The flutes are stuffed with hairy marsupial meat, and the groom is instructed to unplug the flutes, take out the meat and feed it to his bride. The flute a man gives to his son-in-law consists not only of the decorated instrument, but also of the right to play his own named 'cry', a distinctive combination of sounds and rhythms. Blowing into a flute, the men reveal, is like going into a woman, and the sounds the player blows out are the cries of his child.[31]

31. Gillison, *op. cit.*, pp180-182.

Gillison argues that: 'A man's giving his son-in-law his "child" together with the right to play her his way, using his own "cry", is like bestowing his daughter while he himself still "plays" her, while his wind or "penis" or "head" still fills her. In the sense that the kamiba (flute) is "the same" as both the bride and "the Penis of the Moon", the groom who empties and plays it "copulates" at one time with his bride and the Father-inside-Her'.[32] This father is, of course, both the father of the moon, the mythical father, and the father of the bride. This myth of homosexual union between father and son-in-law is further developed by Gillison in very sophisticated ways using detailed ethnography.[33]

32. *Ibid.*, p182.

33. Gillison, *op. cit.* 1991, 1993, 1994.

A number of interpretations are possible, but Gillison points out that Gimi persons are not thought of as being single sex, and that sexual attributes are transferable or exchangeable between persons.[34] The original woman, from whom the boy stole the flute, was not of a single sex, she contained the father inside her, and this was what her making of the flute symbolised. What the decorated flute tells the groom who receives it, is that the bride's vagina only looks empty, but it is in fact filled with the head of her father's child, symbolised by the hairy marsupial meat with which the flute is filled.[35] When the groom pulls the meat out of the flute and feeds it to his bride, he is pulling the mythic Father and the child of the father out of the flute, so that his own wind may enter the flute and he can produce his own children. Gimi ritual, symbolism and myth thus suggests two interpretations of what happens at marriage. On the one hand, the groom copulates with the father of the bride who still resides inside her.

34. Gillison, *Between Culture and Fantasy*, Chicago University Press, Chicago 1993, chapter 9.

35. Gillison, 1991, p183.

On the other, the unplugging of the flute symbolises the transfer of procreative responsibility from the father to the son-in-law, and thus it also symbolises a circumvented coital encounter between them.[36] However, in both interpretations what is important ultimately is the unplugging of the woman, the act or acts symbolically necessary to keep her open, so that she may produce children.

36. Gillison, 1994, p218.

CIRCUMCISION: CASTRATION OR WHAT?

Both the Gimi and the Chagga material shows that the symbolic exceeds the biological, and perhaps that is an insight for which we should be permanently grateful to Freud. Masculinity and femininity have to have symbolic forms, and that paradoxically is why bodies have to be transformed: the work of nature is not enough. There is always something about gender identity and about sexuality which is not strictly speaking on the human scale. In order for reproduction to take place and for social life to be assured, there always has to be something else: it is not enough for physical men and women to come together. They cannot do it, whatever it is, on their own. A symbolic framework is necessary for sexual relations to work. It is in this sense that Lacan is perhaps more use to us than Freud. For a man to be really potent, both physically and socially, there must be something beyond the penis itself, and this something is probably to be identified as the phallus of the father: the father of the moon, as the Gimi might say.[37] What Chagga circumcision and Gimi marriage seem to be about is the fact that what the male subject has to do is to accept the incommensurability of what it is he possesses, and whatever it is that this mythical object represents.

'Having a phallus does not stop one from desiring one'.[38] However what Gimi and Chagga ritual and myth also suggest is that this problem exists for female, as well as male, subjects. The phallus, as a signifier, is distinct from the question of having or not having a penis. This is what the story of the sutured anus tells us, and it is what the Gimi discuss in their myths and act out in their rituals. The symbol of the phallus symbolises the human dimension of lack, and the desire consequent on that lack. 'Castration is thus not a real operation on an organ, but a symbolic dimension of human existence'.[39] This is why the Chagga are more interested in the operation that does not take place than they are in the one that does. It is also why the Gimi take such trouble with flutes. It does make some sense then to think of circumcision as being related to the symbolic trauma of castration, but only in the wider context of initiation rites and transition rituals, and in terms of the long rumination on those rites which is social life itself. In other words, it has to be understood in light of that other unconscious, not that which is repressed or unacceptable, but that which exceeds human knowledge and is genuinely unintelligible. In short, in the context of what it is that we have to give up in order to become women and men.

37. D. Leader, *Why Women Write More Letters Than They Post*, Faber and Faber, London 1996, p37.

38. *Ibid.*, p45.

39. *Ibid.*, p46.

Cut in the body:
from clitoridectomy to body art

Renata Salecl

Today in the same quarter of New York there are youngsters who decorate their skins with body piercing, artists who use body mutilation as a form of art, and African immigrants, some of whom practice clitoridectomy. How can these facts be explained?

Those who practice clitoridectomy, for instance, are usually fully integrated into Western society: they work or go to school, they participate in public life, while they also retain old initiation rituals. Body mutilations like clitoridectomy cannot simply be understood as the repetition of or the return to pre-modern forms of initiation; they should rather be understood as a way in which the contemporary subject deals with the deadlocks of so-called post-modern society. And some practices of body-art, as well as the fashion of body piercing and tattooing, can also be seen as another way of dealing with these deadlocks.

I will analyse the practice of clitoridectomy in comparison to the masochistic turn in body art. But I am far from saying that these forms of body transformations are of equal nature. What makes them comparable is the fact that they are two different types of answers to the same question: what is the place of the subject in contemporary society?

Before making connections between these two practices, one needs to examine the different ways in which the subject identifies with the symbolic order in pre-modern, modern and post-modern society. My intention, however, is not to trace the genealogy of these forms of society, but to take them as three different types of the subject's relation to the so-called big Other, i.e. the symbolic structure. If today people are returning to body painting or even to old forms of initiation, they are not simply copying some old cultural forms: they are reinterpreting these old forms in a new way. But to understand this reinterpretation, one first needs to analyse the initial meaning of initiation rituals such as clitoridectomy.

INITIATION AND INDIVIDUALISATION

The ritual of clitoridectomy in the Third World countries is a topic that from time to time attracts the attention of the Western media and provokes almost universal admonishment from the public.[1] There are usually two types of reaction to clitoridectomy: first, the defenders of universal human rights are for strict prohibition of this ritual; second, those who insist on the right to cultural difference oppose clitoridectomy while stating that

1. The United Nations data shows that there are 130 million women in the world today whose genitals have been mutilated. This practice is widespread in parts of Africa, in some Asian countries, and among the immigrants from these places in the West.

non-Western cultures have their own rituals that might appal Westerners who, nonetheless, have no right to impose their standards on non-Westerners. Things become more complicated when the Westerners realise that the rituals of clitoridectomy are performed not only in Africa or Asia, but also among the immigrants in the middle of New York, London, Paris. Here the legal prohibition of the ritual has no real effect, since clitoridectomy is never performed as a public act, but as a secret ritual. From the Western point of view, it is shocking that something like this should happen in democratic societies.[2] It is also surprising that the development of capitalism in the Third World countries did not contribute to the extinction of clitoridectomy; on the contrary, in some countries this practice has become even more widespread in recent years. How can we explain this fact?

Women who support such initiation rites usually claim that this practice is part of their ethnic identity and has been performed by their ancestors; by carrying on with the initiation rituals, they are essentially contributing to the survival of their tradition. When the members of such ethnic groups migrate to the West, they insist on the right to protect their identity through the performance of clitoridectomy. Women also claim that if they have not been initiated via clitoridectomy, they cannot get married; and mothers who submit their daughters to this ritual usually state: 'If it was good for me, it will also be good for my daughter'.

While Westerners fear that the customs of non-Western immigrants shatter their way of life, the immigrants complain that the Western states' prohibition of certain initiation rituals endangers their ethnic identity. It is thus not only Westerners who see the danger of the erosion of their culture, the immigrant cultures also perceive themselves as endangered by the dominant Western mores.

The case of clitoridectomy creates many dilemmas that go far beyond the simple decision whether one is against this ritual or in favour of it. The question is: what role does clitoridectomy play in the formation of women's sexual identity and how essential is this ritual for transmission of sexual norms from generation to generation? Here, the question is also: how does sexual difference inscribe itself in pre-modern and in modern societies; and how is one to understand a return to the cut in the body that happens in the post-modern society, for example in the case of some practices of body art?

Let me first summarise the explanations given by the supporters of clitoridectomy as to why this ritual needs to be preserved. Although different ethnic groups usually justify clitoridectomy with different mythologies, one can make some comparisons between them. A widespread belief is that clitoridectomy assures women's fertility. In many mythologies the clitoris is regarded as something impure and dangerous for the future child. The clitoris is considered to be a rival to men's phallus. In Ethiopia, for example, some people believe that the uncut clitoris grows to the size of men's penis

2. Although clitoridectomy is prevalent in communities that practice Islam, this ritual is not linked to Islam, much less prescribed by the Koran. In the past, clitoridectomy was sometimes also performed by Catholics, Protestants, Copts, and other religious groups. The Catholic Church never officially distanced itself from clitoridectomy: the missionaries in Africa, for example, did not condemn this practice. Only the Anglican Church, in the 1920s, denounced this ritual and advised its missionaries to prevent it. Cf. Efua Dorkenoo, *Cutting the Rose: Female Genital Mutilation - The Practice and its Prevention*, Minority Rights Publication, London 1994. See also, Martine Lefeuvre-Deotte, *L'excision en proces: un differend culturel?*, L'Harmatan, Paris 1997, and Jean-Thierry Maertens, *Le corps sexionne*, Aubier, Paris 1978. Clitoridectomy was also practised in Europe in the nineteenth century to treat female hysteria. Cf. Jane Ussher, *Women's madness: The Misogyny as Mental Illness*, Harvester and Wheatsheaf, Hertfordshire 1991.

and thus prevents insemination. The Bambara from Mali claim that a man who has intercourse with an uncircumcised woman might die, since the clitoris produces some poisonous liquid. They also believe that at the time of birth one finds in the child both female and male traces. The clitoris is the trace of the male in the female and the prepuce is the trace of the female in the male. In order to clearly define the child's sex, the trace of the opposite sex is extinguished via male and female circumcision.

Other justifications for clitoridectomy stress the importance of group identity. A woman who is submitted to this ritual becomes the equal of other women in her ethnic group - she is thus accepted in her community. The circumcised woman finds 'the feeling of pride in being like everyone else, in being "made clean", in having suffered without screaming'.[3] For a woman, to be different; i.e. unexcised or noninfibulated, produces anxiety: she is ridiculed and despised by the others, and she will also be unable to get married in her community.

Some ethnic groups also claim that clitoridectomy protects women from their excessive sexuality. This ritual thus makes women faithful. Since excised women are supposed to be less sexually demanding, men can have many wives and keep them all satisfied. Others argue the opposite: the excised woman is supposed to be more inclined to have extramarital affairs, since she is always sexually unsatisfied. But, a very common position is that clitoridectomy helps to retain women's virginity, which is especially important in those communities that make virginity the absolute prerequisite of marriage and in which women's extramarital affairs are strongly condemned.

Some defenders of clitoridectomy also claim that this ritual needs to be understood as an aesthetic practice: the infibulated woman's sexual organ is supposed to be much more attractive than the noninfibulated one. And the most beautiful organ is the one that, after the scar is healed, feels smooth as a palm.[4]

Why do women who are submitted to the horrific practice of clitoridectomy not rebel against it; why do they calmly accept mutilation of their genitals; and why do they force their daughters to do the same? The problem is not simply that women live in patriarchal societies in which they have no power to express their disagreement with the rituals. Many cultures that perform clitoridectomy are not classical patriarchies - in some cultures men are perceived as quite powerless and a lot of authority is in the hands of the older women, who are cherished as father-like authority figures and as guardians of tradition, which is why these women are entrusted with the task of performing the ritual of clitoridectomy.[5] Thus the dilemma of why women support clitoridectomy primarily concerns the position the subject has in his or her culture, i.e. the way the subject is entangled in his or her community.

Max Horkheimer points out that, with the advent of the Enlightenment type of patriarchal family, one discerns a process of individualisation that

3. Note that so-called female circumcision is the mildest form of the deformations of female genitals, since circumcision removes only the prepuce that covers the clitoris. Much more severe and also much more widely spread is so-called excision, which removes the whole of the clitoris. Even more common and painful is the ritual of infibulation, which means the removal of the clitoris and the labia. This practice causes numerous infections and many women die because of it.

4. The defenders of clitoridectomy who invoke the aesthetic dimension of this ritual usually say that it should be compared with the Western obsession with beauty ideals, which lead western women to undergo painful plastic surgery operations, use tattoos, etc.

5. On the paradoxical role of men in some pre-modern societies, see Suzette Heald, 'Every man a hero: Oedipal themes in Gisu circumcision', in *Anthropology and Psychoanalysis: An Encounter Through Culture*, Suzette Heald in Ariane Deluz (ed), Routledge, London 1994, and Maurice Bloch, *From Blessing to Violence: History and Ideology in the Circumcision Ritual of the Merina of Madagascar*, Cambridge University Press, Cambridge 1986.

did not exist in the pre-modern family.[6] The modern subject is, of course, linked to his or her tradition, family, national community, but this tradition is no longer something that fully determines the subject and gives him or her stability and security. The modern subject is expelled from his or her community - this subject is an individual who has to find and re-establish his or her place in the community again and again. That modern society no longer stages the ritual of initiation means the subject must 'freely' choose his or her place in the community, although this choice always remains in some way a forced choice. As we know from psychoanalysis, the subject who does not 'choose' his or her place in the community becomes a psychotic - a subject who has an external relationship to the community and is not barred by language.

6. Cf. Max Horkheimer, 'Authority and the Family', in *Critical Theory: Selected Essays*, Continuum, New York 1972.

But this forced choice to become a member of the community also enables the subject to experience some actual freedom, for example to reject the rituals of his or her community. Only when the subject is no longer perceived as someone who essentially contributes to the continuation of his or her tradition and is completely rooted in his or her community, does the moment emerge when the subject can distance himself or herself from this community, for example by criticising its rituals. Western feminists justly take clitoridectomy to be a horrific practice. However, one can arrive at such a position only after going through the process of individualisation, i.e. only when the subject has already made a break with his or her tradition.

When we say that in pre-modern society subjects are not individualised yet and are thus not able to distance themselves from the tradition, this does not mean that when people support clitoridectomy today they are falling back to the level of pre-modern family organisations. On the contrary, the return to old traditions needs to be understood as a way in which subjects deal with the deadlocks of the highly individualised contemporary society. When people propagate old initiation rituals they are not simply nostalgic about the past or unable to oppose their tradition (usually they are quite willing to give up many other old rituals and prohibitions), they are trying to find some stability in today's disintegrating social universe.

There are various ways subjects deal with individualisation in contemporary society. A young punk, for example, seems to respond to individualisation by taking it to the extreme: he or she adopts an ultra-individualised stance and constantly searches for new decorations for his or her body, which make his or her image unique. Punks make a conscious effort to dress differently from the dominant fashion trends, but then he or she also strongly identifies with some peer group. The punk's response to individualisation is thus finally a formation of another group ideology. Although this ideology encourages people to look different from each other, it nonetheless quickly forms new fashion codes.

By contrast, an African immigrant might respond to radical individualisation by strongly identifying with his or her ethnic tradition. In this case, too, group identity, paradoxically, appears as a solution to the deadlocks of individualisation. If individualisation first happened when the subjects made a break with their tradition, now the deadlocks accompanying individualisation incite either a return to tradition or a formation of some new group identity.

THE IMPOTENCE OF AUTHORITY

It is well known that both types of initiation - male circumcision and clitoridectomy - are ways in which pre-modern societies mark sexual difference. In these societies, biological sex is not enough to ensure their reproduction. It is the symbolic cut made by the law, i.e. by language, that enables the continuation of tradition. The pre-modern society imposes all kinds of prohibitions and rituals that make a social being out of the human animal. But in this society the symbolic cut in the body, the inscription of subject's identity, occurs as something real. In the act of initiation, the subject receives a physical mark on his or her body, in most cases through circumcision, but in some cases also through paint on the body or a tattoo. Anthropologists stress that initiation is an extremely traumatic event, especially if it happens in adolescence, since before being initiated the subject does not have a clear identity, while after initiation the subject becomes heavily burdened by his or her sexual function and is thus expected to perform in accordance with it.

The pre-modern subject has doubts about his or her sexual identity, but the gesture of initiation is supposed to alleviate this doubt and through the cut in the body confirm the subject's sexual identity. This mark on the body is therefore the answer of the big Other, of the symbolic structure, to the subject's dilemma in regard to this identity. In the case of the modern subject, we no longer have the inscription of sexual identity on the body, since it is enough that the subject is marked by symbolic castration in his or her inner self. (St Paul, for example, explains that Christians do not prescribe circumcision, because the subject is already cut in his or her soul.) In modern society the big Other still has power, since socialisation usually proceeds via submission to the symbolic law represented by the paternal authority. By contrast, in contemporary, post-modern society, there has been a radical change in the organisation of the family, which also entails a different relation of the subject towards the symbolic order: the return to the ritual of clitoridectomy as well as other forms of the inscription in the body (even genital mutilations) in some practices of body art is not the answer of the big Other, but the subject's answer to the non-existence of the big Other.

Before dealing with this return to the cut in the body, let me first try to give a psychoanalytic account of clitoridectomy. The ethnic groups that support this practice usually claim that by cutting the female genitals they protect women's honour and thus show respect for them. The cultures that perform clitoridectomy perceive Western cultures as degenerate, since they do not honour women. Here, we have two totally different points of view about what women's honour is: for the Westerners, clitoridectomy is an act that mutilates women and violates human rights, and thus also dishonours women; while for people who embrace clitoridectomy, the absence of this ritual devalues women.

How would psychoanalysis explain this logic of honour and respect for women? Freud dealt with the problem of female shyness, which he linked to the lack, the absence of a phallus in women. By being shy, the woman tries to cover the lack and to avert the gaze from it. However, this shyness has in itself a phallic character. So it can be said that the very lack of the phallic organ in woman results in the phallicisation of her whole body or a special part of the body; and covering up this part of the body has a special seductive effect.

There is no significant difference between women's shyness and their honour: 'The respect for women means that there is something that should not be seen or touched'.[7] Both, shyness and respect, concern the problem of castration, the lack that marks the subject. The insistence on respect is a demand for distance, which also means a special relation that the subject needs to have towards the lack in the other.

7. Jacques-Alain Miller, 'Des semblants dans la relation entre les sexes', in *La Cause freudienne, Revue de psychanalyse* 36/1997, p8.

Freud thought that woman is the subject who actually lacks something, which means that in her case castration was effective. As a result of this, the woman has *Penisneid* (penis envy). In psychoanalytic practice, women's 'deprivation' appears in many forms: as a fantasy of some essential injustice, as inferiority complex, as a feeling of nonlegitimacy, as a lack of consistency or a lack of control, or even as a feeling of body-fragmentation. The Freudian solution for this 'deprivation' was maternity. But for Lacan, women's relation towards the lack is much more complicated: the trouble with femininity is not simply linked to having or not having a penis. The lack concerns the subject's very being - both a man and a woman are marked by lack, but they relate differently to this lack. Woman does not cover up the lack by becoming a mother, since for Lacan the problem of the lack cannot be solved on the level of having but on the level of being. Motherhood is not a solution to woman's lack, since there is no particular object (not even a child) that can ever fill up this lack.

Respect, therefore, has to do with the subject's relation to the lack in the other, which also means that respect is just another name for the anxiety that the subject feels in regard to this lack. The respect for the father, for example, needs to be understood as a way in which the subject tries to avoid the recognition that the father is actually impotent and powerless - that there is nothing behind his authority. Here, we come again to the problem of castration. Lacan understands castration as something that is linked to the radical emptiness of the subject. The subject is nothing by him or herself; he or she gets all authority and power only from outside - from symbolic insignias. When we respect the father, we believe that the insignias have real power and thus we cover up the fact that the father is castrated, which means that he is himself an empty and powerless subject.

Respect is therefore an imaginary relationship that the subject has towards another subject, or, better, towards the symbolic status that this other subject temporarily assumes. (Of course, respect does not concern only our relationship with another subject, but also with the big Other, the symbolic structure as such. Paying respect to our homeland, the flag, or the law are all a subject's imaginary means of taking the big Other as a consistent order.)

The modern idea of human rights is based on the Kantian subject. And, especially in the case of human rights, we usually invoke the idea of respect. Human rights concern some part of the subject's inner freedom, which the community or other people have no right to violate. (And here freedom is also meant as protection of the subject's bodily integrity. From this perspective, those who criticise clitoridectomy rightly point out that this practice contradicts the idea of human rights.) If we take into account the aforementioned thesis that respect means the need for a distance toward the lack that marks the subject, the idea of respect that human rights invokes also assumes another meaning. The inner freedom of the subject that human rights protects concerns nothing other than the lack that marks the subject when he or she becomes a speaking being. And when we respect the bodily integrity of the subject, this actually means that we avert our gaze from the fact that the subject actually does not have a naturally given bodily integrity, since this integrity comes into being only when the subject undergoes symbolic castration. Then the subject will be temporarily entrusted with a certain symbolic power, but the lack that pertains to his or her subjectivity will nonetheless remain.

It is well known that human rights were invented at the time of the Enlightenment when the subject lost his or her roots in nature as well as in his or her tradition.[8] From the time of their conception, many political struggles have gone on to conceive human rights in a non-discriminatory way. Today, the very principle of human rights is that the subject should be respected regardless of gender, age and race. This understanding of respect differs greatly from the idea of respect which is embraced by the defenders of clitoridectomy. The latter can respect only a woman who has been initiated and not just any woman. Similarly, some cultures respect women only when they are covered by a veil.

8. More on human rights in the last chapter of Renata Salecl, *The Spoils of Freedom*, Routledge, London 1994.

Contemporary understanding of human rights also includes the idea of freedom of choice. A widespread liberal stand in regard to clitoridectomy, for example, is that women need to be educated about the torturous nature of this practice: but if an educated woman still insists on being circumcised, then the educators usually powerlessly conclude: 'What can we do, this is her choice'. But education does not simply establish a neutral terrain on which the subject can make a free choice, it also imposes a certain dominant ideology on the subject; as, on another level, the subject's ethnic community imposes its ideology on him or her.

Let us now turn to self-torture in body art. These practices are usually understood as an individual's choice to use his or her body as he or she pleases. However, it is only quite recently that the practices of bodily-mutilation became perceived as art. What a specific culture perceives as art always depends on a certain social consensus and not simply on the idea of a personal choice.[9] Self-mutilation came to be understood as an artistic practice and not simply as the private indulgence of a masochist when a change occurred in the social symbolic organisation.

9. Cf. Jacques Lacan, *Ethics of Psychoanalysis*, Routledge, London 1993.

So what happened in contemporary society to allow the cut in the body to be perceived as art? A generally accepted thesis is that in today's society the way the subject identifies with the law or, better, with the symbolic order has changed. The dissolution of the traditional family structure changed the subject's relation towards authority, which means that the subject nowadays seems to be in a position to choose freely his or her own identity, including even his or her sexual orientation. In the pre-modern society it is the initiation ritual that situates the subject in the social structure and assigns to him or her a special place as well as his or her sexual role. In the modern Enlightenment society, we no longer have initiation rituals, but the authority of the law is still at work in this society. The law is linked to the role of the father; and in taking a position against this law, in other words by distancing himself or herself from it, the modern subject acquires his or her 'freedom'. In contrast, in post-modern society we have a total disbelief in authority and in the power of the symbolic order, the so-called big Other. But this disbelief has not simply resulted in the subject's liberation from the law or other forms of social coercion. The post-modern subject no longer accepts the power of the institutions or society's power to fashion his or her identity, but sometimes believes in the possibility of self-creation, maybe in the form of playing with his or her sexual identity or by making himself or herself out as a work of art. However, in this process of freeing the subject from the big Other, one can also observe the subject's anger and disappointment in regard to the very authority of the big Other. It thus appears as if it were not the subject who recognised that the big Other does not exist and that the authority is just a fraud, but that the big Other has somehow 'betrayed' the subject. The father's authority, for example, revealed itself only as a mask of his impotence, the social rituals in institutions appeared more and more as a farce. However, this apparent liberation of the subject from authority can also be understood as a 'forced' choice that the subject had to make when he or she acknowledged the impotence of the authority.

What does this disbelief in the big Other mean? We always knew that the big Other is just a fiction and that people somehow pretend when they follow state, religious, or family rituals. Most of the time we believe only that someone else believes in these rituals, which is why we follow them in order to avoid offending the others. This belief in the belief of the others is well exemplified in the parents' pretence that they are playing Santa Claus because children believe in it. But when children find out that Santa Claus is just a fiction, they go on pretending to believe in it, so that they will not offend their parents, who still think that children believe in Santa Claus. What we have today is precisely the disbelief in the fiction of the big Other. The logic of this disbelief is exemplified in the well-known anecdote from the Marx brothers. When Groucho Marx was once caught in an obvious lie, his response was: 'Whom do you believe - my words or your eyes?' The belief in the big Other is the belief in words, even when they contradict one's own eyes. What we have today is therefore precisely a mistrust in mere words (i.e. in the symbolic fiction). People want to see what is behind the fiction.

But the encounter with what is behind the fiction can be most traumatic for the subject. An example of the fictional character of the Big Other are the rules of politeness in speech. When we meet someone, we usually say, 'How nice to see you.', even if we actually think, 'Drop dead, I really hate you.' If we stop using the polite words, we do not achieve a simple liberation from the fictional character of politeness, but encounter violence, which radically disrupts the social bonds.

Lacan's famous saying is that what is excluded from the symbolic returns in the real. As an example of this return in the real, Lacan takes psychotics. They are the ones who do not identify with the fiction of the symbolic order, but deal with the real. A psychotic, for example, does not believe in the fictional character of God, but has direct contact with God: he hears voices of God, God's eyes are constantly pursuing him.

On another level, today's disbelief in the fictional character of the father's authority caused a return of the father as real - the father who is a harasser, abuses children, has insatiable sexual desires, i.e. a father who very much resembles the character of the Freudian father of the primal horde, who was the possessor of all women and denied his sons access to *jouissance*.

The disbelief in the symbolic fiction and the search for the real thing was also obvious at the time of the tragic death of Princess Diana. Public polls show that the majority of British people think that the monarchy is a relic of the past - an archaic institution that needs to be either abolished or radically changed. The public no longer believe in the fictional character of the kingdom; however, at the time of Diana's funeral, people were terribly upset that the queen did not show enough emotion.They wanted the queen to show physical signs of sorrow, to address the nation and to hang the flag in front of the Royal Palace at half-mast. On the one hand, therefore, we have the rejection of the fiction of the monarchy, but, on the other hand, we have a desperate appeal that the fiction cease to be a fiction and that people see what is behind it.

The public identification with Diana also shows the changes that have come about in the way the public identifies with its idols. In the past, the idols were supposed to be active, they were perceived as having abilities they did not have – like bravery and intelligence. But Diana was a passive idol for the people. Her attitude greatly resembled that of ordinary people who complain about the institution but are actually a part of it, who like to help others, but do not sacrifice their own well-being. If in the past people tended to identify with an idol who was not like them, in the case of Diana they identified with someone who was exactly like them.

One of the ways in which the subject today deals with the absence of the big Other is the turn to narcissistic self-admiration. The lack of identification with some ego ideal (a symbolic role or authority-ideal) resulted in the subject's identification with some imaginary role (i.e. ideal ego) in which the subject finds himself or herself likeable. This narcissistic search for the perfect image results in the subject's obsession with changing his or her body with the help of excessive dieting, exercise and plastic surgery. Another aspect of the subject's concern with the non-existence of the big Other is discernible in the contemporary phenomena of the so-called 'culture of complaint'. Western societies nowadays brim over with people's complaints about all kinds of injustices in their private and public lives: people search for the culprits who deprived them of their enjoyment, wealth, respect, etc. The disbelief in the power of the big Other resulted in the belief that there are various small others (institutions and authorities in the subject's immediate environment) who are guilty of causing the troubles in the people's lives. And the legal as well as financial compensation that the subjects seek is supposed to reinstall the lost equilibrium at least for a moment.

Another reflection of today's disbelief in the big Other is displayed in the practices of body art. Isn't this inscription upon the body an attempt by the subject to deal with the absence of the big Other? Has the contemporary subject taken initiation into his or her own hands?

A documentary entitled *Sick: The Life and Death of Bob Flanagan, Supermasochist* (Kirby Dick, 1996) deals with the theme of masochism and art. The film depicts the performance artist Bob Flanagan, who enjoys masochistic rituals in which, with the help of his mistress - his wife - he cuts his skin, mutilates his genitals, etc. It is crucial that the artist suffers an incurable illness, cystic fibrosis, which makes him unable to breathe without an iron lung. The film is a collage of the artist's performances, most of which were presented in art galleries. The end of the film also records the artist's death and his corpse being photographed by his devoted wife. The most shocking scene includes the act of genital self-mutilation, in which the artist nails his penis onto a wooden board. While he removes the nails, the blood squirts onto the camera. (This scene is hard to watch - many of the male observers identify so strongly with the painful ritual that they scream in panic, some even leave the room).

Now, how can one understand artistic enjoyment in masochistic practices? First, it must be pointed out that masochism and sadism never go hand in hand. As Gilles Deleuze said, a masochist and a sadist do not

10. Cf. Gilles Deleuze, *Masochism: Coldness and Cruelty*, Zone Books, New York 1991.

form a couple.[10] A sadist takes himself as an executor of some higher will, an ideal. He takes himself just as a mere object through whom this ideal enjoyed. And the sadist tortures the victims because he is executing the desire of this higher will. On the contrary, the masochist searches for a torturer whom the masochist him/herself will educate and instruct. In the masochist situation, the victim speaks through the torturer: it is not the torturer who invents the forms of punishment; the inventor is the victim himself.

The torturer is usually a woman who takes on the role of the severe, cold mother. It is essential for the masochist to establish a contract with the torturer that describes in detail the conditions of the torture. The masochist is thus not simply tied by chains but by the power of the contract through which he invests in the torturer the symbolic power of the law. The torturer acts like a cruel mother who humiliates the father figure, who is incarnated in the victim himself. The masochist therefore invests the law in his mother - in the very object of incestuous enjoyment - and by doing so excludes the father from the symbolic. Here, one again needs to invoke the familiar Lacanian thesis that what is excluded from the symbolic returns in the real. In the case of the masochist, the excluded father returns in the guise of the masochist himself, since the masochist takes on the role of the weak, humiliated father who needs to be punished.

For the masochist, castration has not been completed, which means that the symbolic law did not become fully operative. This is why the masochist, in his torturous ritual, caricatures castration and tries to make the law operative through the contract with his mistress. The subject (i.e. the hysteric or the obsessional) for whom the castration was effective is always unsatisfied with the ways he or she tries to fill up the lack: the subject thus complains about the law that supposedly prevents his or her enjoyment; however, the subject finds a special enjoyment in this very dissatisfaction. But the masochist finds enjoyment in punishment imposed by the law that he himself establishes. Since he lacks the symbolic prohibition, the masochist becomes an executioner for himself.

How can one therefore understand the turn to perversion in contemporary art? My point is not that the use of the body in art presents some kind of generalised perversion of our society. If a masochist castrating himself on the stage might be clinically a pervert, this is not the case for the majority of artists who use their bodies in art work. Similarly, one cannot universally take body piercing and tattooing as clinical forms of perversion. Most of the people who in one way or another mark their bodies would much more fall into the clinical category of neurosis than perversion; their acts are an imitation of perversion and not an actual perversion. But, what is the difference between the perverts and the neurotics who just imitate perversion? Both of them stage some kind of drama when they paint or mutilate their bodies. The perverts stage this drama in order to deny castration: via their masochistic ritual, they mock castration, while at the same time this very staging is also an attempt to find a law which would complete castration. In the case of the perverts, castration is thus first denied, then it is mockingly staged as an outside event, which does not touch the subject in their inner beings, but behind this is a failed attempt to make castration operative again. The neurotics, on the contrary, stage perverse rituals in order to come to terms with the lack that has been introduced by castration. Since for the neurotics castration was effective, they create a fantasy scenario to cover up the lack, which is the result of castration; i.e. they try to show how they are not essentially marked by the law, since they can openly play with the castration rituals on the stage.

WHAT IS BEHIND THE IMAGINARY SIMULACRA?

The fact that subjects face a radical change in the belief in the big Other or that they know very well that the big Other actually does not exist, does not mean that the symbolic structure is not operative. Subjects are still very much marked by the symbolic prohibition, although they might no longer identify with the authorities who are supposed to be bearers of this prohibition.

The symbolic structure today appears to be more and more replaced by imaginary simulacra, with which the subjects identify. Life seems like a computer game in which the subject can play with his or her identity, randomly follow fashion rituals, has no strong national or religious beliefs, etc. But the fact that life appears as a screen on which everything is changeable has resulted in a desperate search for the real behind the fiction. The cut in the body thus appears as an escape from the imaginary simulacra that dominate our society.

Young people usually explain their obsession with tattooing and body piercing as ways to escape the pressures of the dominant fashion industry. The media constantly bombard them with images of beauty, and one of the ways to escape this enforced identification is to take a real action - to mark the body in a way that cannot be changed.

In recent years, social theory has widely discussed the issue of identity, which appeared not only as something socially constructed, but also as something multiform and changeable. The discussions on performativity and sexual difference also created the impression that the subject can play with his or her sexual identity. The paradox of the contemporary cuts in the body is that, at the same time, they seem to be a realisation of these theoretical beliefs and a reaction against them. Making a cut in the body does not mean that the subject is merely playing with his or her identity; by irreversibly marking the body, the subject also protests against the ideology that makes everything changeable. The body thus appears as the ultimate point of the subject's identity. Since the subject does not want to simply play with the imaginary simulacra presented by the dominant fashion ideologies, he or she tries to find in the body the site of the real.

For the group of artists united in the project Body Radicals, the body is today the only remaining realm over which an individual has retained power.[11]

> Unmediated, direct access to the inner being through the artist's own blood or the feeling of pain opens up almost Artaud-like perspectives. What is happening is literal. There is no simulation. The symbolic field of the art is collapsing, bodies become black holes into which symbolic significance implodes.[12]

The latter thesis is a very pretentious one, since the Body Radicals still call themselves artists and their artworks are usually presented in art galleries: they may not be accepted by the mainstream art community, but they nonetheless very much want to be recognised in the alternative spaces of the 'symbolic field of art'. This demand for social recognition already proves that in the new forms of body art, we are not dealing with some kind of generalised psychosis or with the total collapse of the symbolic order. However, the use of the body in contemporary art does deal with today's subject's problem in searching for something real in the form of his or her body.

Although the artists united in the Body Radicals use their bodies in very different ways in their artworks, one can find some similarities between them. For the purpose of my analysis here, I will focus only on the work of Orlan and Stelarc.

Orlan's art consist primarily of multiple plastic surgery operations on her face, which are recorded and, with the commentary of her voice, presented in art galleries.[13] When Orlan provides theory about her art, her primary point is that she uses her body as a site of public debate. Her art challenges the standards of beauty, it explores the variety of body-images that are outside the norms and dictates of the dominant ideology. When she plays with the images of femininity, her intention is to practice a transsexuality of woman to woman, which, however, does not follow the usual transsexual desire to have a defined and definite identity. Orlan also claims that, with the help of surgery, one can bring the internal image closer to the external one; she therefore does not need to identify with the image that nature had given her. With the help of surgery, her body is transformed into language ('flesh becomes word'). Orlan also plans to be mummified after her death and placed in an art gallery.

Orlan therefore tries to play with multiple identities, make her body a changeable work of art, and by doing so achieve some kind of immortality. She takes her work as a self-portrait, which is presented as an inscription in the flesh made with the help of the new technologies. Orlan's intention is to impose control not only over her naturally given body image, but also to manipulate the new technologies (like plastic surgery) and use them against the ideals of the dominant ideology.

When Orlan objects to the idea that she is performing some kind of self-mutilation, she comes very close to the defenders of clitoridectomy.

11. The group Body Radical includes artists like Orlan, Ron Athey, Stelarc, Franko B and Annie Sprinkle. While they all use their own bodies as their artistic means of expression, their art and the explanations they give for it differ signifficantly.

12. Cf. Body Radicals home page on the Internet.

13. For an extensive analysis of Orlan's art, see also Parveen Adams, *Emptiness of the Image*, Routledge, London 1996.

Orlan claims that her body transformation augments her power and does not diminish it. Similarly, the defenders of clitoridectomy say that the ritual of circumcision actually gives women power they did not have before initiation. And when Orlan says that she transforms her body into language, she caricatures initiation rituals, which in their own ways also mark the body with language.[14]

If, in the pre-modern type of society, initiation has a very specific role in assigning the subject's sexual identity and in imposing a mark of social prohibition onto the body, one cannot say that, in post-modern society, initiation rituals still play the same role. The insistence on clitoridectomy in the case of some of the African immigrants in the West or among some very developed African countries, for example, can be understood as a specific answer to the deadlocks of contemporary society. The class antagonisms of post-industrial society, the globalisation of capital, the erosion of tradition, all brought the subjects to the point of searching for some stable forms of identity. The African immigrants may still respect their grandmothers enough to allow them to perform the act of initiation, while they have an utter mistrust of other authorities in the society they live in. Here, we also have the case of disbelief in the fiction of the big Other in contemporary society; thus the insistence on old rituals of initiation must be understood as an answer to this disbelief, i.e. as an attempt to find in the body a place of some stable identity.

When the body artists caricature initiation rituals or play with the new forms of tribalism, they are trying to challenge precisely the idea of stable identity, while they nonetheless try to find in the body some piece of the real. In their own way, the body artists are also dealing with the deadlocks of today's highly individualised society: with their cuts in the body, they challenge the idea that the body can give the subject the basis for an identity. So they are actually searching for what is supposed to be behind the body. If the body is just a playground for various identities, what is real here?

For Orlan, the final, unchangeable thing becomes her voice. With the help of her voice, Orlan tries to provide explanations for her art: she thus reads from theoretical texts as her face is cut and comments on the procedure of her surgery. But behind this search for meaning for her changeable face, her voice remains a constant. Orlan's voice is the drive, i.e. the real, that stays the same throughout her performances. Plastic surgery of Orlan's face is painful to watch; for observers it is not only shocking to see Orlan's skin being detached from her face, but also to hear her monotonous voice reciting texts during her surgery. If Orlan were to be quiet, the observers might be able to pretend they were seeing a dead-like, deeply anaesthesticised person being cut on the stage. In this case, the shock for the observers would not be so very different than watching horror movies: when one does not want to see a scary scene in the film, one simply closes one's eyes. Of course, in horror movies one still hears the music and the screams, but

14. Artists Ron Athey and Franko B also caricature various forms of initiation rituals in their performances, in which they primarily play with blood, shit and other bodily discharges.

the voice without the picture is less frightening, since the voice loses power when it is not accompanied by the picture. But in the case of Orlan, it is the voice that is the real site of horror. If one only listens to her voice and keeps one's eyes shut, one does not get relief, since Orlan's voice is the sign of deadliness and of life at the same time. As such, the voice is a death drive that always undermines the subject's identity. Orlan tries to show with her art how she can play with her identity, but her voice nonetheless remains the real, what in her is more than herself.

Some other artists are trying to find a piece of the real beyond the skin with the help of computer technology and in this endeavour they also try to give up on the human voice and replace it with computerised sound. The Australian artist Stelarc, for example, questions the role of the body in the post-industrial age. His thesis is that, with the new developments in technology, the body became obsolete, since it is biologically ill-equipped for the technological level of contemporary society. Stelarc wants to create some kind of new meta-body, which first needs to pacify and anaesthetise the existing body; i.e., with the help of genetic technology, the organs become replaceable, the skin more durable, the body starts acting without expectation, it produces movements without memory, has no desires, etc. In this way, the self can be placed beyond the skin and put in direct contact itself with the virtual world. The body becomes a phantom body, which plays with its images and connects itself with the immortal machinery. Reproduction is substituted by redesigning and sexual intercourse is replaced with the interface between the subject and the machine. We thus no longer have to deal with birth or death: Stelarc wants to make life eternal. In the end, this life would be nothing but a symbolic fiction, a fiction that would eliminate the very trauma of the unsymbolisable real. As such, life would cease to be life, too.

Both interventions in the body - clitoridectomy and some practices of body art - pose numerous questions about the subject in the post-modern world. Some see the main problem of contemporary society in the total erosion of the symbolic network, which results in some kind of generalised perversion or even psychosis. Others take the dissolution of the patriarchal system of social authorities as a possibility for subjects to form their own identities without submitting themselves to the imposed normative ideals. But the changed relation of the subject to the symbolic order in contemporary society should neither be taken as a total catastrophe nor as an opening up of unlimited possibilities of freedom. The disbelief in the big Other has, on the one hand, incited people's return to such cruel initiation rituals as clitoridectomy, and, on the other hand, it has instigated the self-imposed cuts in body art. But is this the only way to respond to the fact that the big Other does not exists? Aren't there other ways of dealing with the inconsistency of the symbolic order?

Perversion in public places

Juliet Flower MacCannell

If violence is in the air these days it no longer seems what it once was, an expression of uncontrollable passions - political and personal. Despite the advent of a much-touted post-war world for the principal nations of the northern hemisphere (with some notable exceptions among the 'third world' type nations of Eastern Europe where an 'irrational' violence is said to linger) public attention to interpersonal modes of violence has begun to hit the front pages on a regular basis.

The violence-in-the news has a formal air - systematic, controlled, even practised within limits. To invoke Lacan's famous sentence about de Sade, it has 'a tone of reason.' Its effect is, nonetheless, to confound the Law.

PERVERSION A LA MODE

A mere fifteen years ago when the media reported on a respectable grammar school teacher in a mid-sized northern California city who, after school, was a highly paid dominatrix ('Ms Brandy'), the tone was that of shock, though a titillated shock. As the police relayed descriptions of the fully outfitted dungeon beneath the teacher/dominatrix's suburban tract house and revealed her clientèle to be members of the local Chamber of Commerce, they also expressed a certain befuddlement: could they charge her with any crime? She was, after all, not selling *sex*, but *punishment* to her 'johns.' And her johns were equally difficult to imagine prosecuting: for how could a masochist be punished by the forces of law and order, since any punishment would have to take the form of the very punishment he was being punished for? More recently, episodes of the popular television series *NYPD Blue* and *Nash Bridges* have featured police detectives unable to figure out whether the people they find tied up and handcuffed are robbery and murder victims, or simply masochists who succumbed to their own demands.

Somewhat greater uneasiness attended the underground rumours of perverse behaviours involving the highest officials in the United States (or their closest friends). The mistress (now deceased) of a well-known business magnate alleged she had documented sadomasochistic acts with public figures (including some in the White House) on videotapes. Some, purporting to have viewed them, released titillating details. With these allegations by Vicki Morgan sadomasochism came out of the dungeon for all of America: perversion threatened to go public on a national scale. (Even the youngest children at the time could hardly fail to escape awareness of and curiosity about the sensationally half-revealed images;

one very small boy of my acquaintance took to calling Vicki Morgan 'Puss in Boots.')

Hypothetically, at least, perversion as an official way of life had become conceivable to middle America. The Reagan administration's swift reaction - a vigorous and successful effort to countervail (or to veil) the *soupçon* of perversion - was comforting, to be sure. Still, something had changed forever the American psyche.

Any tone of puzzled shock has long since disappeared from our media accounts of perverse behavioural styles. Today, it is not *perversion*, but the hint of a once-standard adulterous or *heterosexual* liaison that is deemed 'scandalous.' Several top US military officers have resigned while others have been forced to step aside on being confronted with evidence they have had adulterous or extra-marital affairs. The presidency itself is currently considered 'threatened' by just such an allegation.[1]

Meanwhile, a Sadism Cafe, *La Nouvelle Justine,* has opened in Manhattan, where light spankings are served up by waitresses along with meals. 'S&M is a big hit South of Market' in San Francisco, where 'couple after couple, clad in black leather, silver chains, or barely anything, are taking turns whipping, slapping, and pinching each other all for the benefit of the crowd of drooling tourists, articulated voyeurs and S&M practitioners'. Clubs like 'Bondage a Go Go' and sex toy stores like 'Stormy Leather' report that 'a good chunk of our business is heterosexual, middle-aged couples'.[2] At a birthday party thrown in May 1997 for a political consultant who successfully managed the vote for a new city stadium, the guests, (including leading San Francisco politicians), were entertained with a sadomasochistic act featuring a dominatrix who 'carved a pentagram on a man's back, urinated on him, and sodomised him with a Jack Daniels bottle'.[3] 'Gothic' societies have formed around adopting sadomasochistic paraphernalia.

Lest we too quickly conclude New York and San Francisco are simply the new Sodom and Gomorra, let us note that academic lesbian sado-masochism is now considered a fully legitimate form of feminism with high ethical standards inspired in part by Gilles Deleuze's influential 1967 book, *Coldness and Cruelty*.[4] Deleuze called for a new ethics in which women would conscientiously give up their traditional 'masochism' and 'play at sadism' to afford men an opportunity to change their ways, get out of their traditional sadism, and adopt a new masochism.

Such suggestions as Deleuze's have been amply implemented in the lesbian sado-masochist world, where 'sadism is a pleasure in mastery and not a perversion . . . an active life-preserving aggressivity,' that aims 'to assert control over power and violence in sexuality by using it'. It is 'potentially liberatory, harnessed and theatricalised for greater sexual pleasure and greater understanding of that pleasure'.[5] Self-limited by mutual consent, without having to pass through the unascertainable desire of the Other (Lacan's 'castration'), full enjoyment unhampered by arbitrary power: how, indeed, could anyone demur from this utopian picture of

1. The Pentagon's new sex policy forced Gen. John Ralston, 'a confessed adulterer . . . a candidate for chairman of the Joint Chiefs of Staff . . . to withdraw his name,' *San Francisco Chronicle/Examiner*, 8 June 1997, pA1.

2. Julie Hinds, 'S&M is a big Hit in SoMa' *San Francisco Chronicle*, 8 June 1997, pA1

3. *Ibid.*

4. Gilles Deleuze *Coldness and Cruelty,* Zone Books, New York 1991.

5. Karin M. Cope, 'Sado-Masochism', in E. Wright (ed), *Feminism and Psychoanalysis: a Critical Dictionary*, Basil Blackwell, Oxford 1992, p388.

pleasure-filled existence?

The current publicity surrounding perverse behavioural styles may index the extending of this new ethic. Or it may merely be a fad. To determine its nature requires investigating the degree to which perversion is the new ethic in our contemporary politics, economies and psyches. We would still need to decide, though, whether an increasingly familiar phenomenological 'sadism' and 'masochist violence,' glamorised in the media, have any lingering connections to a perverse *unconscious* not under rational control.

The interplay between public life and the structures of perversion - the disavowal of the law and its violation, the staging of violence with alternately submissive and dominant partners - clearly merits exploration because it seems to mirror a process that can no longer easily be termed either conscious or unconscious. Perverse 'sadistic violence' practised on a willing 'victim' - is it violent or not? Can we distinguish 'playing at' sadomasochistic violence from an allegedly 'true' sadomasochistic pervert's acts, whose cool and reasoned cruelty poses so important a challenge to the law?

Since the pervert always requires a theatre, we might take a scenic route into perversion and its connection to the form of social relations today.

Two different scenes of instruction follow.

SCENE I. IN THE LACANIAN CLASSROOM: PARANOID VIOLENCE

The Subject-Object Dialectic in the Unconscious Recently, I began teaching a course on treating psychosis at a Lacanian School. I began by emphasising that unconscious psychic structures may exist without being manifested. As I was telling my students (many of whom work with psychotics and the mentally ill homeless) that someone may have a psychotic unconscious and yet function perfectly and even very effectively within society for quite some time, the class became visibly disturbed, though obviously incredulous.[6]

I persisted in my theoretical exposition, pointing out that, after all, Schreber had been functioning so well just before he became ill that he was about to assume a role equivalent to Chief Justice of the Supreme Court. The manifestation of his delusion showed he had fundamentally and unconsciously foreclosed believing in the law. Yet here he was, about to become one of its most prominent public representatives. For Schreber, for the paranoiac, the law - the beliefs we hold in common, the fictions we collaboratively produce, the stories we tell each other to support and sustain our mutual co-existence against the unpredictable Other - were null. The inevitable, irreparable collision between the positive existence of the law and his own inner constructions, built on a void where the symbolic law should have been, induced Schreber's breakdown.

What is this symbolic 'law' ('castration') Schreber foreclosed? Symbolic law is what enables mutual co-existence: it is a partition that intervenes

6. Willy Apollon, Danielle Bergeron, and Lucie Cantin, *Traiter la psychose*, GIFRIC, Quebec 1990, p17.

between the pair ego/other. To the paranoid unconscious, the ego/other pair is constructed out of a dialectic of self and other as-mutual-objects of envy and competition - mutually destructive objects:

> [T]his dialectic always carries the possibility that I may be called upon to annul the other, for one simple reason. The beginning of this dialectic being my alienation in the other, there is a moment at which I can be put into the position of being annulled myself because the other doesn't agree. The dialectic of the unconscious always implies struggle, the impossibility of coexistence with the other, as one of its possibilities.[7]

7. Jacques Lacan, *Seminar III: The Psychoses*, tr. R. Grigg, W. W. Norton & Company, New York and London 1993, pp39-40.

The paranoiac cannot even be said to have a subject, so pronounced is his avoidance of the Other. (Lacan puns that the 'S' of his diagram is replaced by *Es* - the German 'It' in the paranoid unconscious.) By contrast, 'normal neurotics' who unconsciously grant that the law protects them by means of a painful but bearable separation of subject from object, have a modicum of unfounded faith that peaceful co-existence is possible within the law. They can suffer the presence of an other, however unknowable. Lacan put it this way:

> The distinction between the Other with a big O, that is, the Other insofar as it's not known, and the other with a small o, that is, the other who is me, the source of all knowledge, is fundamental. It's in the gap, it's in the angle opened up between these two relations, that the entire dialectic of delusion has to be situated.[8]

8. *Ibid*., p40.

In the neurotic unconscious, subject and other are mutual question marks: what does s/he want? In the psychotic unconscious, voided where the law should be, the infinitely unknowable Other who 'causes' us as subjects is unendurable. Only the other, me-as-other, who contains/envies the object (of enjoyment), exists.

The paranoiac, because he *knows* exactly what the other is, has or wants - himself-as-object - finds the concept of the Other intolerable. He *knows* that in the Real, there is no law, no shelter, no shield against the lethal other, small o.

Schreber sees in the mirror both a Supreme Court Judge, a representative of the law, and his murderous rival. He disguises himself to himself by wearing women's jewels and finery whenever he looks in the mirror - to deceive the persecutory other? His breakdown is inevitable. Yet, up to the crisis, he had been able to work, and work well, sustained by means of an inner construction of his own devising until it gave way. After the crisis, he repairs the original elaborate delusion that had held him together, his self-made system, and then needs to publish it to save the whole world from the unchecked violence he *knows* to be the essence of the other.

As I went over these points to the psychoanalysts in training, I noticed them becoming uniformly anxious, as each turned increasingly inward to wonder about their own unconscious structure.

SCENE II. IN THE UNIVERSITY CLASSROOM: PERVERSE VIOLENCE

The Subject As Object. By contrast, my literature graduate students at the University of California responded completely differently from the psychoanalysts in training when I began presenting my proposals on perversion. Where the latter had become unnerved at the suggestion that psychosis was a structure that can exist without overt manifestation in those whose behaviour appears 'normal,' the literature students in my seminar 'On Perversion' started out by eagerly identifying themselves with and as perverts: 'Perverts are good, right?' one student declared early in the class. As they expressed their earnest feeling that perversion was about an *agency* that 'straight' life denied them; I could see the challenge before me. Not only did they initially discount the unconscious, the thought of its independent agency was foreign to them.

I gently began examining perversion as an unconscious structure that was neither good nor bad, nor fundamentally tied to homosexuality (which is a question of object-choice by the ego, and a matter of indifference to psychoanalysis: homosexuals come in the same varieties as heterosexuals - neurotic, psychotic and perverse). In time, the students' responses to my lectures on hysteria, sexual difference and the work of Lacan, Deleuze, and André on perversion, suggested to me that my listeners were not nearly as perverse as they might have liked.

In this second classroom scene, the complications of analysing the perverse came to the fore. Apart from some clinical books (which often insufficiently distinguish perversion from homosexuality), we have little to go on to determine the relation of sadism to violence. Little, that is, besides the fictional writings of de Sade.

Lacan did his foundational work on perversion by setting out from Sade's work, and his insights have been convincingly updated by Serge André.[9] From them we learn that the sadist, like the psychotic, does not accept the law. But, unlike the psychotic, the basis for the pervert's rejection is less unbelief than a *reasoned* conclusion. His scepticism stems from 'knowing' that 'the form of the law is its only substance'.[10] The sadist wants to demonstrate the insubstantiality of the law - to discount, pre-empt, humiliate and expose the law as merely formal. Sadism acknowledges the law and dispenses with the need for it in one stroke.[11]

The pervert Dolmancé appears in Sade's stage-lit *Philosophy in the Bedroom* as a paragon of rationality. Controlled to the point of apathy, he demonstrates why taking the law as merely formal is most consequential: it allows a sheer mutuality, among a set of equals, to take the place of, and to take over for, any centralised authority over enjoyment. As the impresario at the advent and enactment of this purely formal law, Dolmancé's role is to demystify that Other who traditionally brings a partitioning law in its wake - God and the Woman. The atheist Dolmancé ably demonstrates that 'woman,' like the God he provokes, is reducible to a measurable dimension:

9. The algorithm of Sade's fantasy: Lacan, 'Kant avec Sade' tr. J. Swenson, *October 51*, 1989 is re-analysed brilliantly by Serge André, *L'Imposture perverse*, Seuil, Paris 1993, pp22-31.

10. Lacan, *op. cit.*, p59. Lacan speaks of Kant, but the remark contextualises his reading of Sade.

11. 'He' is generic: André studies two lesbians, Rose (a hysteric) and Violette (a pervert), pp89-144, and 221-22. Violette affirms and denies castration, declaring that s/he *has* the phallus *and* that s/he *is* the phallus.

the capacity to enjoy the other. She holds no mystery: her desire is fully plumbed. The girlish 'victim' Eugénie instantly drops her modesty and abandons her virginity in favour of equal participation with her fellow bedroom occupants in the *Philosophie*, plunging with zest into the general *will-to-jouissance*, 'the V'*[Volonté]* 'that dominates the whole affair,' Lacan calls it.[12] Dolmancé proposes *will-to-jouissance* as a new 'social' contract (Deleuze would say 'institution') to replace all prior forms of social relation. He induces rather than seduces the participants with it. (Seduction means giving one's word, and words for the pervert are strictly logical demonstrations correlated with *acts*.[13])

12. Lacan, *op. cit.*, p63.

13. Deleuze, *op. cit.*, p25.

Will-to-jouissance: What does this mean for the Sadean character? It mimes the unfathomable desire of the 'Other' that founds social reciprocity, but it is so radically nuanced toward *knowledge* as to revolutionise the social relation itself. It 'solves' the mystery of desire; it is a collaborative construction in which everyone present *knowingly* participates. Its 'natural law' is of a *jouissance* that poses no limits. Indeed, immersed in the *will-to-enjoyment* immanent in the acts ordered up by Dolmancé, not one participant in the scene gainsays their self-evident collective power to achieve unlimited enjoyment for all. Nor, since their pain is always ultimately converted to pleasure, can any one believe in the ultimate violence - death at the hand of the other. (Nor in castration - for Freud, fear of death and of castration are the same.)

The subject-object dialectic, so overwhelming to the paranoiac, is effectively declared null and void by Sade's mouthpiece. The partner of the pervert will consecutively *be* the fully enjoying subject and the fully enjoyable object: 'I have the right to enjoy your body and you have the right to enjoy mine'. All can enjoy all at no cost to one or the other. The object, for the pervert, will *replace* the rival other entirely by the object of enjoyment he stands for. This object will become a fetish penetrated with enjoyment, its place held alternately by both self and other.

The sadist looks to the other, then, not as a *semblable*, but as an unequal, destined to be more himself than himself. This 'dominant' other will be, however, someone with whom the 'submitted' partner will exchange places. No matter how monstrous the dominant, the 'submissive' sadist-as-object has the ultimate right to trade places and to become himself the subject of enjoyment.

But can he? By analysing the fantasy and the placement of the object in its scene, Lacan gave us access to the pervert's *unconscious* . There, the story is different. In the fantasy underlying Dolmancé's sadistic script, the full, 'raw' subject of enjoyment inflates to the dimensions of that *sur-homme* designated by André's perverse Violette - the One beyond gender who can enjoy so much more than mere men and women can.[14] The other (small o), proportionally diminished, is cut down to the dimensions of the (small) object a. The fantasy's secret wish, which *precludes* the 'even trade' Dolmancé promises, is the wish to *remain forever a mere object.* 'Sade rejects the pain of

14. Violette identifies with neither woman nor man - both are miserably castrated - but with *'le plus que masculine'*: *'Violette ne se présente pas comme un homme, mais comme un sur-homme'*, S. André, *op. cit.*, p125.

existing into the Other, but without seeing that by this slant he himself changes into an "eternal object"'.[15] Why? Only as fully petrified, apathetic, *object* can he escape the fate of all subjects - to be subject to death, to pain, to the invasive violence of the other. Sade's fantasy denies his own torture at the hands of Madame de Montreuil as much as it claims his full enjoyment.

15. Lacan, *op. cit.*, p65.

The pervert, trumpeting an entirely new basis on which ego and other, subject and object can be bonded, unconsciously reveals that his dream is only an unconscious desire, a way of making up for the fact that he is already the object of the Other's invasive *jouissance*. His attempt to convert himself from object of the other's abuse to object/subject of enjoyment, so desperate, has created great sympathy for the persecuted Sade.

To bring out the unconscious of the pervert more, Lacan employed structural terms (subject/object) and conspicuously political imagery. They help distinguish between two unconsciouses - paranoid and perverse. They, in turn, contrast with the hysteric's. Structurally, in the paranoiac unconscious, the object remains a principal player. The paranoiac looks in the mirror and sees the object that torments him - himself. He *is* the other, his reflected rival who is also the object of his envy. Likewise for the pervert, but with a crucial difference: the object *replaces* the subject. For the hysteric, jouissance, the *object* of unconscious desire, is always (happily) 'lost' to the veiling symptom.

Lacan's political fables illustrate this point about the perverse unconscious another way. For Lacan, the paranoid unconscious is a parable of a master and a slave, whose dialectic's final stakes are the death of the subject or its object.[16] Taking his cue from Sade's formally 'Republican' pamphlet in *Philosophie dans le boudoir*, Lacan places the object of the perverse unconscious into a scenario of the 'Rights of Man'. These 'Rights' are supposed to supplant the master-slave dialectic by a simple declaration: no one may henceforth be the property of another; the power of life and death over another is banned. Who could blame an enlightened and liberated bourgeoisie for concluding that suspending the master's right to life or death over his slave puts an end to arbitrary actual violence and inaugurates the reign of 'Perpetual peace'? Such an inmixing of the political does not, however, necessarily follow from the philosophical dream of Sade. (Lacan sceptically remarks that despite the pervert's rhetoric of liberation from the Master - death or castration - he remains 'a serf of pleasure.')

16. 'The master-slave dialectic reappears here', *Seminar III*, p40.

For in the quadripartite structure of the unconscious, a subject-object (or ego/other) dialectic is crossed by a subject-Other relation. What the pervert unconsciously denies is less the purchase of formal law than the power of the entire field of play of Other to touch him. That field is the site of death, pain: the field of castration, the real threat that flesh might be cut, blood might really flow. The pervert instinctively refuses all but stage blood.

Sadism's essential hallmark is that violence is only a dramatic device, it does not credit the existence of the Real Thing. Unconsciously it remains in the grip of that Thing lurking just behind the object.

THE PERVERSE STRUCTURE *AND* REAL VIOLENCE

The violence of and by the big O Other is called 'castration' by Lacan and *law-creating violence* by Walter Benjamin. It is the law of society, the dimension linking Subject to Other, as distinct from the twisted tie bonding ego to object.

This law the pervert fundamentally disavows. Sade's writing, to be sure, touts the 'Law,' but of Nature, not *the Law* in the way we understand it from Rousseau, Hegel, and Marx on down to Benjamin and Lacan. Klossowski showed Sade's as a law of pleasure, a Natural Law of creation and destruction rendered so extreme as to vitiate the very category of the subject. Law that breaks with this Natural Law, founding itself as a *pure* violence, is the province of the wholly Other. It makes the subject.

For Lacan, who interpreted the origins of Judaeo-Christianity this way, law-creating violence is the *law of language* that accompanies and founds all human society.[17] Origin and by-product of speech, the Deity - God's law - is the most common way of representing the alterity and founding violence of what institutes society.[18] But even the atheistic Enlightenment found Rousseau offering the law of the stranger in the *Social Contract* as a substitute: the law can never come from within a group; its lawgiver *must always be* a foreigner to the society instituted.

Figured as a transcendent alterity - God, Society, the State - and apprehended as a violent force intervening between you and your fellows, law-creating violence is one way of characterising the violence language has done to one's nature. Castration. The violence Lacan portrays in *Television* as 'carving out' a body from a mass of animal substance.[19] That this separating, shattering violence is also the very same as that law we discussed earlier, the law of Partition (paternal metaphor) which shelters us from the other's murderous intentions cannot be iterated often enough. Like partition, the violence of the law is no mere dramatic effect, no *deus ex machina*. It never shows itself. God's justice, in Benjamin's *Critique of Violence*, has no phenomenality.

BLOOD RITUALS

How, then, can psychoanalysis respond to contemporary staging of violence?

One of the most publicised aspects of 'modern primitives' is the flagrant and extreme piercing, scarifications, brandings and corseting now commonplace among working- and middle-class youths in every major urban environment, with countless imitators in small towns and peasant settings everywhere. Even the rich and famous are caught up in it. Some are rituals legible as secondary effects of the law; others are not.

It seems that blood must be spilled. But spilled within in a perverse scenario

17. *Introduction to the Names of the Father Seminar*, tr. J. Mehlman, in *Television*, tr. D. Hollier, et al., W. W. Norton & Company, New York and London 1990. He interprets the Ten Commandments as the laws of speech in *Seminar VII: The Ethics Seminar*, tr. D. Porter, W. W. Norton & Company, New York and London 1993, pp68-9.

18. From the demanding, threatening and exasperating Yahweh to the Hegelian State, which periodically disrupts the happiness of its citizens, the terrifying Other's intervention reminds us of the fragility and necessity of the Law.

19. '[Man] thinks as a consequence of the fact that a structure . . . language . . . carves up his body, a structure that has nothing to do with anatomy.' Lacan, *Television, op. cit.*, p6.

or in a scene of imaginary castration?

Mask

André studies those 'men's groups' who, in private ceremonies, require the shedding of blood. Initiation rituals (even secret handshakes) are imaginary representations and public demonstrations of a reparation applied to a failed symbolic castration. They resolve the castration complex when there has been a failure of Oedipus. For example, institutionalised coitus between an adult male and a non-initiated youth, common in warrior peoples, has a youth's femininity 'dying' as he is 'reborn' to himself as virile.[20] The violation effectively 'completes' a castration process in the form of an imaginary, not symbolic, simulacrum. Real blood must flow, as a sign of the mortal danger the Other brings:

20. S. André, *op cit.*, pp218-50. Institutional pederasty was required for pre-hellenic Greeks, tribal Germains, Cretans, Macedonians, New Guineans, et al.

> West Point, N.Y. - About 50 West Point seniors were punished for taking part in a 'blood branching,' in which pins designating their branches in the Army were pushed through their uniforms into their chests. Calling it a 'stupid rite of passage,' Lieutenant Colonel Rick Machamer, director of public affairs for the military academy, said yesterday that the cadets face demerits, extra duty or restrictions for the ritual.[21]

21. *San Francisco Chronicle*, 25 November 1997, pA3.

This is 'sacrifice': compensation for a missing paternal metaphor. It demands real violence that mimes but attenuates the horror of the 'carving out of the body' by language's original law-creating violence. The tone of the sacrificial *mise en scène* is less to deny the reality of violence than to remind us of it. Blood must flow. Just not too much blood.

In true sadism the purpose of staged violence is different. It is to show that the Other's violence can be limited contractually. The sadist displays violence and even puts 'castration' on stage, but as *never more than* a scene, never more than a perverse imposture. He mocks castration, like death, by denying it. He refuses it altogether precisely by admitting it as a mere *fiction*.

Self-mutilations naturally fall toward the masochistic side and further complicate the conflation of sadism and masochism in today's 'sadomasochism' which Deleuze denounced so roundly as a 'misbegotten name, a semiological howler'. A recent article treated a case of masochism with surprising equanimity:

> Amy's parents wouldn't recognise the bookish daughter who once earned straight A's and sang in the choir at a Texas boarding school. The smiling 20-year-old is in a South of Market club surrounded by other pierced,

> tattooed, branded and scarred patrons. She's wearing a red corset with the waist cinched to an uncomfortable 20 inches. She has a ring through the septum of her nose and two more in each nipple. She recently got a second tattoo on a shaved patch of skull . . . Amy is part of a growing subculture that is exploring the line between fashion and mutilation, design and destruction, choice and compulsion . . . Pain is part of the attraction . . . 'I like pain,' she says, as if telling you she likes ice cream. Her 21 year old friend Ivy is . . . branded . . . she has faint lines like railroad ties on her legs and wrists from more than six years of cutting herself. 'I like pain. I like blood,' she says. 'I like testing *my* limits'.[22]

22. Joan Ryan, 'A Painful Statement of Self-Identity,' *San Francisco Chronicle,* 30 October 1997, pA1.

The girls' blood flows to re-mark the sacrificial way castration has been written on their bodies. But the ritual scarification of an Amy or an Ivy, whose 'initiation' ceremonies could never parallel those of males, may also be a masochistic twist to sadistic perversion. Their high profile, public, 'fashionable' female masochism is hardly the masochism Deleuze hoped would escort male sadism back to a place within the law. There is a dash of perversion as the girls scoff at the law as mere form: 'I like testing *my* limits.'

Deleuze says there is an 'aestheticism to masochism' whose hallmark is 'coldness' rather than Sadean apathy. This couldn't apply more than in the case of the late Bob Flanagan, who purposely made an aesthetic-masochistic example of himself. Flanagan suffered from Cystic Fibrosis, a degenerative disease whose victims rarely live to, let alone past, adolescence. Flanagan died in his mid-40s, one of the oldest known survivors, 'a distinction largely credited to his masochistic lifestyle and the strength he derived from learning to live with, and tolerate, pain'.[23] Flanagan became a performance artist who movingly described (and videoed) the ways his longtime dominant partner and collaborator, Sheree Rose, enabled him to feel alive by subjecting him to whippings and pain.

23. Craig Marine, 'You Always Hurt The One You Love' in *Sick: The Life and Death of Bob Flanagan, Super Masochist, San Francisco Chronicle,* 2 November 1997, pC7.

Something more of the real is involved with Flanagan's masochism than we easily feel comfortable with. When Craig Marine tries to describe Flanagan's theatre of pain, he has quite a bit more difficulty than Joan Ryan has discussing Amy's and Ivy's scars. Depicting one scene of a penile subincision (an alternate form of ritual circumcision that involves splitting the penis end to end) Marine's text demonstrates amply how the law of language, metaphor and figure, shelters us from direct experience of the violence a masochist goes to extreme pains, so to speak, to acknowledge:

> Let's see if we can describe this one scene for publication. You've got Mr Two By Four, Mr Hammer, Mr Nail and Mr Distinctly Male Appendage. There is a meeting of the aforementioned - a rather violent one at that. There is an extraction, and plenty of resulting blood on the camera lens.[24]

24. *Ibid.*

Flanagan does not deny death. He resists it. He stages its horror not only to remind himself of its power, as in male initiation, but to mobilise his body to fight against it. Kirby Dick, the documentary's maker, says: 'I view it as a form of cross-training. Bob came to know the limits of pain and methods of tolerating pain. A large part of masochism is mental training'. Flanagan's idiom of masochism permitted him, overwhelmingly threatened by the Real, to formulate a response where the Other's jouissance had him in its grip. Flanagan's self-'violence' fought death's drive with its own weapons where the Sadean scoffs yet unconsciously submits.

So Flanagan's is the inverse of the pervert's scene.

PERVERSION IN PUBLIC PLACES

We can and will return every effort to violate the norm to the catalogue of cultural stuff we hold in common. Thus, the vogue for publicly perverse behavioural styles is taken as an opportunity to retrieve normality from sadism's formal dismantling of the law. Pundits now say, 'S&M is still at the far limits of the sexual envelope [but it is] filtering down into the mainstream . . . We're a large populist culture. We'll take anything and normalise it'.[25] An unmistakable ethical propriety and a faith in personal agency appears in comments like these: tolerant, urbane, witty. They show a general public comfortable with sadomasochism and perversity as mere styles. So little anxiety attaches to these remarks, though, that we must wonder whether indeed the radical nature of the perverse unconscious has been rendered obsolete, or is being naively misrecognised.

25. *San Francisco Examiner*, 8 June 1997, pA1.

A look at the rhetoric accompanying the S&M and BDSM[26] practices (private and commercial) the Berkeley students brought to my attention shows a discourse of progressive social ideals: brotherly love, mutual respect, interpersonal trust, restraint and self-control - the same things we generally (though not psychoanalytically) think of as required for communal co-existence. Indeed, my California students were certain that S&M culture offered them an agency, a sense of community and of decency that the worn-out forms of neurotic sexuality could not. It accommodates such odd crossovers as the Christian singer Pat Boone's showing up in full leathers, tattoos and a dog collar for the American Music Awards in January 1997.

26. Bondage is restriction and control; Dominance is psychological reversal and giving up power; Sadism is talking and taking power; and Masochism is transforming pain.

BDSM practices have come to stand as codified models for a trust that long ago fled a society awash in tales of out-of-control crimes and punishments. What sadomasochism offers is a welcome relief - 'guarantees,' signed contracts - to young moderns bereft of once taken-for-granted co-ordinates of civil society. Couples today, entering their second or third serial marriage, wanting to do it right this time, can now purchase by mail order from Colorado a ready-made pre-nuptial agreement for remarriages. It promises the partners they will be able to live together tension-free by specifying in advance everything that usually causes friction in re-combined households: whose cats are kept, whose given away; which partner is responsible for seeing that the automobile's tank is filled; how often the laundry gets done and by whom. In a similar spirit, so-called 'perverts' can pick up their pre-printed sadomasochistic contracts at Good Vibrations, a female-owned family-style sex emporium in San Francisco.

The hallmark of these S&M contracts is that the threat of violence is contained or controlled within it by explicit rules. They are documents to establish 'trust' - the very thing that we, at the mercy of ordinary human verbal, and sexual, intercourse, will never find guaranteed.

A laundry list of rules and regulations is, we also know, the sign of the Sadistic superego - not of the law and, so far as I know, no human society has ever come with money-back guarantees. Still, I wonder. The immensely popular adoption of perverse sexual forms and of styles associated with 'neo-tribal' or 'modern primitive' subgroups certainly leads us to conclude that the world has indeed rolled joyously over a sadistic edge. As BDSM has gone public, coming out of private clubs and made a tourist attraction, the utopian side of Sade's vision does seem on the point of being fully realised. In today's scene, gay men and lesbians play BDSM games together without being segregated by 'gender': 'femmes' can experiment with being 'tops,' 'butches' can date 'daddies,' and anyone can pick any role - 'Daddy'-'Mommy'-'Boy'-'Girl' - to play with anyone else.[27] Sade's theatre appears not only to have triumphed, Dolmancé's dream of a new form of social relation that neutralises all real violence is being institutionalised.[28]

Willy Apollon and Serge André distinguish pervert from neurotic this way: the neurotic fantasises about perversion; the pervert acts. Yet as the 'heterosexual, middle-aged couples' who consume sadomasochism's commodities purchase their paraphernalia and their tickets to Bondage à Go Go, the line separating fantasy and act becomes uncertain: is a fantasy your own when you've bought it off the shelf? Is then acting it out the same as the pervert's passage to act? If we set up the question of violence and perversion on the model of this neurotic structure, we end up dealing only with outcomes, or comings out, or comings apart, and not with *causes*, the Thing psychoanalysis must discover. If we only count the pervert 'wannabe' as an hysteric induced to having their enjoyment stage-managed by a pervert, we would still not have located where the real pervert is, nor its partner.

Perhaps Sade's 'utopian' vision has been implemented through that new social contract his Dolmancé anticipated? Perhaps his dream is being realised? Has the human creature begun at last to shed its 'subjectivity' not for the *Es* of the psychotic, but for an enjoyment without limits?[29] This may be too fast. More traditional interpretations are possible.

Our collective fascination with 'perverse' behaviour and style may index a collective hysterical fantasy more than an actual rise in the pervert ratio in the population. The public staging of perversion-as-entertainment recalls a long-standing dream of blissful existence outside the pale of civilisation and the confines of the law. The eighteenth century dreamed of savage life just as an industrial age that would forever eliminate that getaway plan was

27. Thanks to Stephanie von Schnurbein and Carl Reyes for invaluable research assistance.

28. The investment in making war into a series of non-threatening images - e.g., Grenada and the Gulf War - is a sadistic structure.

29. When the censor rated his *Bent,* NC-17 for 'scenes of excessive sensuality,' director Sean Mathias objected: 'I didn't know sensuality needed to be limited.' Edward Guthmann, 'Director Mathias Has a Long, Intense History with *Bent,' San Francisco Chronicle*, 2 December 1997, pD1.

dawning. Neurotic 'perversions' are scenes of a *jouissance* lost to civilisation (or industry) and their discontents - to some Thing - and available only in fantasy. If we take the pervert as one who acts out his or her own fantasy, but who must confirm its logic by inducing the hysterical other to go along, we can begin to assess in socioeconomic terms the commodification of perversion and its proliferation of pre-staged fantasies for sale. Why is it selling so well? For despite its denial of the Other's violence, perversion can ultimately do nothing, really, to prevent it from breaking out, no matter how carefully it fences in, contracts with, regulates the 'Other.' Just why does the hysteric get involved in the pervert's scenario?

To avoid knowledge of that Thing, perhaps? Are we in complicity with a deeper perverseness, a greater loss of agency than our thematisation of 'ready-to-wear' perversion, 'made for TV' and 'for sale to tourists' indexes? Taking on the perverse stand without meaning it is a political danger not only in the old-fashioned Adorno/Marcuse/Horkheimer sense of a 'repressive desublimation.' It lies with the fundamental problem that, by averting knowledge of the *Cause* (the violence of the Other; *la Chose*) the real violence potential even in the Law, the permanent violence of the unbarred Other goes unchallenged.

To restate the issue: is perversion in public places today the triumph of Sade's *conscious fiction*, installing a new, workable social contract without need for the Subject/Other relation marked by the institution of the law? Or is it the ironic realisation of Sade's *unconscious fantasy* - the desire to become the 'eternal' object and thereby cease suffering from intolerable abuse? Are hysterics, too, like the miserable Sade, unconscious witnesses to our own subjection, to our torment by an uncontrolled and unacknowledged Other? Who is the abusive Other today? And what ethic could contest It? The perverse (im)posture and its consumers may end by participating in a denial of serious abuse. An Other who violates its own laws will see the Sadean comedy (in French, English and Freudian meanings) finally turn tragic.

A return to some well-worn political, economic, and sociological concepts may permit some purchase. Alongside the spread of sadism, masochism and the ideals of violence-lite, we are also undergoing an unprecedented and revolutionary extension of the means of aesthetic production. Computer driven technologies are setting the work of art into an age of electronic *production* that may exceed the domain Benjamin carved out - the work of art in the age of mechanical *reproduction*. If the master-slave issue is not yet overcome by the sadist's formal scepticism, part of the reason may lie with the unlimited freeplay of the imagination now available technically, but in which, however, the apparent conquest of the master-slave field is being reversed.

Only an ethics can face the situation. At our disposal, we have Levinas' religious ethic of the Other; Deleuze's neo-masochist ethics; Zizek's ethics of Lost Cause, which gets close to my concerns, and Badiou's general reflection. Traditional religion and spirituality in the workplace are much in the news. But to understand the new, wily ways of the Other unwittingly freed from constraint in the sadist's unconscious, we must pay stricter attention to the pathway Lacan took from 'Kant avec Sade' towards ethics: aesthetics. Lacan's confrontation with the ethics of art and of sadism is still the best account of the 'aestheticisation of violence' and the investment in 'violence-lite' and 'phoney wars' now around us.

The object in the aesthetic relation. When Lacan embarks on an ethics of psychoanalysis in *Seminar VII* he encounters two versions of relation to the object that similarly discount or formalise the relation to the law. The *perverse* we have already discussed.The *aesthetic* partakes of the general problematic of sublimation. Lacan discovers that the two oppose each other structurally, if not phenomenologically.

Yet Lacan had set out to reach the aesthetic, as a form of 'creative destruction,' by way of Sade. He first looked to courtly love poetry for the apparent sadism of the Lady, and perhaps also because Laure de Sade - Petrarch's Laura - was Sade's supposed ancestress. An aesthetic Superego shares some features superficially with the Sadistic one.[30] But a major distinction is to be made between Sade's notion of creative destruction (the material principle of Nature's cycles) and the aesthetic 'destruction' Lacan happens upon. Lacan gently mocks us with an image of failed creativity: 'We haven't even been able to invent even a single new perversion'. I question if there is an aesthetic Superego at all.

30. Julia Lupton, 'Sublimation,' in Wright, *op. cit.*, pp416-17 and Slavoj Zizek, *The Metastases of Enjoyment: Six Essays on Women and Causality*, Verso, London 1994, pp89-112.

Let us see how Lacan laid out the structural relation of subject and object in the aesthetic before setting it into the new context of electronic production. In contrast to the realm of the unconscious - neurotic, psychotic or pervert - the aesthetic marks out a unique relation to the object that does not have to do, strictly speaking, with the unconscious.[31] That the object not remain for the artist what it is for the neurotic, forever unreachable, nor become the persecuting object of the psychotic is already the risk the artist takes each time. But what does the artist risk vis-à-vis the sadistic object? Does art entertain an intimate relation with sadism? After all, art too designates the object as fully enjoyable. It brings 'delight.'

31. See my forthcoming book, *Things to Come*, Minnesota Press and 'Love Outside the Limits of the Law,' *new formations*, 1994.

The aesthetic demands a fundamental 'clearing' of the field of the Other in order to establish a fresh relation to the object. This entails a risk. Wiping away the Other and the Law that have stood between and partitioned subject from object - sweeping out the whole of tradition, metaphor, and unstated social agreements - leaves the object again a free-standing entity, renewing its threat to the subject. The subject's sense of awe (wonderment and fear) before the object is restored. The crucial difference between the artist and the sadist, then, is that in brushing aside the 'law' the artist risks encountering the Thing, the Real in all its violence and brutality. Where the sadist consciously imagines he can control the Thing, but unconsciously plots his own subjective destitution to escape It, the artist risks everything in order to raise anew and quite differently the law of partition that shields us from It. The work of art reconstructs, on the basis of a void in the law, a new form of shelter, a beauty that forms a 'barrier so extreme as to forbid access to a fundamental horror'.[32]

32. Lacan, *op. cit.*, p63.

This miracle is operated, Lacan tells us, by granting the object dignity, raising it to an untouchable Thing. Again, the sadist seems close: both sadist and artist value the object; for each, the object is penetrated with jouissance. But the sadistic unconscious falls short. It cannot divide subject from Thing. Having formally discredited the laws of language and speech, the sadist is impotent to re-establish a sanctuary from the Other.

The aesthetic, too, contests the law of the signifier, but unlike perversion, it also partakes of its function. Art retains its direct relation to jouissance, yet still manages to put its experience of enjoyment into circulation. Like the signifier's, this circulation cannot be controlled in advance, nor can its itinerary through time and space be pre-determined by contract, rule, or regulation. Lacan devised the term *sinthome* to coincide with this aspect of the artistic sign, designating the artwork as a *signifier* and not as an *object*. But it is a signifier penetrated with jouissance and not, as the signifier of language is, marking the loss of jouissance.

Art - Freud's *sublimation* - functions to re-place, put back in place, a kind of law of the Other. Its fiction differs from the law-lite of the sadist, however, because it includes knowledge of the violence of the Other. Without hiding the shock of the Real that inspires it, without giving that violence an alibi, as sadism does, art goes about constructing new barriers, new and necessary partitions, new forms of relation to the past and to tradition. It constructs a new difference between subject and object and, more importantly, a new distance from the violent potential in their relation. It does so especially where the paternal law, God and society, are in default, or lie discredited. Hence, perhaps, the misguided accusation in the US today that artists are perverts (e.g. Mapplethorpe, or Karen Finley).

THE VEL

> Who's the boss - you or the pain?
> Come on, show me who's the boss?[33]

33. Jay Wiseman, *SM 101: A Realistic Introduction*, Greenery Press, San Francisco 1996, pp170-171.

When Lacan speaks of the 'aesthetic' clearing necessary to re-fabricate a barrier between subject and Thing, for him it's only a metaphor. Let's take it literally - as a *playground* where the crucial new relation to the object takes place. A pre-emptive strike against the arts and their playgrounds is underway, its pressure announcing more than simple 'natural' market forces, rising real estate prices, and popular targets for professional moralists in government, religion and art criticism. Rhetorical attacks, arts administrative protocols, and sheer economic demands are combining to pre-empt a mental free space, a space where no one, unlike the sadist, need *ever* work for the *jouissance* of the Other.

The shutdown of 'creative play spaces' arrives at the same time as an acceleration in the conversion of 'creative production' to the electronic.[34] If the artistic relation is ever completely commandeered for what Disney has generously given us a name - 'imagineering' - we may find ourselves more open to the revenge of the Thing than ever. If the energies of art-making are taken up for someone else's profit (the *jouissance* of the Other captured in a financial image) the cardinal aesthetic itinerary I describe above risks being fundamentally hijacked.

34. No neo-Luddite, I use computer compositing for my own installation art.

I do not mean that artists should not make money, but that the exhaustive conditions under which artists work to secure a new and crucial relation to the object are being mimicked industrially for quite other than the aesthetic aim of refounding the subject's relation to the object. For why else should tampering with the conditions of production of the work of art correlate with a high profile for sadomasochism (or its hysterical converts) in the age of electronic production? Is the essential work art does for us with respect to the law being blocked here?

Of course, the computer/graphics/software business has taken extraordinary pains to configure itself as the opposite of heavy industry. It classically exhibits the Marxist problems of any industry taking off (intense exploitation of capital and labour), and its spectacular growth has often found governments willing to cut this enormous wealth-generating machine some slack, relaxing labour, overtime and financial laws, and lifting certain traditional safeguards protecting workers and investors.[35] But the industry has innovated in a direction that is by all accounts reasonably enlightened. Because everyone is working in a 'creative' industry, everyone understands that they should give more than the usual to the 'project.' In return, however, the workers are offered sabbaticals, or given time off for 'think tanks' in research parks, stock options, and so on. The factories they go to work in are sometimes called 'campuses.'

35. Iain Boll and James Brook, (eds), *Resisting the Virtual Life*, City Lights Books, San Francisco 1997.

Notwithstanding, the conditions of production of the aesthetic means of production are viewed by those employed in them as harsh - from Burbank to the Silicon Valley, throughout the global economy. There is an undeniable demand for excess from workers, it is even written into their contracts, justified by the point that projects in these settings are creative, and thus consume the same kind of energies as the work of sublimation, enormous creative energies. Yet: situating the creative process within what is essentially a field of economic warfare (competition) is still to model it on the demand for jouissance by the Other, not on resistance to it. With this twist, we may collaboratively be producing the model for a unique new exploitation of the human soul, possibly deeper than ever before devised. Freely decided upon, this model nevertheless forces open the royal road between the jouissance of the Other and the subject, and closes the 'angle between Other and other' Lacan saw as essential to our *humanity*. We will have given up on sadism's egalitarian dream by giving in to its unconscious desire.

Such exploitation anyone subject to it might understandably flee, if only in their unconscious.

South of Market, where the BDSM clubs are located in San Francisco, is also the site of 'Multimedia Gulch,' the 'creative' end of the software business. One of the most telling comments from the young people flocking there for S&M these days unknowingly reproduces Lacan's *vel* of 'Kant avec Sade.' It is a 'people's critique' of the extreme working conditions encountered in this alluring new, high-paying industry: 'It's a choice. You can have money - or a life'.

Cars and scars

Parveen Adams

I start with a quotation from Lacan's Seminar on psychosis:

> Imagine a machine that has no mechanism for overall self-regulation, so that the organ designed to make the right leg walk was unable to coordinate with the one that makes the left leg walk unless a photo-electric receiver transmits the image of another machine functioning in a coordinated way. Think of these little automobiles that you see at fairs going round full tilt out in an open space, where the principal amusement is to bump into the others. If these dodg'em cars give so much pleasure, it is because bumping into one another must be something fundamental in the human being. What would happen if a certain number of little machines like those I describe were put on the track? Each one being unified and regulated by the sight of another, it is not mathematically impossible to imagine that we would end up with all the little machines accumulated in the centre of the track, blocked in a conglomeration ... A collision, everything smashed to a pulp.[1]

1. Jacques Lacan, *The Psychoses* (Seminar III, 1955-56), Routledge, London 1993, pp95-6.

This is a fable of imaginary dissolution which could be thought of as a description of the space of Cronenberg's film, *Crash*. Perhaps *Crash* does represent a dissolution of the imaginary into a psychotic world whose figures fumble to reinvent the distinction between subject and object. For Freud at least, the symptoms of psychosis mark the attempt at just such a *re*construction of the world rather than its collapse. But the marriage of cars and people in *Crash* isn't really this kind of reconstruction. It is true that in the film, as in the fable, cars bump each other and smash each other into wrecks. But we might say that in fact *Crash* supposes that this process has not gone far enough. I am far from making the claim that the space of the film is psychotic as such. Yet the imaginary dissolution is unmistakeable as the disturbance in the relation to 'otherness'. To make sense of what is going on in the encounter between men and machines in *Crash*, I want to suggest the idea of penetrability in terms of a continuously open wound and also to suggest that this image represents a dissolution of otherness itself, a dissolution which is lethal.

First let's consider two different and opposite responses to the film. Both concern sexuality but while some see a straightforward heterosexuality, others are outraged by its flagrant perversity. Joan Copjec holds to the first position. She writes:

> *Crash*, the film, is less about the drive than it is about sexual relation;

> the coupling of flesh and chrome is merely the mise-en-scène for the coupling of the man and the woman ... the film is a symptom; the drive has been repressed and returns in this false representation of satisfaction.[2]

2. Joan Copjec, *Umbr(a)*, On The Drive, Buffalo 1997, p13.

Of course it is the case that there are scenes of sex which could be read as a conventional, if somewhat accident prone, heterosexuality. Characters in the film question each other about orgasm. But what is really at stake is the intensity of an experience beyond the partial drive. This experience seems indeed to work against any organisation of sexuality and to deprive it of its economy; the drive seems to propel itself towards the unknown, leaving fragments of sexuality in its wake. The drive speeds off, seeming to be the very illustration of Lacan's proposition that every drive is a death drive. Perhaps this is to be explained through Freud's invocation of the navel of a dream. Freud famously spoke of the navel of the dream, the place at which the interpretation of a dream must come to a halt, a place which marks the limits of representation. Of course it is this place that also marks the limit of the navel of the drive. What is at stake then in the sexuality of *Crash* is an experience beyond representation, an experience of a pure libido. The film explores this gap.

What Joan Copjec had in mind when she criticised the film's representation of sexuality was the Lacanian axiom, 'There is no sexual relation'. She accuses the film, in effect, of representing something false - the jouissance that the man and the woman find in each other. But we should consider carefully and in Lacanian terms exactly what kind of jouissance we are dealing with. Perhaps the jouissance of *Crash* is quite different from the everyday satisfactions of phallic jouissance. Perhaps it belongs to the register of the Other jouissance, or even of perverse jouissance.

Let me explain these terms. Lacan distinguishes between phallic jouissance and the Other jouissance in his formulas of sexual division in which men and women are quite definitely differentiated from each other. *Man's* desire, concerned with phallic jouissance, is constrained by the prohibition on incest, by the 'No' of the Father. This desire therefore 'never goes beyond the incestuous wish' as Bruce Fink puts it. *Women* are also subject to the signifier, to the paternal prohibition, and therefore experience phallic jouissance, but the woman is not subject in the same way to these same limits as the man. As Fink says 'not all of a woman comes under the law of the signifier'.[3] She also comes elsewhere. This elsewhere, which has moved beyond the place of phallic jouissance, is what Lacan calls the Other jouisssance, where sexuality has been sublimated from the phallic. It is this Other jouissance that Lacan alleges is shared by mystics. In fact neither phallic nor the Other jouissance seems appropriate to *Crash*. What about perverse jouissance? Is the film masochistic or sadistic? If Lacan is to be believed it would seem unlikely.

3. Bruce Fink, *The Lacanian Subject: Between Language and Jouissance*, Princeton University Press, Princeton NJ 1995, p112.

Let us first consider whether we could describe *Crash* as sadistic. Lacan quotes from de Sade's text, 'Lend me the part of your body that will give me a moment of satisfaction and, if you care to, use for your own pleasure that part of my body which appeals to you'.[4] Sade was thus concerned with the part-object. It could easily seem that this aspect of sadism is relevant in *Crash* where also the body is always breaking into pieces. But Lacan's idea of sadism is really quite different from *Crash*. Sadism always acts upon a whole and would-be perfect body. It may intend to inflict damage and pain but it must start (and as a form of repetition) and start again from this body. Hence all the miraculous cures in de Sade - at the end of some encounter victims are cut, bruised and bloodied if not worse, but with the application of some mysterious unguent, everyone is restored. In effect, the victim is indestructible. Lacan links this figure of indestructibility to the eternal suffering in Sade's fundamental fantasm. Now certainly *Crash* has no equivalent to this indestructible victim; on the contrary, the characters seem always on the verge of injury, moving inexorably towards the fatal encounter of that thing which augments another logic - the 'inevitable accident' which somehow describes a register that is not phallic jouissance, or the Other jouissance, or perverse jouissance but describes the space in which Death begins to appear as the object of something we no longer call desire.

4. Jacques Lacan, *The Ethics of Psychoanalysis* (Seminar VII, 1959-60), Routledge, London 1992, p202.

I will elaborate this later on. At this stage in the argument we can continue the differentiation between sadism and the desire which unfolds in *Crash*. Far from the indestructible victim, far from the magical unguents which make possible the repetition of the sadistic scene, what is at stake in *Crash* is quite different. The body retains its mortal frailty; the proximity of body and car, flesh and steel, skin and bone, dominates sexuality not at all as sadism, but as the world of the wound. Indeed the film's sexuality is textured like a wound, gaping, open, unsutured.

This elaboration suggests that *Crash* is no more masochistic than it is sadistic. Masochism is commonly thought of as involving pleasure in pain and certainly the economy of masochism falls under the sway of the pleasure principle. But there is a beyond of the pleasure principle which allows Lacan to write of 'the unspeakable field of radical desire that is the field of absolute destruction'.[5] What is at stake here is not pleasure, but jouissance. Indeed, pleasure is the barrier to jouissance. Anyone who has seen *Crash* will recognise that it sets out to smash that barrier.[6]

5. *Ibid.*, pp216-7.

6. The argument that *Crash* is not masochistic can also be made by considering the place of the object (*a*) in each. The masochist puts himself at the place of the object to ensure the *jouissance* of the Other. He puts himself just there, where the Other lacks. He thus fills the gap with the object. Now in Lacanian theory the object is both that which covers the gap *and* it is also the gap. What looms large in *Crash* is not the object in its function of cover, but its aspect of the hole. It's as though the attempt were to abolish the object altogether.

Now again, it is crucial to distinguish the signification of the wound from the mark of the whip in masochism. We would normally interpret the latter as a little castration, represented by the cut, by the cut *as* representation, as differentiation, as the Other's signature. The world of the wound is quite different; it is not a kind of writing on the body so much as an unwriting of the body. It is already the other side of representation. All a wound can do is get bigger or smaller, close up or open. It is not so much just the navel of meaning; here it becomes the birth-canal of death.

Indeed normally the closing of the wound, the work of suture, the reinscription of the scar brings the body back towards representation. But in *Crash* the wound is not healed but merely transformed by scars. The scar is also a wound. The characters in *Crash* revel in the exploration of scars, these transformations of skin and tissue, these crusts of a new and hybridised body. Though the scar be healed, it nevertheless opens you up continuously to the previous time of the open wound, to a continuous reopening of the wound. A scar is not fixed.

The sexuality of *Crash* proliferates through the scar and the wound. Two-thirds of the way through the novel J.G. Ballard writes, 'The world was beginning to flower into wounds'. Indeed, in the novel the wounds of Vaughan's body begin to re-open shortly before his own sought-for, fatal crash:

> Vaughan picked repeatedly at the scabs running across his knuckles. The scars on his knees, healed now for more than a year, were beginning to re-open. The points of blood seeped through the worn fabric of his jeans. Red flecks appeared on the lower curvature of the dashboard locker ... Blood mingled with the dried semen on the seats, marking my own hands with dark points ...[7]

7. J.G. Ballard, *Crash*, Vintage 1995 (1973), pp191-2.

The film doesn't represent the literal re-opening of wounds but finds its own way to portray its logic of the wound. The scar is about a fascination and an excitement, about the moment when libido passes beyond representation. Libido unbound. But what does that mean? It is far from any idea of freedom as might be suggested by the term unbound. It is unbound in the sense of having no object, or rather having nothing as its object. Now to be finally unbound libido must break down all barriers or it would remain constrained. It must even break down the last barrier, that which marks the boundary between life and death. This is the last scar which is to be opened - the place where Desire and Death bisect each other.

* * *

I must now justify the rough sketch of the film that I have presented to you. Stéphane Bouquet writes in *Cahiers du Cinema*, a lyrical and appreciative review of *Crash*, under the title 'Sweet Movie':

> A man, a woman, a car, and there we have a very good film, a powerful experience of cinema ... an immersion in a radical and new universe. A man, a woman, a car, it doesn't matter which of them provided that there is a triangle. Sometimes the man changes, or the woman; sometimes, there are two men together, or two women. What is important is neither sex nor identity, but the moment when beings meet, bump each other, run into each other.[8]

8. *Cahiers du Cinema*, (my translation), No 504, p24.

Stéphane Bouquet treats that first time in the film in which human beings 'run into each other', that is, the accident in which Ballard kills Helen Remington's husband - a scene which includes a moment of disruptive sexuality - as the *primal scene* of *Crash*, a primal scene in Freud's sense. A scene played over and over again, albeit in different combinations. I quote:

> *Crash* is thus a film constructed on repetition, but a repetition which is a-dramatical, non-progressive, serial ... There is no acceleration, no urgency, no stake to be suddenly revealed. There is the same rhythm always, this same slowness, frankly welcomed in a film which could have easily allowed itself to be intoxicated with speed. Quite simply, people make love, and love again, amidst more or less damaged cars.[9]

9. *Ibid.*

Bouquet gives the film this erotic dimension and also the dimension of the hybridisation of automobile and human. He reads this aspect in terms of Cronenberg's concern with the effect that the car can have on the imaginary. He speaks of the scene where Vaughan orchestrates a real replay of James Dean's fatal accident:

> Vaughan works to derealise the car, to project it into the space of fantasy, to circle it with a heroic aura, by reconstituting celebrated accidents in open air clandestine theatres. In a long, detailed and splendid sequence (*bleu nuit*), one sees him replay James Dean's accident in reality, presenting the cars and the protagonists of the drama, reproducing the crash, and emerging from it, as if the force of the automobile had been to install an imaginary space where desire could never encounter the reality principle.[10]

10. *Ibid.*, p25.

Bouquet's review contains precise and vivid accounts of the traumatising medical imagery and of the cold objective way in which the film is shot, its pure exteriority. I don't quite disagree with any of this. And yet I find that it is not enough. I certainly hope to show that this is no 'sweet movie'.

It is not just a question of disagreeing with other critics. For it will also be part of my argument that one of the difficulties in analysing the film is that the effect it has on the spectator is to conceal something. Certainly Bouquet's review gives a perfectly adequate account of one's feelings at a first experience of the film. But his commentary on the triangle, the question of repetition, and the imaginary space of domination over reality, need to be reformulated.

A man, a woman and an automobile. Yes. But what is the identity designated by the term automobile? It is not the automobile *qua* inanimate machine. Nor will any old automobile do. It is not just sheet metal but crumpled sheet metal that might do. A battered automobile. Or a bruised, bloodied and battered human. Indeed the third term isn't necessarily on the side of the automobile; it can perfectly well be human. Actually, it's not the one or the other as such that is needed. What is necessary is the wound that will connect them both. The film overflows with wounds. Partly through what Bouquet calls the 'traumatising medical imagery', the pins, the prostheses, the apparatuses to hold in place the wounds which cannot close. Indeed the film is dominated by the wound. So it is not necessarily a question of a man, a woman and a car. It is the wound which is primary. Then why bother to speak of a triangle so redolent of the Freudian Oedipal triangle? Of course one usually thinks of a wound in terms of castration in many narratives but in *Crash* a wound is just a wound. Indeed the remarkable thing about *Crash* is that it does not refer to the Oedipal nor to castration. The wound in *Crash* is less bound up with the sexual organ, male or female (though we might think of it as both the origin and the residue of the organ), and more to do with the Freudian drive for Life.

Furthermore look at the idea of the imaginary space of desire that Bouquet talks of - Vaughan, he says, works to project the car into the space of fantasy. But does the film really work at the level of the imaginary domination of reality? It seems to me that *Crash* is much more ferocious than this; it seems to me that it bears closely on the Real and on the quite terrible *jouissance* in which all subjectivity is submerged.

Finally consider how repetition actually works in the film. There is no one register of repetition in general; how we understand it depends on what repetition bears upon. In Lacanian terms - whether the repetition was at the level of the Imaginary, the Symbolic or the Real. Now the characters copulate over and over again in more or less damaged cars. But how are we to interpret this repetition? If it were at the level of the Symbolic it would go on repeating itself as if it were repressed material within analysis, as speech which continues to insist, even while facing resistance. But this is not the level at which the repetition of *Crash* works. I want to suggest that in fact the repetition exists at the level of the Real and that this puts the spectator of the film at the edge of the symbolic and its ordering of reality.

Surely Bouquet is right to make the first crash in the film its primal scene, the point from which all other crashes are repetitions. The primal scene is always accompanied for the child with elements of violence and excitement for which the child has no model of assimilation. According to orthodox definitions of trauma, that which is traumatic involves a violent shock and implies a wound. Yet in *Crash* the ingredients of trauma fail to work. Somehow *Crash* deals with trauma that doesn't traumatise.

What kind of thing is the repetition of trauma? It is founded on a return of jouissance, yet paradoxically this *jouissance* is not available to the subject. For repetition itself produces the loss of *jouissance*.[11] This is the domain of the death drive where the trauma repeats and something is lost over and over again. In *Crash*, on the other hand, with each repetition a little more is gained.

Usually the something that insists and insists again has a life of its own, quite outside the pleasure principle. *Crash* is a film that seeks the repetition

11. Jacques Lacan, *L'Envers de la Psychanalyse* (Seminar XVII, 1969-70), Editions du Seuil, Paris 1991, pp51-2.

and submits to the ever-repeating loss of repetition. Why then is it not traumatic? Because the film alters our psychical situation by depriving us of all the usual parameters of psychical depth. Many viewers have commented on the way in which we are made to attend to the surface of the film. I call this effect 'flatness' and I will show later how the film achieves it at the expense of psychical depth. The flatness of this filmic world puts the viewer at the very edge of the psychical situations known to psychoanalysis, including all the psychopathologies it traditionally describes. This is what enables the reading of the film in terms of a wound which does not succumb to the interpretation of castration.

Spectators will deal with their experience of the film in their own ways, but the logic of the film remains unequivocal: repetition follows repetition in order that the wound is kept open. The wound is the boundary between life and death, but also refuses to be the boundary and allows life and death to communicate in an alarming space. The wound marks the spot where death nearly realised itself in an accident. But the wound is not just a premature memorial; it also, and ferociously, aims at pure libido and immortality - to be achieved through the intensification of sexual energy released by car accidents, into the unbound beyond. The sexuality of this death requires the death of the sexed subject as its price, just as it offers the immortality of the Real to its victim. This is a description from the outside; the characters of the film and its spectators live from within the experience, which is that the end of one's subjection to desire is almost reached and that eternity will soon start after just one more accident.

Let's consider more closely how what I am calling the wound relates to life, death and sexuality. This wound connects the life and death drives in the film. My thesis is that fundamentally it plays the part of Lacan's *lamella*, the libido as indestructible life. This is Lacan's account of the *lamella* in *The Four Fundamental Concepts of Psychoanalysis*:

> The *lamella* is something extra-flat, which moves like the amoeba. It is just a little more complicated. But it goes everywhere. And as it is something ... that is related to what the sexed being loses in sexuality, it is, like the amoeba in relation to sexed beings, immortal - because it survives any division, any scissiparous intervention. And it can run around.[12]

12. Jacques Lacan, *The Four Fundamental Concepts of Psychoanalysis* (Seminar XI, 1963-4), The Hogarth Press and the Institute of Psychoanalysis, London 1977, p197.

The *lamella* is certainly running around in *Crash*. You see it arising in all the scenes of death. If the crash produces the wound, the wound is the very token of palpitating life. You can see how the attempt at the experience of sexuality in the Real relies on the wound. To make up for the insufficiency of the partial drive there is the wound, the lost part of sexuality, indestructible life. Death is set aside; immortality is secured in the legend of the mortal who perishes by death-by-accident.

Death has a function in *Crash*, paradoxical as it may seem, to ensure life. What is at stake here is pure life, the *lamella*. While the crash secures a death, something creeps and crawls out of it. Death nurtures life. This is the significance of the wound. The crash creates the wound and residue of indestructible life which survives death. This wound is to be found on the body of the car as well as on the human body. We can now understand the way in which *Crash* relates automobile and body. On both of them the wound must figure. It reminds me of Vaughan's desire to drive an automobile which had actually been in a fatal crash - he would do it up just enough to get it going. The original wreck is ideal for Vaughan's whole project which involves the death that would fuel a legend. A human dies in a car accident; the wrecked body of the car retains the sexual energy released at death; another human harnesses this energy in the entrails of the car by 'merging' with it in the sexual act; this human in turn dies in a car accident and achieves the indestructible life of a legend. Vaughan seeks to overcome death and attain indestructible life by becoming a legend. He continuously seeks jouissance in after-the-crash encounters; but it is his final crash that will make the *lamella* go spinning off. Vaughan had spoken of the incredible sexual energy released only by crash deaths. He waits his turn. This far exceeds the limits of the imaginary realm of domination over reality.

We can now ask how the endless scenes of sex work to keep the wound open. Sex, cars and scars. It couldn't be more explicit than in the scene between Ballard and Gabriella, a young woman with the strangest gait, encased in metal calipers, showing a deep cleavage, a substitute female genital, in one of her legs, a giant cleft leftover from some accident. Bouquet is correct in his reference to Calvary here – '*un calvaire physique*' - to sum up the play of torsions, distorsions and contorsions of her body and we will return to the echoes of religion that extend through out the film. This wound is what holds Ballard's attention and finally it is the wound that he penetrates.

Of course this takes place in a car. The scene horrifies with its materialisation and visualisation of the analogy between body and machine. Gabriella's body is like a second car awkwardly encased within the first. Her limbs, half artificial, half natural, threaten at the joints, creak and resist and scream, as Ballard lifts and bends parts of her body in his rapture at its awkward hybridity. Gabriella herself experiences all this with awful enjoyment. It is *enjoyment of the wound* at its purest.

This scene is set fairly late in the film since the ground has to be laid for its proper reception. In spite of which it is one of the most difficult scenes to read and experience. I don't want to detail all the scenes that result in the privilege of the wound. I'll just mention one early scene with Ballard and Helen Remington after the crash. They are together in a car and a certain repetition whets her sexual appetite. Following her observation that he has replaced his wrecked car with an identical model, he loses control of the car and narrowly misses another accident. The repetition provides the thrill of the fatal accident - the traumatic encounter with the Real, this time in miniature - that is all that is needed to fuel their sexual appetite.

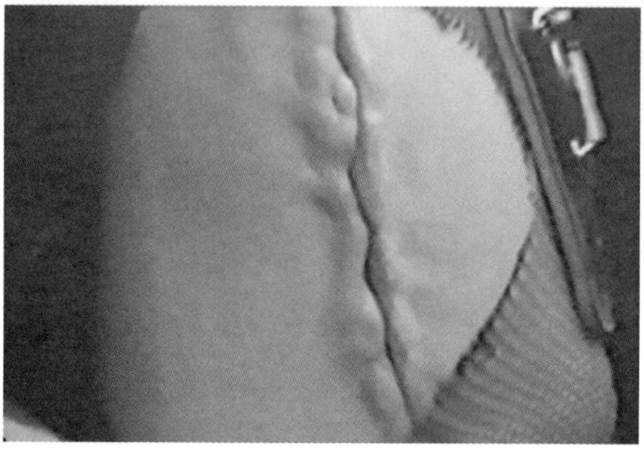

Crash, David Cronenberg

This is about cars and excitement. What about scars? Where are the scars to be looked for? The answer is - in the bodies of both cars and humans and as both the effects and the signs of crashes. This is graphically portrayed in the centre-piece of the film, a double and related *tour-de-force* - a scene of carnage, the multiple car crash, the background against which in the car-wash scene that follows, Vaughan and Catherine's bodies copulate strangely in the throes of a struggle for life. Wandering through the scene of the multiple crashes, we see smoking ruins of cars, we look through windows at trapped bodies staring vacantly in shock, we look at the injuries of freed and living passengers and at the injuries of dead ones. Here, a disbelieving Vaughan discovers himself outstripped in satisfaction as he finds the stuntman Seagrave's scalped and dismembered body, breasts and long-haired scalp torn off and ejected in various directions. Seagrave had gone ahead with the Jayne Mansfield crash - and so successfully! A success not only at the level of verisimilitude - the 'large tits' which he had wanted so that the crowd could see them 'get cut up and crushed on the dashboard', the head embedded in the windscreen, the dead little chihuahuas on the back seat - a success measured by the exact repetition of Jayne Mansfield's crash. In fact Seagrave replicated the Jayne Mansfield crash to perfection since the crucial ingredient, his own death, was included. The film is indeed about the re-emergent failure to integrate some impossible kernel of the Real - till you succeed with your death in being born a legend. Seagrave was the first to star on the opening night after his rehearsals for death and thus enjoy the ultimate copulation of fragmented body and metal.

Crashes excite. Vaughan is clearly excited. But Catherine has also been wandering around the scene of disaster with a growing sensitivity and excitement about cars. She sits on a bench next to a dazed and bloodied woman with bubbles of blood on her face. She allows Vaughan to place her first against the bonnet of a wrecked car, and then inside it, to photograph her inclusion in the scene. This moment marks her incision into Vaughan's world of accident.

Where is the wound in this sequence of crashes and car wash? The answer is that it is both multiple and dispersed. There are many wounds,

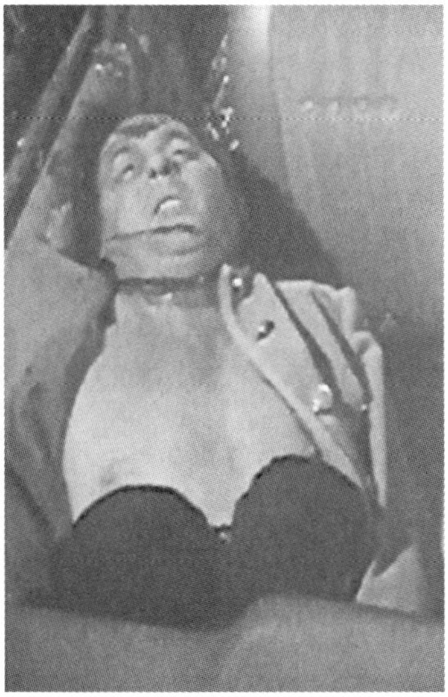

Crash, David
Cronenberg

but the whole scene is a wound and my sentence earlier about that which creeps and crawls out of the crash materialises here. The wound is the opening of the gap of the Real. Life ebbs and flows through the wound.

Catherine has remained unscarred so far, but she will emerge from the car-wash encounter with her body covered in bruises. The copulation with Vaughan transmits the wound. We could call this scene *the* image of hybridisation. The open car quite literally closes around them before it moves forward to be battered with torrents of water and embraced by bristling brushes. What is being done to the car is what is being done inside the car. We hear and see battery and assault. Can we call this violence? This is the New World Passion on the back seat of a 1950s Lincoln. The cross and the scourge are not the instruments of this Passion. Certainly it is a Passion which marks the body but it concerns the refashioning of the human body in the likeness of colliding machines. What Vaughan does with Catherine's body has been prefigured in the scene with the airport hooker. (That was the first time Ballard was at the wheel watching the *scene* of passion in his rear-view mirror.) Vaughan forces the limbs at the joints, for the body is articulated like a machine and he controls its movement. The body has a steering column, a set of gears and he 'drives' it. The effect is of cars in slow motion collision - engaging and ricocheting off each other's parts.

The scene with Catherine is extended in time and in intensity. It is shot in a way that conveys the unmistakeable inseparability of bodies and cars in desire. Here we have the wear and tear of the leathered driving seat, erupting just behind Ballard's right ear. Bodies crash with the same rhythm as the violent swirls of the waterstorms hurled at the battered Lincoln. Out of the unholy marriage of cars and bodies in the accident sequence is born a backseat Passion. This unholy marriage has death as its witness. It is the proximity of the death-by-car-accident (that which will make the legend and defeat death) that releases the life force and intensifies *jouissance*.

After the Passion the martyred body of Catherine laid out on her bed, a body now bruised, mottled and marked. Ballard's tender exploration of these. A scene that feels religious. It is as though she had undergone an initiation rite of the wound. Now the wound doesn't signify castration but rather the life substance that is usually subjected to castration. And so it is men who have to outfit themselves with wounds before they can enjoy together. There *is* a progression in the film in the sense that the nature of the fundamental relations clarify themselves, and the extraneous features gradually drop away. Gender, object choice, sexual aim, all these fundamental marks of identity began to fade into the background. The relation to the wound is what insists. After the penetration of Gabriella's wound by Ballard, the wound detaches itself as the very condition of *jouissance* hence the power of the men's tattoos in that most difficult scene between Ballard and Vaughan.

Perhaps you will now agree that the sex scenes maintain the openness of the wound. As I said earlier, despite the primal scene and the repetitions of the events in the film, we are not dealing with trauma as we know it. What the film creates is trauma that is not traumatising. It shows us what a world where trauma failed to operate would be like. That is to say, it lays bare trauma as a condition of our psychical and social life.

* * *

Let us now return to the question of the cinematic effects of *Crash* on the viewer's psychical situation. As I noted earlier, a strong effect of the film, one which is often commented upon, is a certain *flatness* of the film. To what precisely, is this effect due? And what does it mean? I want to suggest that it is a cinematic effect which corresponds to a psychical situation. That situation in turn is related to the depth of space (or to its lack) which is the register, indeed almost the index of the subject's relation to the Other. This can be elucidated by some remarks which Lacan makes about the subject, the Other, and space in his unpublished Seminar *Crucial Problems of*

Crash, David Cronenberg

Psychoanalysis.[13] Obviously these remarks are based on the Lacanian assumption that the subject is always defined in relation to the Other, and that space is not a pre-given container of that relation but is rather an effect of that relation. The idea that subjects react with each other within a neutral ground of geometrical space is quite alien to Lacan. For him the subject is firstly a subject of the signifier, a subject which is an effect of language. This well-known proposition defines two dimensions of the subject, provides as it were the surface of the subject. But what gives depth to the subject, what is the three-dimensional space of the subject, lies in the subject's relation to the Other. Indeed the depth of space is precisely the field of the Other.

13. Jacques Lacan, *Seminar XII*, 1964-5.

It is clearly here that we can see a fundamental relation between spatiality and the mechanism of identification. In psychoanalysis the term identification refers to the process whereby the subject takes up an attribute of the Other and comes to be determined by it. While most accounts of identification are concerned with the content of identification, I am concerned with the way in which identification comes about. Lacan modifies his reference to the three-dimensional space of the field of the Other by adding 'except that it is not space, it is time'. That is to say, before the subject can enter into three-dimensional *space*, there are a series of things it has to do in *time*. For it is this element of time that allows the subject to appear in the field of the Other in the first place.

In the 1940s, Lacan had developed a theory of what he called logical time, based on the logic of the game of prisoners where each of three prisoners has on his back either a black or a white disk and the first one to work out the colour of the disk on his own back is to win his freedom. For Lacan the time of the game is not chronological but is differentiated by three moments - the moment of seeing, the time of comprehending and the moment of concluding. Much later Lacan went on to use these moments to map the movement of analysis. In the Seminar on *Crucial Problems* he uses the three moments to map the movement of identification, claiming that the culmination of these three moments is to be found in any identification.

Now it is this identification that *Crash* denies the spectator, by using techniques which thwart comprehension and scatter its elements to the four winds. And thus the spectator is thrown back again and again on the moment of seeing. Without the identification with the Other there can be no access to the everyday three-dimensional space of the Other. There is barely the subject as surface and this makes for the flatness of *Crash*. I want to suggest that there is a type of shooting that Cronenberg employs that is closely connected to this flatness. It involves a limited, narrow direction of view where you remain in the same place even though you are moving and where what you see doesn't vary - you see one side of the car body and an unvarying strip of open road. It is clear from his interview with Chris Rodley that the scenes I am talking about are also important for Cronenberg:

> ... sometimes the simplest things are the most difficult to do. The way I

put the camera on the cars, for instance. The framing is not quite normal ... I *do* want to suggest people wrapped up in their cars: their relationship to their cars. So the framing is unusual, but in a very simple way.

It's really a matter of exactly where you put the camera. Not that simple. Each day, after choreographing the first scene to be shot, that would be the first thing I would do. I put it more *outboard* of the car body so that the windshield pillar was halfway through the frame, and the other half is looking right down the car body. That meant building rigs. You don't see that much because it takes a lot of time and it's hard to do. Shooting on a platform means that you can dolly while the cars are moving. We had six Lincolns; one of them cut in half, one of them made into a pick-up truck so that I could dolly and put lights on from behind.[14]

14. Chris Rodley (ed), *Cronenberg on Cronenberg*, Faber and Faber, London 1992, p202.

* * *

Some final remarks. All versions of the urban involve a certain relation between the subject, danger and technology. In the nineteenth century the excitement of the city was involved in its immediate danger. In the 1950s the gradual rendering of the city into the safety of the suburbs required that danger re-appear frequently as the car, as in the game of chicken. But this use of the car as danger couldn't be further from what we are speaking about with *Crash*. The world of James Dean is about the use of skill and nerve to avoid catastrophe. Even if the body is put at risk, the reward is the body unscathed. The inertia of reality is activated by introducing the threat of death. The economy of desire here is the pleasure principle in all its simplicity. Danger is used as a way of highlighting or outlining objects and of glamourising subjects. The world of *Crash* is completely different; perhaps it corresponds to a radical change in the nature of repetition, and therefore of addiction. If addiction was used in the 1950s to heighten overly domesticated and suburbanised object relations, in the 1990s it seems it may have been used to bring the world of desire to an end, or to find the end of the world of desire.

It would be an eschatology of desire, a concern with 'the last things' of desire. As if the subject has seen through the illusions and substitutions of the object and wishes to be precipitated beyond desire and beyond the object ... into the ending of desire. It is akin to being within the death drive in which the apparatus of the subject is progressively smashed to pieces, while the residue of the subject regresses, warm and sleepy, to an inevitable assignation with death. This is the space of the death drive, an analytic road movie. But it is not, as Cronenberg has seen, a phenomenological violence. Violence is an experience of inhabited tissue, of an experience which life suffers in its attempt to maintain itself. This is after violence; it is the wreck of the abandoned. First there were abandoned buildings, then there were abandoned cars. Now in this late, very late landscape there are abandoned limbs in an abandoned narrative. The text will be complete when we are not there.

Why did I eat daddy?

Alain Abelhauser

Ignorance of the law is no excuse; noone is deemed to be ignorant of the law.

If this kind of formulation can still be uttered other than mockingly, this is because the law is not only a collection of rules making possible the social bond, and enabling human groups more or less to manage their conflicts and their violence. It is because the law is also a determining instance in the structuring process of the human subject - the third instance, the only one that enables the subject to situate himself or herself in the 'dialectic of desire'. No one is deemed to be ignorant of the law, then, among those who are human in constituting themselves (at least in the neurotic mode) as speaking and desiring subjects.

But where does this third instance come from? How did it get put in place, at the very beginning? There is no getting round the question - a question of origins, *par excellence* - once we propose to take account of this subjective structuration, and are not satisfied with the hypothesis of God. Everyone knows that psychoanalysts, and Freud first of all, were quick to ask themselves this question. And everyone knows too that in order to reply to it, Freud, going beyond his fascination with Moses the founder, Moses the trustee of the tables of the law, had no hesitation in fomenting his own founding myth - *Totem and Taboo* - that of the murder of the father of the primitive horde. What is he explaining here? That the law did not exist as long as 'the social order' was the fact of the desire of one, or the other, the dominant male of the tribe of primates, the father of the horde, thought of as confiscating the females for his own exclusive use. That this kind of violence could not but induce its reciprocal kind, a mirror violence which leads the young, his sons, to kill him, and prompts one of them to take his place to begin everything over again, brings everything back to the identical situation, from generation to generation. And that it must be assumed that on one occasion, at least, the murder of the dominant one led to something other than making way for a successor. It led to the dead man becoming a totemic figure, and brought it about that *in the name of this dead man, in the name of this father*, a law - and a prohibition - were laid down, which from that time forth govern the division of women and the conduct of relationships between brothers, between *subjects* of this law.

Fine. But what then are the conditions which must have been realised for a rupture like this to come about? It is not enough for Freud to invoke a contingency - it happened once, that's all there is to say. He puts forward the view - and this is where the weak spot in his reasoning lies - that it is the guilt suddenly experienced by the parricidal sons gathered round the father's body which must have led them to this necessity of founding a law which from then on should avoid any repetition of such an act. May this never happen again!

That's where the snag is. And indeed it often happens that the only reply that can be provided to a question like this - a question of origins, as we said - is a circular one. For the Freudian explanation does not hold up, not at least if it is left as it is: in the end it consists in postulating that an affect, guilt, is at the origin of the law, while acknowledging in another way that it is only in reference to the law that the affect can truly be experienced - while assuming that one cannot be guilty unless the law already exists. The chicken certainly explains the egg, but it is also the egg that the chicken comes from.

Of course it is possible to open up this logical loop, and Freud doesn't fail to do this, by having other notions intervene: for example ambivalence and the conflict of desires. In this account, the sons made the dead father the support of the law because they felt guilty for having killed him, and this was because they loved him even while they hated him, and because once their hatred had been expressed and sated, the time came for love to take back all its rights, and to express itself in the 'heart-broken' form of guilt. But in spite of everything, it is clear to see that as long as one remains at this 'level' of explanation, what is not operating is the only thing that would really make it possible to give an account of this absolutely radical rupture which Freud is trying to explore: the passage from the plane of a certain desiring logic to that of the structure of that desire - that is, to the only thing which enables human desire to be constituted - the prohibition and the structuring recognition of the Other.

* * *

At this point in the debate, it may be helpful to mention a short book by Roy Lewis, recently translated into French, which makes a completely irreverent contribution to the question, but one which to my mind is also extremely funny and enlightening.[1]

What We Did to Father features a tribe of ape-men burdened with an evolutionist father, Edward, who occupies himself, with enthusiasm and self-sacrifice, in guiding his kin along the risky road of progress. It is all very well for his sons to kick at it, all very well for his brother, Vania the traditionalist, to protest that in coming down from the trees, the hominoid is heading straight for ruin - nothing to be done, the discoveries will come one after another, the changes will mount up, evolution will speed up. Edward conquers fire, which he will soon make use of not only to protect the horde and keep them warm, but also to dislodge a whole pack of bears from the caves and thereby procure for his own people the comfortable, secure abodes which they didn't dare to dream of.[2] Then, still thanks to

1. Roy Lewis, *What we did to Father*, Hutchinson, London 1968; trans. into French by Vercors and Rita Barisse as *Pourquoi j'ai mangé mon père*, Actes Sud, Paris 1990.

2. This is the only criticism I would make about the book: Edward conquers fire by going and taking it from a volcano. Roy Lewis, an anthropologist and anything but naive, cannot however have read the little piece by Freud called 'The conquest of fire', which he would have found useful and amusing. The hypothesis there is that man appropriated fire from the moment when he knew how to resist the compulsion to extinguish it by pissing on it. Which leads me to put forward the idea that it was in fact woman, not man, who conquered fire, as is evidenced in a contorted way by the myth of the Vestal Virgins.

fire, he learns to harden the points of spears, and this, together with the perfecting of the size of the flint, will open up new opportunities for hunting. Clearly, in making the transition crudely from a more or less vegetarian regime to an essentially meat diet, the subhumans will have to spend long hours masticating these new foods, not to mention the time spent on miserable digestive processes: all wasted time, which could be more usefully dedicated to study or meditation! No problem - Edward discovers meat cookery, and the barbecue organised every evening will also be the opportunity to refine social rituals, to discover figurative art, music and dance, and to organise big public debates on the meaning and the risks of evolution. Vania, even as he enjoys the kebab feast, thinks that the hominoid, in thus distancing himself from nature, will lose his soul. Edward maintains that in fact there is no choice: evolve or disappear. For him the whole question is rather about which direction to evolve in, and above all how to pinpoint their own degree of evolution: Lower or Meso-Pleistocene? He protests, at any rate, against the dangers of excessive specialisation, thinks that the adept *homines habiles* will best preserve all their future chances by becoming perfect generalists, and declares his unreserved support for a general distribution of technological progress, for inter-ethnic exchanges and collaboration, and for free access for all to the benefits of Science.

Time passes, and the sons grow up; one morning, the father brings them together for a big hunting outing. But it is no ordinary game that they set off to pursue. When they have reached a place at a little distance from the encampment of another tribe, the father conveys to them his order to go and abduct a few charming young girls. The sons, of course, protest: why complicate things like that; why not sleep with our sisters, as we always have? The father will hear no opposition: after the natural sciences, it is time to tackle the social sciences: 'Exogamy starts here', he says. 'There is no desire which does not sooner or later become a duty. Do yours!'

Time continues to pass: the sons have gone back to the horde, each of them provided with a wonderful spouse with brand-new genes; some of their sisters have been abducted in their turn; every day living conditions are further improving; they have all discovered talents of their own. One is a great hunter, an expert in trapping and beating; the second is a great artist, soon to be famous for the boldness of his mural frescoes; the third, a geologist and a born industrialist, efficiently helps his father and collaborates in the discovery of the flints which make it possible to make fire when you want; the fourth has more difficulty: passionate about ethology, he tries to domesticate dogs, pigs and horses, but his efforts have little success. It has to be admitted that evolution is lagging a little behind: the horse he wants to break in is still a 'Hipperion'! As for the youngest one, the narrator, he doesn't contribute much to the horde; his reflections are primarily speculative. For instance, it seems to him that when they begin by 'killing' the animal figures painted on the walls of the cave before they go off to hunt, the hunt is that much better; or, to take another example, he thinks that this strange world in which we wander in thought at night is perhaps the world where the shadows of beings have to go when the beings have been killed and devoured. In a word, he is in the process of putting into shape the foundations of *symbolic efficacity*, but he doesn't yet realise this.

Then everything really does speed up. In the course of his experiments, Edward has set fire to the surrounding savannah. They must expatriate themselves, negotiate a new territory with other tribes, to whom Edward, faithful to his principles, and despite the ferocious disagreement of his family, confides all the horde's secrets and acquired knowledge. The sons are more and more afraid for the future: isn't this frantic search for progress going to send them all headlong to their ruin? Is it still possible to reason with their father? - who, beneath his apparent kindness, seems to be challenging them to stop him in his quest. And he takes a further step: he invents the bow. It's too much. Up till then, the narrator had not managed to stop himself from thinking that it was not necessarily a bad thing to send beings into the world of dreams, and from this point his decision is made: a trial of the very latest paternal invention will be fatal to him. A great banquet is organised to celebrate his memory, according to the gradually acquired custom. The narrator's speech on this occasion is edifying: he pays a staggering tribute to this father, the inventor of so many things, and among others - and I quote - 'of social institutions as fundamental as parricide and patriphagy.'

* * *

Since Freud's study of the *Witz*, we have known that every joke should be taken seriously; and since his text on Jensens's *Gradiva*, we have known how a 'historical fantasy' can be useful ... or a prehistorical one. And doesn't this one answer some of the fundamental questions asked by both psychoanalysis and anthropology?

'What is a father?' Lacan reminds us of this question in 'The subversion of the subject and the dialectic of desire'.[3] 'A dead father', he has Freud reply. What does that mean? Quite simply this: that a father is a being put in the position of fulfilling, or being asked to fulfil, what psychoanalysis calls the *paternal function*, namely that which belongs with the Desire-of-the-mother, that which enables the subject to break with all dual, imaginary forms of relationship, and that which leads him finally to find his bearings as subject of a genuine desire. And that this function - this Name-of-the-father - can be attained only through death, to be understood not so much as death in reality, but as the sign of the transition to another plane of functioning. In other words, to counter the threatening, engulfing side of death, what is needed is something other than another subjective desire, which is to say that it is necessary to take away his subjective dimension

3. Jacques Lacan, 'The subversion of the subject and the dialectic of desire in the Freudian unconscious' (1960), in *Ecrits: A Selection*, trans. Alan Sheridan, Tavistock, London 1977, pp292-325.

from the one who guarantees the law and the prohibition - which is what death does. In this, the father present in reality can only appear as for the most part lacking - as is amply demonstrated by the creations of children's imagination that Freud pins down under the term *family romance*, as well as by that other rebound of belief to which it is customary to give the name God-the-father.

Thus the death that Lacan speaks of is what procures for the father this Name without which he cannot be set against the original savagery of desire and confer upon it that structured form which turns out to bring the subject to life. But it certainly isn't a matter of just any 'death'. It is not real death but death psychically *realised* - death that the subject discovers and recognises - death which gives absence its organising scope and gives lack its definitive inscription in the kernel of being. It is that death which, for Freud, puts in place the totem, the mythical guarantee of lineage and filiation. For Lacan, it is the death which founds the symbolic, the principle of the signifier - the signifier which retains from this origin its first property of excluding the real, which is what is acknowledged in the famous formulation of the 'signifier as murder of the thing'. Put in other terms, it is symbolic death, to be understood also as the symbolic of death.[4]

And this is how the value Freud gives to the totemic meal should be understood: very specifically as the operation which makes a father the absent one *in whose name* things are henceforth decided. So the basic question is not to know *why someone kills their father*, but rather, as Lewis puts it, *why you eat him*, since it is this devouring, this banquet - which has nothing cannibalistic about it, in the end, to the extent that it consists of creating some Other, some lack, some symbolic - which really constitute him as father. Now Lewis, without seeming to be touching on it, gives a number of indications with regard to this basic question which, if you know how to understand them, seem to give a perfect account of this radical disruption which Freud himself had trouble in explaining.

Why did I kill my father? The reply, according to Lewis, is simple to the point of being childish: 'Because he was intolerable'. And then also - and here we have a very nice paradox - because he had to be stopped from going further in the path of progress. And that it is precisely this attempt which decided in favour of definite progress, which put in place the keystone which would henceforth make it impossible to go back on the direction of evolution: as always, it is when you want to avoid something that you turn out to make it happen!

And why did I eat my father? Well, the reply implicit in what Lewis says is just as simple: because I/we had no choice. Because he was asking for it. Because he put us, his sons, in a position where we had no other way out.

However disappointing it may seem, it is there that we have to find the solution to the question of origins: what then is it that, for a subject, puts in place the third instance, the symbolic? The answer is that the symbolic, for a subject, is always already there, or rather that it is through a process of

4. Cf. Jacques Lacan, *Le Séminaire, Livre VII, L'Ethique de la psychanalyse, 1959-1960*, Editions du Seuil, Paris 1986, in which symbolic death is defined as the subject's discovery of the pure truth of his or her mortal condition. It is what happens to Antigone, condemned to be buried alive, in other words to live her own death in advance.

reciprocal determination that both symbolic and subject emerge simultaneously. It is only by eating daddy that I really become a subject, and it is only because I am already in the process of taking a subject-position that I think of eating daddy.

But there is an element missing for grasping the operation of this reciprocal determination, the element which makes it possible to tie up the subjective phenomenon with the symbolic dimension. This element is present, but not formalised, in the Freudian myth; it is conceptualised in Lacan; and it is invoked in a way that could not be clearer by Lewis. It is what Lacan calls the *objet a*: the remains, the refuse, the object which is radically lacking to the subject, the object which causes the subject's desire, the object around whose missingness the subject is constucted. What makes it possible for the subject to gain access to the symbolic dimension is having lost something - this object - because both the lack which generates desire and the demand which conditions language depend on this loss.

In the Freudian myth, the object has a place: that of the father's corpse with the sons gathered round it, that of the dead man. And it is not for nothing that Lewis made the father into this character who is adorable and intolerable, both at once. That way he gives him the primary feature of the object: just that, to be intolerable to the subject. It is only in the face of *the dead one*, suddenly imposing on the subject the presence of an absence henceforth revealed, that the dimension of *death* is then unveiled - of death alone capable of founding that paternal function which is itself necessary to guarantee the law and its recognition.

Translated by Rachel Bowlby

Where does power come from?

Mladen Dolar

I shall take two very short quotations as slogans or proverbs, one by Foucault and the other one by Lacan. The first is a direct and blunt statement from one of Foucault's numerous interviews: 'Power doesn't exist'. [Le pouvoir, ça n'existe pas.] The statement seems so blunt that the English translator (in *Power/Knowledge*) deemed it necessary to interpret: 'Power in the substantive sense, *"le" pouvoir*, doesn't exist'.[1] The second one, by Lacan, states simply: 'The Other lacks'. [L'Autre manque] One can find it in this minimal form in one of Lacan's last statements, but there are also numerous variations throughout his work (most frequently as 'the lack of the Other').[2]

1. Michel Foucault, *Power/ Knowledge*, Colin Gordon (ed), Colin Gordon, Leo Marshall, John Mepham, Kate Soper (trans), The Harvester Press, Brighton 1980, p198.

2. The seminar of January 15, 1980 (repeated in a curious letter for *Le monde* shortly thereafter): 'L'Autre manque. Ça me fait drôle à moi aussi. Je tiens le coup pourtant, ce qui vous épate, mais je ne le fais pas pour cela. [The Other lacks. I don't feel happy about it myself. Yet, I endure, which fascinates you, but I am not doing it for that reason.]' Lacan, 1980, p12.

This starting point may seem meagre, but it may allow us to take a shortcut to the core of these two great theoretical endeavours of our time. What both sentences have in common, on the face of it, is a direct and straightforward statement of a non-existence, but a non-existence that causes formidable problems: for both entities which are claimed not to exist have nevertheless very palpable effects; their non-existence doesn't simply make them nonentities. Moreover, power for Foucault and the Other for Lacan are both submitted to very close theoretical scrutiny and subjected to most meticulous conceptual elaborations; they stand at the very core of their respective works and keep recurring in them as the obsessive threads that can even serve as handy clues for their immediate identification in the hazy realms of *Zeitgeist*. What kind of theory can one make of a non-existing entity and why should one engage in such a paradoxical enterprise? What consequences - theoretical and practical - follow from this non-existence? And most of all, for our present purpose, do the claims of non-existence possess the same meaning in both cases, or do they follow a different logic? I will try to show that the latter is the case.

Let us start with Foucault. All of Foucault's work can be seen as revolving around this paradoxical point, a certain kind of non-existence of what was ultimately the principal object of his analysis. So in what sense does power not exist? Is the 'substantive sense' a sufficient qualification? There one should take measure of the originality and the novelty of Foucault's position, which seems to separate him from most of the structuralist generation as well as from the quasi-totality of traditional political theories.

In the interview, Foucault hastened to add some precautions that he never tired of repeating throughout his work:

> What I mean is this. The idea that there is either located at - or emanating from - a given point something which is a 'power' seems to me to be based on a misguided analysis, one which at all events fails to

> account for a considerable number of phenomena. In reality, power means relations, a more-or-less organised, hierarchical, coordinated cluster of relations.[3]

3. Foucault, 1980, *op. cit.*, p198.

This is just one specimen from dozens of similar declarations that Foucault made, particularly when pressed by different interviewers.

There is a profound difficulty in approaching this paradoxical entity 'power' if one tries to do justice to its specific nature - and Foucault himself only gradually became aware of the whole extent of this challenge. The predicament is probably much greater than in tackling those two other basic Foucauldian entities, knowledge and the subject. In the end of his life, Foucault summarised his endeavour rather roughly in the big triad 'knowledge - power – subject'.[4] Power seems to be an entity that encompasses the other two and that defies delimitation. The predicament can first be pinpointed as a constant series of negations: what Foucault is doing a great deal of the time is declaring what power is not. A necessary first step of an account of power is a 'negative theory of power', as it were, which would clearly separate the possible new theory from virtually all previous attempts. If one is to take a step into an uncharted direction, one must delimit oneself from the known.

4. See Foucault, *Beyond Structuralism and Hermeneutics,* The Harvester Press, Brighton 1982, p208. These are also the three steps that Deleuze schematically follows in his admirable book on Foucault.

So, to start with, power is not a place, a definable location, a locus in the social that could be limited to a particular point or site. This was the classical and the most common illusion of the political theory that saw power situated in a particular person, the sovereign, in a particular group of people or social class, or in a privileged institution, the state. Power could then be seen as emanating from this point downwards, displaying a neat pyramidal structure, and the ensuing natural counter-strategy was the endeavour to get hold of this particular locus at the top in order to exercise power in turn, or to try to ultimately eliminate it (cut off the king's head, abolish the state along with class domination etc.). According to this seemingly self-evident view power is something that can simply be possessed by someone and exercised from this privileged point.

Furthermore, at an even more rudimentary level, power is irreducible to either violence or law. The two entities are opposed - the rule of law being, supposedly, the end of the rule of violence - and implicated in each other - for the law takes support in violence by assigning a monopoly over it to certain institutions. If power presents a problem, it is insofar as it cannot be reduced to direct violence, physical coercion or simple repression. 'Power is exercised only over free subjects and only insofar as they are free ... Slavery is not a power relation when man is in chains. (In this case it is a question of a physical relationship of constraint.)'[5] Neither can power be reduced to the law as 'the founding word' of society, its basic contract that holds it together and provides legitimacy for its distribution of power, nor to particular forms of legality brought about by specific procedures of consensus and participation. The legal or juridical part of the story may be

5. Foucault, 1982, *op. cit.*, p221. Cf. 'A man who is chained up and beaten is subject to force being exerted over him. Not power. But if he can be induced to speak, when his ultimate recourse could have been to hold his tongue, preferring death, then he has been caused to behave in a certain way. His freedom has been subjected to power. He has been submitted to government. If an individual can remain free, however little his freedom may be, power can subject him to government. There is no power without potential refusal of revolt'. Foucault, *Politics, Philosophy, Culture,* Lawrence D. Kritzman (ed), Routledge, New York, London 1988, pp83-4. It is strange how Foucault, an anti-Hegelian if there ever was one, reproduces here the very Hegelian setting of 'master and slave' as the minimal pattern of any power relation.

very important, but it is far from being the whole story. Moreover, power cannot be reduced to something more fundamental lying behind it and of which it would be but a mask, e.g. the economic sphere, productive forces and relations of production. It is not an epiphenomenon or a superstructure whose basis is somewhere else. There is no hidden depth of power, it is all on the surface and what is on the surface is all there is to it. Neither can it be reduced to an origin, transcendent or 'natural', from which it would derive and which would endow it with authority. There is nothing behind power and power is always already there, supported only by itself.

With this argument - very briefly summarised and oversimplified - Foucault gradually discarded virtually all the classical and common approaches to power and the bulk of standard political theories. They are not completely wrong, of course, it is just that they fail to account for a large number of diverse effects and mechanisms of power, and furthermore, their key concepts (sovereignty, legitimacy, state) are not the foundations they claim to be, but they are involved, as very important parts and regions, in strategies of power that, however, don't stem from them, but enclose, comprehend and incorporate them.[6] One could say that these entities do have an existence, whereas power, as we have seen, does not; it permeates and constantly displaces them.

But these discarded entities - the monarch, the sovereignty, the state, the law - had one thing in common: they all made a totality out of the social, they made it into a whole. Taking these entities as a starting point, one could delimit the social and consider it a totality as well as discern its underlying power structure. Whereas for Foucault, and this is the first important consequence, power doesn't form a totality, it doesn't totalise the social, it rather makes it a non-whole, not-all, something that cannot be delimited. If these entities formed a totality, it was always by a certain logic of exclusion or external division - one excluded the monarch from the social as a transcending point; one excluded the law as a symbolic foundation and authority, opposed to the social texture it founded; one divided the social into opposing spheres, e.g. state and civil society, the state being the agency totalising the social, etc.[7]

Foucault's step, on the other hand, is based on a logic of inclusion: there is no outside power and if it operates by constant divisions, those divisions are internal to it - or more precisely, the division into internal and external is thereby made superfluous and non-pertinent. So power has no exteriority and is thus by its nature 'non-totalisable'. Nor does it have an essence or an interiority, and this is why the 'what' question has to be replaced by a 'how' question - not 'what is power?' but 'how does power work?' It is neither a substance nor a subject in Hegelian terms, neither an agency nor a place, and it is ultimately not a concept at all, insofar as a concept presupposes an ordered totality. As non-totalisable, it is also non-conceptualisable - not in any traditional sense. One could say that *Foucault has no concept of power*, or that power emerges in a paradoxical

6. Cf: 'I don't want to say that State isn't important; what I want to say is that relations of power, and hence the analysis that must be made of them, necessarily extend beyond the limits of the State. In two senses: first of all because the State, for all the omnipotence of its apparatuses, is far from being able to occupy the whole field of actual power relations, and further because the State can only operate on the basis of other, already existing power relations. The State is superstructural in relation to a whole series of power networks that invest the body, sexuality, the family, kinship, knowledge, technology and so forth'. Foucault, 1980, *op. cit.*, p122.

7. Cf: 'What we need, however, is a political philosophy that isn't erected around the problem of sovereignty, nor therefore around the problems of law and prohibition. We need to cut off the King's head: in political theory that has still to be done'. Foucault, 1980, *op. cit.*, p121.

status of a non-concept (and I perhaps need to add that this is not meant as a critique). This produces a side-effect: he has constantly to multiply its attributes (proliferation, multiplicity, dispersion, prolixity, inciting, enhancement, diversification, production, fermentation, heterogeneity, innumerable - attributes very often appearing in plural). But this is an external mark and consequence of the radical stance that power is a non-concept. It has many names because it is, strictly speaking, unnameable.

To be sure, power can have totalising effects, but these are to be seen as divergent processes of totalisation as opposed to totality, i.e. as processes that cannot reach their end or stabilise themselves, processes of permanently shifting borders, always partial, unstable and constantly undermined. (As Deleuze put it: 'One, Totality, Truth, object, subject are not universals, but singular processes of unification, totalisation, verification, objectification, subjectification, processes which are immanent to certain dispositives.'[8])

A further consequence of the pure exteriority of power is that Foucault discards another line of thinking that was common in many approaches to power, the approach that envisions power in terms of 'ideology and consciousness'. The problems of the type of consciousness that makes power relations possible, its inherent illusions, its essential blinding, the false consciousness that enraptures individuals and turns them into subjects, the intertwining of recognition and miscognition - these problems do not arise for Foucault at all, for they would entail - in the widest sense - a space of interiority and a mechanism of repression, the entities he is trying to do away with. To be sure, there is a constant problem of how to translate a disciplinary program into a subjective conduct, but the problem has to be solved without recourse to the ideological representations and the traditional themes of consciousness, its interiority and self-comprehension. This is why the problem of the subject, once it explicitly arises in Foucault's later work, is posed in entirely different terms: the terms of practices of self-relation, the practical self-production of the self rather than a universality of subjectivity or its self-reflection. 'Care for the self', figuring in the title of his last book, is not a type of consciousness, but a type of practice. And most importantly, it is not something external to power, opposing some realm of interiority or the psychic to power relations, but rather a relation of power to itself, a power bending in on itself, as it were, an internal loop of power (as is visually demonstrated in the somewhat mysterious drawing by Foucault reproduced in Deleuze's book.[9] An internal loop to be conceived as being at the very opposite end from the self-reflective turn of the classical self-consciousness, a self-referentiality devoid of self-reflexivity, and thus of any notion of recognition or mirroring. (Produced in an entirely different way, it comes very close to Deleuze's notion of '*le pli*', the fold.)

This is why the Foucauldian subject - very different from the subject in psychoanalysis - is not derivative of the relation to the Other, neither in its imaginary form, for it doesn't emerge in the dialectics of recognition/

8. Gilles Deleuze, 'Qu'est-ce qu'un dispositif?', *Michel Foucault philosophe*, Seuil. Paris 1989, p188.

9. Gilles Deleuze, *Foucault*, Minuit, Paris 1986, p128.

10. Michel Foucault, *La volont, de savoir*, Gallimard, Paris 1976, p209.

11. This shows the extent to which Foucault's attempt to think power is opposed to Althusser's account of power relations (which had its notorious period of glory and has passed into a sad oblivion since). In spite of the common insistence on material practices and 'rituals' as the site of power, the distance to Althusser is obvious. First, the whole issue of ideology and of becoming a subject by the mechanism of interpellation is for

miscognition, nor in its symbolic form, for it is in no way reducible to the function of a lack. This is also why Foucault avoids the notion of desire and proposes to replace it by an analysis based on 'bodies and pleasures'.[10] Desire, for Foucault, implies a 'negative ontology' of a lack and of an object supposedly detained by the Other, an object that would be able to fill the lack. Pleasure instead of desire, body instead of castration, the positivity of event instead of the lack, the multiplicity of power relations instead of the Other.[11]

If such is the nature of power, there is an important historical lesson to be drawn from it. Namely, if this nature of power was not recognised, it was not due simply to the lack of insight. Rather, its mechanisms, although ubiquitous, became fully deployed only in a certain historic juncture. With the advent of disciplinary society (roughly coinciding with the advent of modernity), power itself underwent a major historic change. There is an essential discontinuity, a rupture that has shaped the fate of power and that inaugurated our era. This is what Foucault tries to pinpoint on different levels throughout his work: the exclusion of the mad with '*le grand renfermement*' as opposed to their liberation framed by the new disciplinary techniques; the spectacle of public punishment as opposed to incarceration; power that displays itself as opposed to power that controls; the dispositive of alliance as opposed to the dispositive of sexuality; power that takes - goods, ultimately one's life - as opposed to power that produces and enhances, the bio-power that promulgates life. In each of those instances, there is a shift from a negative functioning of the norm to its positive and immanent deployment, from the norm as a restriction to the norm as a progressive incorporation and constant proliferation, from exclusion to inclusion. The norm is now seen to be immanent to, and constitutive of, the field of its application; its supposed restrictiveness constitutes what it is supposed to repress. It does not negate or repress from an external position, but it presents the moment of its inner 'condition of possibility'; it does not restrict something which was already there before, but rather brings it about.[12]

The whole issue of 'governmentality', the subject of Foucault's scrupulous reflection in his later period, aims precisely at this point of dissociation between sovereignty and legality on the one hand and the pervasive power mechanisms on the other. What is at stake is a power aiming at the disposition of things, a multiform tactics with a finality of its own beyond issues of law and sovereignty - the new techniques of governing, enhancing and controlling populations, statistical methods, calculations of risk.[13] The emergence of the 'reason of state', *la raison d'État*, and its curious new logic, along with the emergence of the new entity, the police (in the seventeenth-century sense of the word), are the two most marked signals of a modality of power that has moved well beyond the obsessions with sovereignty and law into a previously uncharted area. So the paradoxical non-totalisable nature of power only becomes fully deployed with the

Foucault misguided insofar it implies the dubious conceptual pairs of ideology/ science, recognition/ miscognition etc. Second, to take the state apparatuses as the locus of power and its material existence is to presuppose the state as the decisive framework of power, to think of power as a function of the state. Third, the complementary division into ideology and repression (ideological vs. repressive state apparatuses) obfuscates the issue by perpetuating some classical conceptual divisions (consensus *v* constraint). Fourth - and this goes for the whole of Marxism - to take the class struggle as the principal antagonism is to misread the multiple, heterogeneous and ubiquitous nature of 'agonism', (Foucault, *op. cit.*, 1982, p222), which cannot be reduced to one big general split or central contradiction that would found all power relations. To be sure, the picture is much more complex and the Althusserian position can be convincingly defended on many points.

12. Cf. Pierre Macherey, 'Pour une histoire naturelle des normes', in G. Deleuze, 1989, *op. cit.*, for an excellent account of this shift.

13. Cf: Foucault, 'Governmentality', in Burchell et al (eds), 1991, p94-5.

disciplinary society (although the different breaks that Foucault studies are not simply homologous and cannot be reduced to a simple common denominator - they have been brought about in multiple and heterogeneous ways). Most political theory remained stuck with the notions of sovereignty, legality and state, thus unable to understand the novelty of disciplinary mechanisms or to account for the most important ways in which modern power is exercised. As Foucault put it: 'Maybe what is really important for our modernity ... is not so much the statisation of society, as the 'governmentalisation' of the state'.[14] Here lies Foucault's enormous endeavour to invent power as a new phenomenon and to think its specificity beyond its antiquated models - an object that hasn't been thought before.

14. *Ibid.*, p103.

If there is a negative aspect to Foucault's theory of power, establishing what power is not, then this aspect has to be seen as a preliminary step towards establishing power in its positivity. Indeed, the point of rejecting the traditional approaches was precisely an attempt to think power in its pure positivity, since to posit power in terms of sovereignty or law was also to endow it with an essential negativity, to take it basically as a 'power that says no', an agency of repression. The point of Foucault's famous critique of the 'repressive hypothesis' was to reverse perspective and to envision power as production, a proliferation, an inducement, an enhancement, an increase, rather than negation, exclusion, prohibition or limitation. So the negative side of Foucault's theory aimed precisely at discarding the negativity that the traditional theories introduced as pertaining to power. The real difficulty emerges with thinking power as positive. This is at stake in Foucault's insistence on events as opposed to structure. For him, the main problem is in principle not a search for some hidden structure behind surface events, regulating them with a secret hand, disguised in some deeper layer or assigned to the unconscious. Nothing is hidden and there is nothing behind the curtain.[15] In this respect, Foucault is at the opposite end of the spectrum from someone like Levi-Strauss, and this is also why on several occasions he decidedly proclaimed himself anti-structuralist.[16] To think the event is to think the heterogeneous in its exteriority and singularity, which cannot be reduced to a hidden rule of a structure and its differential oppositions. To be sure, events form series, repetitions, encounters, regularities of dispersion, connections, of their own, but these are of an entirely different nature from symbolic laws and 'structuralist structures'. The task of analysis is not to reduce events to a hidden matrix of intelligibility or to present them as instances of some universal laws, but rather to 'lighten the weight of causality and maintain their contingency.[17] The event, being unhidden at the very surface, is nevertheless what is the least self-evident, and it takes a whole new strategy to do justice to events. It is much harder to stick to the surface than to dig in the depths.

15. It is curious that both Deleuze (1986, p61) and Macherey (1989, p218) use this paramount Hegelian dictum to summarise Foucault's position, and one can find some rough equivalents in Foucault himself as well. Hegel's own exemplary formulation is to be found in its emphatic form as the parting shot of the chapter on understanding in *The Phenomenology of Spirit*.

16. 'One can agree that structuralism formed the most systematic effort to evacuate the concept of the event, not only from ethnology but from a whole series of other sciences and in the extreme case from history. In that sense, I don't see who could be more of an anti-structuralist than myself', M. Foucault, 1980, *op. cit.*, p114.

17. Foucault, 1991, *op. cit.*, p77.

Foucault often insists that power is not an entity but a relation, or rather a cluster of relations, 'actions on actions', and one could infer from this that its elements are purely relational, without an inherent identity, just as the elements of structure are purely differential and consist only in clusters of relations. But the difference between the two is essential: the model of power is war rather than language, its vocabulary is that of struggles, strategies and tactics, and if power relations can never be stabilised in a differential logic, it is because of their inherently agonistic nature (agonism being 'a relationship which is at the same time reciprocal incitement and struggle; less a face-to-face confrontation that paralyses both sides than a permanent provocation').[18] The agonistic struggle cannot be abated in the serenity or transparence or the aesthetic appeal of the structure, which can at best be a provisional stage of an ongoing conflict.

18. Foucault, 1982, *op. cit.*, p222.

Seen from a broader perspective, the notion of event was central not only to Foucault, but to a number of undertakings that marked a certain turn in the development of structuralism - as was most notably elaborated by Gilles Deleuze and later by Alain Badiou. Very briefly and schematically, one could say that the first epoch of structuralism was preoccupied with the realm of the symbolic and its newly-discovered and far-reaching properties, which defined the very concept of structure, and this was long the principal trademark of 'the structuralist revolution'. At a certain point, however, roughly from the late 1960s on, the early semiological interest started to give way to an implication overlooked during the first enthusiasm, namely that the elaboration of the symbolic necessarily yields a remainder, a residue, the *non-symbolisable* (and the resistance to symbolisation can be seen as the backbone of event). So the fascination with the sign, the signifier, its logic and its paradoxical status, was suddenly overshadowed by another concern, the question of *a new invention of the real*. The Lacanian concept of the real, focused on the object a, was perhaps the first inkling of this turn; it reshaped his entire theoretical edifice and was to determine his entire later period.[19] The concept of event (magisterially promoted by Deleuze at the end of the 1960s) was another way of doing this; it resulted from similar structuralist presuppositions and was an answer to the same problem, although it extended the consequences in another direction.[20]

19. The twin notions of *matheme* and *lalangue*, for example, can be seen as the retroactive effect of this dimension of the real on the notion of the symbolic, the rethinking of the symbolic 'in view of' the real, as it were.

In Lacanian terms, Foucault's endeavour, in a nutshell, could be read as an attempt to show that power cannot be based either in the symbolic (the Law, the Name-of-the-Father, the Master Signifier) or in the imaginary (modes of consciousness, the constitution of the ego, specularity, recognition/ miscognition). His project could be described as an attempt to think 'the Real' without the Symbolic and the Imaginary, in an effort to produce its 'logic' without recourse to the other two, indeed to show, ultimately, that the other two are superfluous and necessarily lead to delusions and impasses. For Lacan, on the other hand, the central endeavour remained not to discard any of them (hence his insistence on the great triad of the real, the symbolic and the imaginary), but to think the way they are necessarily tied together, although they are entirely heterogeneous and even mutually exclusive, following completely different kinds of logic, to think the way they are tied in a knot that defines human experience and that underlies

20. I ignore here the possible and tricky connections with the Heideggerian concept of *Ereignis*, which was developed along entirely different lines. The connection bears a lot of weight in the work of Derrida, which can be seen as another answer to the same problem.

the bottom of power relations (hence his curious preoccupation with the Borromean knot).

Foucault's adoption of the 'logic of event' also resulted in his abandoning, at a certain point, some of his earlier concepts, most notably the episteme and to some extent the discourse, in favour of a new concept of dispositive. Dispositives are no longer discursive formations, but rather the clusters of events that indiscriminately mix the events pertaining to enunciation (magisterially analysed in *Archéologie du savoir* in 1969) and those pertaining to the realm of the bodies, and the visible. The lines of knowledge, power and subjectivity form variable chains, and although they form precarious 'diagrams', they can never be circumscribed in the stability of a system or abated to a matrix of intelligibility. They present certain regularities, but yield no universalities. Their contingent and heterogeneous nature is irreducible, there is no Other to secretly regulate them.

It is well known that Foucault's verdict on psychoanalysis gradually became very harsh. The entire project of the history of sexuality, in his later years, may be seen as an attempt at a genealogy of psychoanalysis, an alternative account of its object, an effort to determine power relations it is based on and which it unwittingly perpetuates. Psychoanalysis, for him, ultimately sustains and maintains at its core both the clinical gaze, with its well-known genealogy, and the mechanism of confession, deeply embedded in the whole history of Christianity - for both of which it presents the subtlest and the most insidious transformation. Finally, psychoanalysis is blind to the historic and recent nature of sexuality, which is not something to be unearthed and liberated, but rather constitutes itself as a dispositive of power in a fundamental complicity with disciplinary mechanisms. The analyst could ultimately be seen as the embodiment of the Other, the bearer of the gaze and the agency to which one confesses the truth about oneself - in a form purified of the more obvious and crude features of preceding confession figures.

Foucault also went against the grain of the time and opposed virtually the entire 'structuralist generation' by gradually systematically avoiding and rejecting the concept of the unconscious, since it was for him ineradicably linked with the hidden truth about sexuality and thus with the whole 'politics of truth', the production of truth, the regime of truth that can be traced back to Christianity and further to antiquity. If we try to pin down the essential difference between Foucault's account of power and the rival account in psychoanalysis - it could perhaps be put this way: for the Lacanian reading of psychoanalysis, the basic assumption is that *there is the Other* that is 'always already' there, and this is what can account for the mechanisms of power, while for Foucault no such assumption is necessary: quite the contrary, if there is 'an effect of the Other', it has to be explained as an effect, i.e. something produced by multiple strategies of power relations and their dispositives, an entity precarious and unstable and always derived. That there is 'always already' power doesn't mean that there is 'always already' the Other, quite the opposite. If the event is pure exteriority, it has no Other - the Other presupposes something it is the Other of, 'the Same' of an interiority or an identity. Yet, if for psychoanalysis the Other is 'always already' there, how are we to understand our initial dictum that 'the Other is lacking'?

For Lacan, the Other arises the moment we are confronted with the symbolic structure. If the Other is 'always already' there, implied by the structure - and at this point one could even tentatively speak of a 'realism', as opposed to Foucault's nominalism - any notion of subjectivity arises in the dialectical move of assuming it by insertion into its order. It is the hypothetical authority that upholds the structure and the supposed addressee of any act of speech, beyond interlocution or intersubjectivity, the third in any dialogue. This elementary assumption was present throughout Lacan's work, acquiring different shades of meaning at different periods and growing more and more sophisticated. It turned out, for example, that any notion of structure, far from being simply differential, a balanced matrix of permutations (as in Levi-Strauss), necessarily gives rise to a 'Master Signifier', a structural function that power gets hold of, but which is in itself empty, devoid of meaning, a pure positivisation of a void. The theory of four discourses, his most elaborate account of power, took its starting point there.

For Foucault, the account of power postulates that the Other from the outset is necessarily circular, presupposing what it should explain. Thus, it can be seen as a lapse into those traditional modes of political thinking based on sovereignty and law - for the Other is ultimately the Other of the symbolic law; the Father, be it as his mere name, is necessarily present to regulate it, and power is still centered on the Master, be it as the 'empty' structural place of the 'Master Signifier'. The new theory may be more complex, but it is a new disguise of old theories and cannot account for the newly discovered multiplicity of power relations and strategies and the heterogeneity of dispositives. The well-known Foucauldian nominalist stance emphatically precludes the assumption of the Other as a starting point or as an explanatory device.

One line of critical approach to Foucault would be to consider whether, at certain points, he nevertheless makes assumptions that cannot be quite covered by his methodological declarations. Is he compelled to covertly introduce the Other - not just as an effect produced by the mechanism, but as something that itself produces effects? Furthermore, doesn't he make some assumptions about the structure of subjectivity that are quite different from his proclaimed notion of the subject as the practice of the self?

There is a certain paradox that may puzzle the reader of *Discipline and Punish*: a peculiar discrepancy between the methodological proclamations and the result. There may well be a dispersed diversity of micro-relations, yet the diagram of the Benthamite Panopticon, the center-piece of the argument, unites them so effectively into a common pattern that it can be easily translated into a number of different domains. 'Is it surprising that the prison resembles the factories, schools, army barracks, hospitals, which all resemble prisons'.[21] If Foucault raises the rhetorical question, which actually closes the chapter on the Panopticon, one could venture an answer: yes, it is surprising, even astonishing, that the multiplicity of dispersed and heterogeneous micro-relations converges into one single image of power which is entirely imbued with the figure of the Other. One could pose a naive question: doesn't Foucault's strategy of dispersed micro-relations eventually converge in a much more massive presence of the Other than psychoanalysis would ever dream of? A pattern of power where the Master (the King, the Father) may well be absent, replaced by architecture and geometry, reduced to pure function and fiction, yet his empty place makes his presence all the more pervasive and intractable. The contingent events appear to be ruled much more by the invisible hand of the Other than was ever the case in psychoanalysis. Is there a lack, or at least a crack, in this massive Other at all? Hasn't ubiquitous contingency eventually produced a figure of inescapable necessity? Didn't the Other, discarded at the outset, return in the end, triumphantly and surreptitiously, as a figure all the more haunting and powerful? A number of critics and commentators have pointed out that the image of disciplinary power presented by Foucault was so overwhelming and staggering that it hardly allowed for resistance or even some margin of leeway. Perhaps it isn't surprising that Foucault had great difficulties in explaining what counter-strategy of resistance might follow from his work, and the eventual introduction of the notion of subject can be seen, among other things, as an attempt to resolve this predicament: the subject, which arises from subjection but is nevertheless irreducible to it, presents an 'internal loop' of power that counteracts power.

There is another aspect that unwittingly brings Foucault close to psychoanalysis, in spite of the unbridgeable gap. The status of the Panopticon is that of a fiction - first in the sense that fiction is what makes it work: 'A real subjection emerges mechanically from a fictitious relationship'. Or a bit further: '... it gives to the spirit the power over the spirit', without physical constraint.[22] And then also in the sense that this fiction doesn't actually describe real life in nineteenth-century prisons at all, but is nevertheless indispensable for their description.[23] It is not an 'ideal type' to be opposed to actuality, the difference 'is not one between the purity of the ideal and the disorderly impurity of the real'.[24] Neither is it the difference between illusion and reality, but rather a part of fiction that is necessary to account for reality itself or, rather, to bring about a certain reality. '... these programmes induce a whole series of effects in the real ... they crystallize into institutions, they inform individual behaviour, they act as grids for perception and evaluation of things'.[25] So the programme doesn't describe what really happens: rather, what makes it happen. It is a paradoxical entity that relates absolutely heterogeneous terms, something 'suprasensible', '*un non-lieu*', a fiction that produces real

21. M. Foucault, *Surveiller et Punir*, Gallimard, Paris 1975, p229.

22. *Ibid.*, pp204, 208.

23. 'If I had wanted to describe "real life" in the prisons, I wouldn't indeed have gone to Bentham. But the fact that this real life isn't the same thing as the theoreticians' schemas doesn't entail that these schemas are therefore utopian, imaginary, etc. One could only think that if one had a very impoverished notion of the real'. Foucault, 1991, *op. cit.*, p81.

24. M. Foucault, 1991, *op. cit.*, p80.

25. *Ibid.*, p81.

effects and functions as a 'historical a priori', a 'grid of perception'. Can one give a better definition of fantasy? The mechanism cannot be conceived without an essential aspect of fantasy that refracts all micro-relations and at the same time unifies them - why would one fall prey to this fiction if it weren't supported by an economy of enjoyment? And if the subjects become subject to self-surveillance, if they have to chain themselves, if they only emerge as subjects by being subjected and attached to power, then they have to be conceived as split subjects, they have to be endowed with a 'psychic economy' that Foucault never really questions. What kind of 'psyche' must the subjects have for the fiction to produce 'real' effects? What makes them espouse fictions at all?

The mechanism of confession, the object of much of Foucault's later reflection, also relies on the incidence of the Other. For confession presents a problem not as something that has to be extorted by torture, but quite the contrary, as a telling the truth about oneself that comes as a liberation, a temptation it is hard to resist. One is trapped by the liberating power of truth. Confession supposes the Other as the true addressee of speech, the Other whom one cannot and must not deceive, the Other one must measure up to and in relation to which one is always deficient. It is a simple and effective mechanism that maintains the Other as the necessary function of a very simple situation and that can be used in a number of dispositives - from mediaeval monastic techniques to modern concerns of *scientia sexualis* (this paradoxical 'enjoyment in the truth of enjoyment', as he put it,[26] medicine, psychology and, finally and above all, psychoanalysis. Isn't the analyst the ultimate embodiment of that agency to which one must confess and which thus maintains a relation of power? Isn't the unconscious the paradigm of an ultimately always sexual truth that one must unearth in order to be free and thus properly enchained?

26. M. Foucault, 1976, *op. cit.*, p95.

If we are to attempt a defense of psychoanalysis against this persuasive charge, should we plead guilty or innocent? It is of course true that psychoanalysis is based on a 'dispositive' that links the Other, the 'confession', sexuality, the truth and the unconscious, yet this is only one side of the matter. For if this tie and its effectivity are taken as psychoanalysis's initial assumption, it is precisely in order to undo it. Insofar as this tie pertains to the very nature of the symbolic, Foucault had great difficulties delimiting it to a particular historic juncture. He first tried to pin it down to the recent emergence of 'bourgeois' sexuality, but taking this as a 'working hypothesis' in the first part of his history of sexuality, he was soon compelled to reach further back, first to Christianity, then to antiquity, but the source of this knot formed by sex, speech and truth remained elusive.

We must start by pleading guilty: psychoanalysis does indeed use this mechanism as its lever; and in its theory, it has a precise name: transference. It is a mechanism, a junction, which is also at stake as a 'necessary supposition' in any relation of domination and which, in Freud's famous dictum, actually links analysis with those two other impossible professions, governing and education (one can hardly resist the temptation to translate them into Foucauldian terms of 'power and knowledge'). So psychoanalysis does assume the hidden suppositions at work in both domination and education; to speak with Freud, it doesn't shy away from the 'faulty assumptions' of traditional theories nor simply reject them as useless. But the process of analysis is precisely a process of a painstaking undoing of them and can only be terminated when these ties are severed. The analysis of transference turns out to be the central part of psychoanalysis, indeed it may be said to coincide with analysis *tout court*.

Power presents a problem the moment when a tie of submission persists after the ties of physical constraint have been cut. So far, both accounts agree. Transference may be seen as the psychoanalytic name for this tie, which is always founded on a supposition, an unwarranted assumption - Lacan therefore speaks of a 'subject supposed to know' as a pivotal point of transference, necessarily supplemented by another supposition, let's say of a 'subject supposed to enjoy' (hence Lacan's analysis of *agalma*, in the seminar devoted to transference, as the miraculous object supposedly possessed by Socrates). For there is an enjoyment to be gained and to be lost (which may strangely be the same thing) in this supposition, and this is what lies at the root of subject's entanglement in the first place. It is through this supposition; that the Other emerges at all, the supposition that it 'makes sense', or that there is a sense to be made, that there is a knowledge, that there is an enjoyment for which the Other possesses the keys. This is the kernel of both power and knowledge.

But there is another twist: the subject is not simply subject to this mirage or delusion, dependent on an omnipotent Other, be it also of his/her own creation, but it emerges precisely at the point where a lack in this omnipotent Other appears - at the points where it doesn't 'make sense', where knowledge and enjoyment fail. The failure of the Other is there from the moment that there is the Other (hence the twin mechanisms of alienation and separation). One could say, briefly and somewhat enigmatically, that fantasy - as the basic 'delusion' framing reality - is a response to that lack in the Other coextensive with the emergence of the subject (the point demonstrated by Lacan at great length in his graph of desire).[27] It is an attempt to sustain the Other, while psychoanalysis is precisely an attempt to undo it, to dismantle and 'deconstruct' its support ('working through' the fundamental fantasy is one of Lacan's definitions of analysis). Once the support of fantasy (fundamental, as it were) is taken away, we are indeed stuck with dispersed, divergent, multiple and heterogeneous events - the point where Foucault wants to start, but which in psychoanalysis appears as the result of a long trajectory. It is a trajectory one cannot forbear and merely keep the result, for it holds the keys to both the necessity and the contingency of power and to a strategy of resistance to it. Furthermore, if the events are to be taken as the Foucauldian version of the real (as opposed to the symbolic

27. I have tried to develop these points more systematically and at more length in 'Cogito as the Subject of the Unconscious', in Slavoj Zizek (ed), *Cogito and the Unconscious* (Sic vol. 2), Duke University Press, 1998; and in 'The Subject Supposed to Enjoy', the introduction to Alain Grosrichard, *The Sultan's Court*, Verso 1998.

and the imaginary), this shows the distance separating him from Lacan. For fantasy was not simply an illusion - of an illusion of a centre and of a sense, covering up a central void, but also contained a confrontation with the real, a traumatic kernel of enjoyment, an impossible coming to terms with it. This is why, for Lacan, the real can only be equated with the impossible, a pure negativity, while for Foucault it appears as a pure positivity. It is taken, in one instance, as that which cannot 'appear' at all, while in the other it pervades the entire field of events.

It is odd that Foucault never mentions the problem of transference in his later attacks on psychoanalysis, while he was very well aware of it in his earlier days. Thus it is rather curious to read, with retrospective knowledge, the following passages written in 1966 at the conclusion of *Les mots et les choses*:

> Neither hypnosis nor the alienation of the patient in the fantasmatic personality of the doctor are constitutive of psychoanalysis; but ... it can nevertheless only be deployed in the calm violence of a singular relationship and of the transference it calls for ... But psychoanalysis uses the singular relationship of transference to discover, at the extreme limits of representation, desire, law, death, which mark, at the extremity of analytical language and practice, the particular figures of finitude.[28]

28. M. Foucault, *Les mots et les choses*, Gallimard, Paris 1966, pp388, 389.

So at that point, transference was seen as an essential opening to what is beyond representation (where desire and law still figured as marks of contingency and heterogeneity), not as closure into the deceptive realm of subtle domination, insidious entrapment into the deceitful regime of truth.

This is where the crucial theoretical alternative must be placed - whether to do away with the figure of the Other, and along with it with the figures of desire and law, as the ultimate and the most refined disguise of domination, a safeguard against the paradoxical nature of events; or to maintain them, but showing that the message they contain is quite the opposite of what was traditionally assumed. It is true that transference is based on a supposition of telling the truth about sexuality, but the unconscious is precisely the experience that no such truth exists, that the truth that appears in the symptoms, in parapraxes, on the margins, is always fragmented and deficient, failing and haunted by a lack, and if it appears only in failed attempts, it is because it is in itself non-whole and lacking, the truth always 'half-said' (*mi-dire*, says Lacan). It is true that psychoanalysis is placed entirely under the sign of the Other, but only to discover that the Other doesn't exist, that it is itself lacking.

'Power doesn't exist', says Foucault, which one can translate, for the present purpose, into 'there is no Other on which power is based'; the implication being that power is always contingent, dispersed, subject to the uncertain results of particular struggles and conflicts, temporary outcomes of an irreducible 'agonism'. The adequate approach that follows from this can therefore only be based on a strict nominalism. 'The Other doesn't exist', says Lacan and it seems that he aims at the same thing. Yet the logic of this statement is quite different and much more paradoxical: without the Other, there is no 'effect' of power nor the 'psychic economy' that makes it possible. The analysis cannot start without this presupposition, although it aims at its abolishment. Power works only if and as long as we assume the Other and pawn a part of our being to it, so that it appears as both necessary and contingent. This is why one is never in a position to say that it would suffice to get rid of the Other as a deceptive entity and start with the knowledge that it doesn't exist anyway, to economise it, reduce it to an effect of diverse micro-relations. One can only think power in the space between the necessary hypothesis about the 'always already there' of the Other, which opens the space of power relations, and the insight that 'the Other lacks'. The insight into its 'non-existence' cannot make the shortcut around its 'existence', its 'always already there', and perhaps the difficulty of Foucault's position - possibly its ultimate unsustainability - stems from his attempt to avoid and circumvent this paradox.

KANT WITH (OR AGAINST) SADE?

Slavoj Zizec

'Kant IS Sade' is the 'infinite judgement' of modern ethics, positing the sign of equation between the two radical opposites, i.e. asserting that the sublime disinterested ethical attitude is somehow identical to, or overlaps with, the unrestrained indulgence in pleasurable violence. A lot - everything, perhaps - is at stake here: is there a line from Kantian formalist ethics to the cold-blooded Auschwitz killing machine? Are concentration camps and killing as a neutral business the inherent outcome of the enlightened insistence on the autonomy of Reason? Is there at least a legitimate lineage from Sade to Fascist torturing, as is implied by Pasolini's film version of *120 Days*, which transposes it into the dark days of Mussolini's Salo republic? This link between Sade and Kant was first developed by Adorno and Horkheimer in the famous Excursion II ('Juliette or Enlightenment and Morals') of the *Dialectics of Enlightenment*: their fundamental thesis is that 'the work of Marquis de Sade displays the "Reason which is not led by another agency", that is to say, the bourgeois subject, liberated from a state of not yet being mature'.[1] Fifteen years later, Jacques Lacan (without knowing about Adorno and Horkheimer's version) also developed the notion that Sade is the truth of Kant, first in his Seminar on *The Ethics of Psychoanalysis* and then in the *écrit* 'Kant with Sade'.[2]

I

The first difference between Adorno and Horkheimer's and Lacan's 'Kant avec Sade' that strikes the eye is that, for Adorno and Horkheimer, Kant's practical philosophy is a sentimental/moralistic compromise that stands for a retreat from the radical consequences of Kant's criticism, while for Lacan, 'Kant avec Sade' is the truth of the Kantian ethical philosophy itself, of his 'critique of practical reason'. In short, Adorno and Horkheimer follow here the standard Young Hegelian opinion, stated in a most forcefully acerbic way by Heinrich Heine, that Kant's *Critique of Practical Reason* accomplishes a retreat from the unique anti-metaphysical all-destroying thrust of the *Critique of Pure Reason*: in his moral philosophy, Kant makes a compromise with compassion for ordinary fellow humans (like his faithful servant Lampe who obediently holds the umbrella for his master when it rains), providing them with necessary illusions (moral 'postulates') that enable them to lead a satisfying everyday life.[3] For Adorno and Horkheimer, this split is inherent to bourgeois society, where 'cold' objective market relations and the utilitarian logic of instrumental manipulation are supplemented with pathetic morality and sentimental philanthropism.

1. Max Horkheimer and Theodor W. Adorno, *Dialektik der Aufklaerung*, Fischer Verlag, Frankfurt 1971, p79.

2. See especially chapter VI of Jacques Lacan, *Le seminaire, livre VII: L'ethique de la psychanalyse*, [1958-59], Editions du Seuil, Paris 1986; see Jacques Lacan, 'Kant avec Sade', in *Ecrits*, Editions du Seuil, Paris 1966, pp765-790.

3. Doesn't the same hold even for Derrida who, in his *Spectres of Marx*, Galilée, Paris 1993, in what is arguably the lowest philosophical point of his oeuvre, in order to prove that, in spite of the ruthless radicality of deconstruction, he is also a good caring human being, enumerates in ten points what is wrong with today's world (from the sad plight of the homeless in our cities to narco-cartels ... - see pp134-139). In a strict parallel to the Young Hegelian criticism of Kant, Laclau's critical analysis of Derrida (see Ernesto Laclau, 'The Time is Out of Joint', in *Emancipation(s)*, Verso, London 1996) emphasised how the Levinasian ethical attitude of 'openness to the spectral Other', to the unique Event of its emergence, cannot be strictly deduced from the basic premise of deconstruction (the constitutive displacement, i.e. the coincidence of

conditions of possibility with the conditions of impossibility) - from the same premises, one can also draw the exactly opposite conclusion, i.e. the need for a strong force of domination which - temporarily, at least - contains the threat of dissemination.

Bourgeois ideology, in its everyday 'normal' functioning, thus retracts from its own consequences - and, for Adorno and Horkheimer, the great merit of the bourgeois poets *maudits* or thinkers like Sade or Nietzsche is that they leave off this moralistic sugar-coating and accept fully the consequences of the capitalist instrumental attitude. So, to put it succinctly, for Adorno and Horkheimer, the Sadean position is the true ethical implication of modern subjectivity (or, more radically, of the entire Enlightenment process from its early mythic origins), formulated in a consequent way, freed of all sentimental sugar-coating.

Kant thus goes only half-way: on behalf of the subject's autonomy, he abolishes the dependence of Reason, inclusive of ethical Reason, on any heterogeneous content (like the traditional, premodern ethics that relies on some substantial positive notion of Supreme Good), but he still wants to save the notion of ethical duty. He himself silently admits the fact that he cannot ground the priority of Good over Evil, of compassion over cruelty, in the inherent formal structure of Reason itself, when he is compelled to claim that the Call of Conscience which requires us to do our Duty is a simple 'fact of Reason', something found in ourselves, a raw irrational fact. The sadist pervert's reduction of the sexual partner to a mere object, to a means to his own unlimited pleasure, is the hidden truth of the Kantian ethical injunction to treat other human beings with respect, to allow them a minimum of dignity.

Adorno and Horkheimer locate Sade in the long tradition of the orgiastic/carnivalesque reversal of the established order: the moment when the hierarchical rules are suspended and 'everything is permitted'. This primordial *jouissance* recaptured by the sacred orgies is, of course, the retroactive projection of the human alienated state: it never existed prior to its loss. The point is that Sade announces the moment when, with the emergence of bourgeois Enlightenment, pleasure itself loses its sacred/transgressive character and is reduced to a rationalised instrumental activity. According to Adorno and Horkheimer, the greatness of Sade is that, on behalf of the full assertion of earthly pleasures, he not only rejects any metaphysical moralism, but also fully acknowledges the price one has to pay for it: the radical intellectualisation/instrumentalisation/regimentation of the (sexual) activity intended to bring pleasure. Here we encounter the content later baptised by Marcuse 'repressive desublimation': after all the barriers of sublimation, of cultural transformation of sexual activity, are abolished, what we get is not raw, brutal, passionate satisfying animal sex, but, on the contrary, a fully regimented, intellectualised activity comparable to a well-planned sporting match. The Sadean hero is not a beast, but a pale, cold-blooded intellectual much more alienated from the true pleasure of the flesh than is the prudish, inhibited lover, a man of reason enslaved to the *amor intellectualis diaboli* - what gives pleasure to him (or her) is not sexuality as such but the activity of outstripping rational civilisation by its own means, i.e. by way of thinking (and practising) to the end the consequences of its logic. So, far from being an entity of full, earthly passion, the Sadean hero is fundamentally *apathetic*, reducing sexuality to a mechanical planned procedure deprived of the last vestiges of spontaneous pleasure or sentimentality. What Sade heroically takes into account is that pure bodily sensual pleasure and spiritual love are not simply opposed, but dialectically intertwined: there is something deeply 'spiritual', spectral, sublime, about a really passionate sensual lust, and vice versa (as the mystical experience teaches us), so that the thorough 'desublimation' of sexuality also thoroughly intellectualises it, changing an intense pathetic bodily experience into a cold, apathetic mechanical exercise.

Here, again, as is clear to Adorno and Horkheimer, Sade paradoxically rejoins Kant: didn't Kant also despise the false morality supported by sentimental compassion or any other pathological feeling of satisfaction, didn't he also preach as the only proper ethical attitude that of apathy, of doing one's duty only for the sake of duty? By drawing all ethical consequences from the formalised instrumental Reason, i.e., by emphasising its ethical neutrality and apathy, by pointing out how, if one sticks strictly to Reason alone, it is impossible to ground even the most elementary prohibition of murder, Sade's work is thus, according to Adorno and Horkheimer, not to be dismissed as the expression of the morbid sickness of our civilisation. On the contrary, in the work of writers like Sade, 'sickness itself becomes the symptom of healing',[4] that is, its fearless exposure of the falsity of compassion and other philanthropic values opens up in a negative way the space for a society that would no longer need similar ideological masks to conceal its own brutal actuality.

4. Max Horkheimer and Theodor W. Adorno, *op.cit.*, p102.

II

How, then, does Lacan stand in regard to the Adorno and Horkheimer version of 'Kant with Sade' (i.e. of Sade as the truth of Kantian ethics)? For Lacan also, Sade consequently deployed the inherent potential of the Kantian philosophical revolution, although Lacan gives to this a somewhat different twist - his point is that Sade honestly *externalises* the Voice of Conscience (which, in Kant, attests the subject's full ethical autonomy, i.e. is self-posited/imposed by the subject) in the Executioner who terrorises/tortures the victim.[5] The first response here is, of course: what's all the fuss about? Today, in our post-idealist Freudian era, doesn't everybody know what the point of the 'with' is - the truth of Kant's ethical rigour is the sadism of the Law, i.e. the Kantian Law is a superego agency that sadistically enjoys the subject's deadlock, his inability to meet its inexorable demands, like the proverbial teacher who tortures pupils with impossible tasks and secretly savours their failings? Lacan's point, however, is the exact opposite of this first reaction: it is not Kant who was a closet sadist, it is Sade who is a closet Kantian. That is to say, what one should bear in mind is that the focus of Lacan is always Kant, not Sade: what Lacan is interested in are the

5. In clinical terms, one can say that Sade radicalises Kantian obsessional economy into a full-blown pervert position.

ultimate consequences and disavowed premises of the Kantian ethical revolution. In other words, Lacan does not try to make the usual 'reductionist' point that every ethical act, as pure and disinterested as it may appear, is always grounded in some 'pathological' motivation (the agent's own long-term interest, the admiration of his peers, up to the 'negative' satisfaction provided by the suffering and extortion often demanded by ethical acts); the focus of Lacan's interest rather resides in the paradoxical reversal by means of which desire itself (i.e. acting upon one's desire, not compromising it) can no longer be grounded in any 'pathological' interests or motivations and thus meets the criteria of the Kantian ethical act, so that 'following one's desire' overlaps with 'doing one's duty'. Suffice it to recall Kant's own famous example from his *Critique of Practical Reason*:

> Suppose that someone says his lust is irresistible when the desired object and opportunity are present. Ask him whether he would not control his passions if, in front of the house where he has this opportunity, a gallows were erected on which he would be hanged immediately after gratifying his lust. We do not have to guess very long what his answer may be.[6]

Lacan's counterargument here is: what if we come upon a subject (as we do regularly in psychoanalysis), who can only fully enjoy a night of passion if some form of 'gallows' is threatening: if by doing 'it', he is violating some prohibition? An Italian film from the 1960s, with Virna Lisi and Marcello Mastroianni, hinges on this very point: the hero can only retain his sexual potency if doing 'it' involves some kind of danger. Towards the end of the film, when he is on the verge of marrying his beloved, he wants at least to violate the prohibition of premarital sex by sleeping with her the night *before* the wedding - however, his bride unknowingly spoils even this minimal pleasure by arranging with the priest for special permission for the two of them to sleep together the night before, so that the act is deprived of its transgressive sting. What can he do now? In the last shot of the film, we see him crawling on the narrow ledge of the high-rise building: a self-imposed task to enter the girl's bedroom in the most dangerous way, in the desperate attempt to link sexual gratification to mortal danger.

So Lacan's point is that if gratifying sexual passion involves the suspension of even the most elementary 'egotistic' interests, if this gratification is clearly located 'beyond the pleasure principle', then, in spite of all appearances to the contrary, *we are dealing with an ethical act*, then the subject's 'passion' is *stricto sensu* ethical.[7]

Lacan's further point is that this covert Sadean dimension of an 'ethical (sexual) passion' is not read into Kant by our eccentric interpretation, but is inherent to the Kantian theoretical edifice.[8] If we put aside the body of 'circumstantial evidence' for it (isn't Kant's infamous definition of marriage – 'the contract between two adults of the opposite sex about the mutual use

6. Immanuel Kant, *Critique of Practical Reason*, Macmillan, New York 1993, p30.

7. '... if, as Kant claims, no other thing but the moral law can induce us to put aside all our pathological interests and accept our death, then the case of someone who spends a night with a lady even though he knows that he will pay for it with his life, is the case of the moral law'. Alenka Zupancic, 'The Subject of the Law', in *Cogito and the Unconscious*, Slavoj Zizek (ed), Duke UP, Durham, North Carolina 1998, p89.

8. The most obvious proof of the inherent character of this link of Kant with Sade, of course, is the (disavowed) Kantian notion of 'diabolical Evil', i.e. of Evil accomplished for no 'pathological' reasons, but out of principle, 'just for the sake of it'. Kant evokes this notion of Evil elevated into a universal maxim (and thus turned into an ethical principle) only in order to disclaim it immediately, claiming that human beings are incapable of such utter corruption; however, shouldn't we counter this Kantian disclaimer by pointing out that de Sade's entire edifice relies precisely on such an elevation of Evil into an unconditional ('categorical') imperative? For a closer elaboration of this point, see Chapter 2 of Slavoj Zizek, *The Indivisible Remainder*, Verso, London 1996.

of each other's sexual organs' - thoroughly Sadean, since it reduces the Other, the subject's sexual partner, to a partial object, to his/her bodily organ which provides pleasure, ignoring him/her as a whole person?), the crucial clue that allows us to discern the contours of 'Sade in Kant' is the way Kant conceptualises the relationship between sentiments (feelings) and the moral Law. Although Kant insists on the absolute gap between pathological sentiments and the pure form of moral Law, there *is* one a priori sentiment that the subject necessarily experiences when confronted with the injunction of the moral Law, the *pain* of humiliation (because of man's hurt pride, due to the 'radical Evil' of human nature); for Lacan, Kant privileging pain as the only *a priori* sentiment is strictly correlative to de Sade's notion of pain (torturing and humiliating the other, being tortured and humiliated by him) as the privileged way of access to sexual *jouissance* (Sade's argument is that pain is to be given priority over pleasure on account of its greater longevity - pleasures are passing, while pain can last almost indefinitely). This link can be further substantiated by what Lacan calls the Sadean fundamental fantasy: the fantasy of another, ethereal body of the victim, which can be tortured indefinitely and nonetheless magically retains its beauty (see the standard Sadean figure of a young girl sustaining endless humiliations and mutilations from her depraved torturer and somehow mysteriously surviving it all intact, in the same way Tom and Jerry and other cartoon heroes survive all their ridiculous ordeals intact). Doesn't this fantasy provide the libidinal foundation of the Kantian postulate of the immortality of the soul endlessly striving to achieve ethical perfection, i.e., is not the fantasmatic 'truth' of the immortality of the soul its exact opposite, the *immortality of the body*, its ability to sustain endless pain and humiliation?[9] Judith Butler pointed out that the Foucauldian 'body' as the site of resistance is none other than the Freudian 'psyche': paradoxically, 'body' is Foucault's name for the *psychic* apparatus insofar as it resists the soul's domination. That is to say, when, in his well-known definition of the soul as the 'prison of the body', Foucault turns around the standard Platonic-Christian definition of the body as the 'prison of the soul', what he calls 'body' is not simply the biological body, but is effectively already caught into some kind of pre-subjective psychic apparatus.[10] Consequently, don't we encounter in Kant a secret homologous inversion, only in the opposite direction, of the relationship between body and soul: what Kant calls 'immortality of the soul' is effectively the immortality of the other, ethereal, 'undead' *body*?

9. Regarding this point, see Alenka Zupancic, *op.cit.*

10. See Judith Butler, *The Psychic Life of Power*, Stanford University Press, Stanford, California 1997, pp28-29.

III

It is via this central role of pain in the subject's ethical experience that Lacan introduces the difference between the 'subject of the enunciation' (the subject who utters a statement) and the 'subject of the enunciated (statement)' (the symbolic identity the subject assumes within and via his statement): Kant does not address the question of who is the 'subject of the enunciation' of the moral law, the agent enunciating the unconditional ethical injunction - from within his horizon, this question itself is meaningless, since the moral law is an impersonal command 'coming from nowhere', i.e. it is ultimately self-posited, autonomously assumed by the subject himself. Via the reference to Sade, Lacan reads this absence in Kant as an act of rendering invisible, of 'repressing', the moral Law's enunciator, and it is Sade who renders it visible in the figure of the 'sadist' executioner-torturer - this executioner is the enunciator of the moral law, the agent who finds pleasure in our (the moral subject's) pain and humiliation. A counterargument offers itself here with apparent self-evidence: isn't all this utter nonsense, since, in Sade, the element that occupies the place of the unconditional injunction, the maxim the subject has to follow categorically, is no longer the Kantian universal ethical command *Do your duty*!, but its most radical opposite, the injunction to follow to their utmost limit the thoroughly pathological, contingent caprices that bring you pleasure, ruthlessly reducing all your fellow humans to the instruments of your pleasure? However, it is crucial to perceive the solidarity between this feature and the emergence of the figure of the 'sadist' torturer-executioner as the effective 'subject of the enunciation' of the universal ethical statement-command. The Sadean move from Kantian Respect to Blasphemy, i.e. from respecting the Other (fellow being), his freedom and autonomy, and always treating him also as an end-in-itself, to reducing all Others precisely to mere dispensable instruments to be ruthlessly exploited, is strictly correlative to the fact that the 'subject of the enunciation' of the Moral Injunction, invisible in Kant, assumes the concrete features of the Sadean executioner.

What Sade accomplishes is thus a very precise operation of *breaking up the link between two elements which, in Kant's eyes, are synonymous and overlapping*:[11] the assertion of an unconditional ethical injunction; the moral universality of this injunction. Sade keeps the structure of an unconditional injunction, positing as its content the utmost pathological singularity. And, again, the crucial point is that this breaking up is not Sade's eccentricity - it lies dormant as a possibility in the very fundamental tension constitutive of the Cartesian subjectivity. That is to say, the intervention of the subject undermines the standard pre-modern opposition between the universal Order and the hubris of a particular force whose egotistic excess perturbs the balance of the universal Order: 'subject' is the name for the hubris, the excessive gesture, whose very excess grounds the universal Order; it is the name for the pathological abject, *clinamen*, deviation from the universal Order, which sustains this very universal Order. The transcendental subject is the 'ontological scandal', neither phenomenal nor noumenal, but an excess which sticks out from the 'great chain of being', a hole, a gap in the order of reality, and, simultaneously, the agent whose 'spontaneous' activity constitutes the order of (phenomenal) reality. If, for the traditional ontology,

11. See Monique David-Menard, *Les constructions de l'universel*, PUF, Paris 1997.

the problem was how to deduce chaotic phenomenal reality from the eternal Order of the true reality (how to account for the gradual 'degeneration' of the eternal Order), the problem of the subject is that of the imbalanced excess, hubris, deviation, which sustains the Order itself. The central paradox of the Kantian transcendental constitution is that the subject is not the Absolute, the eternal grounding Principle of reality, but a finite, temporal entity - precisely as such, it provides the ultimate horizon of reality. For that reason, one should reject the standard reading of the Kantian transcendental constitution according to which, the subject is the agent of universality who imposes on the chaotic multitude of sensible impressions the universal form of Reason: in this case, the subject is directly identified with the force of universalisation, and what is missed is the fact that subject is simultaneously *clinamen*, the out-of-joint excess, i.e. the paradoxical point at which an extreme excess itself, an element which sticks out, *grounds* universality.

The exemplary case of the 'pathological', contingent element elevated to the status of an unconditional demand is, of course, an artist absolutely identified with his artistic mission, pursuing it freely without any guilt, as an inner constraint, unable to survive without it.

The sad fate of Jacqueline du Pré confronts us with the feminine version of the split between the unconditional injunction and its obverse, the serial universality of indifferent empirical objects that must be sacrificed in the pursuit of one's Mission.[12] It is extremely interesting and productive to read du Pre's life story not as a 'real story', but as a mythical narrative: what is so surprising about it is how closely it follows the preordained contours of a family myth, the same as with the story of Kaspar Hauser, in which individual accidents uncannily reproduce familiar features from ancient myths.[13] Du Pré's unconditional injunction, her drive, her absolute passion was her art (when she was four years old, upon seeing someone playing a cello, she already immediately claimed that this is what she wanted to be). This elevation of her art to the unconditional relegated her love life to a series of encounters with men who were ultimately all substitutable, one as good as the other - she was reported to be a serial 'man eater'. She thus occupied the place usually reserved for the *male* artist - no wonder her long tragic illness (multiple sclerosis, from which she was painfully dying from 1973 to 1987) was perceived by her mother as an 'answer of the real', as divine punishment not only for her promiscuous sexual life, but also for her 'excessive' commitment to her art.

12. See Hilary and Piers du Pré, *A Genius in the Family. An Intimate Memoir of Jacqueline du Pré*, Chatto and Windus, London 1997.

13. On the other hand, it is sometimes also productive to read myths as 'real stories' - in this way, if one reads a myth with total 'realist' naivety, the point of the narrative emerges clearly.

IV

On closer analysis, one would have to link the notion of respect to that of castration: *respect is ultimately always respect for (the Other's) castration*. When we respect another subject, we do not do it on account of some outstanding property of this subject, but, on the contrary, on account of some fundamental lack that defines its very being – 'respect' means that we maintain a proper distance, that we do not approach the other too closely, i.e. so close as to dissolve the semblance that conceals/envelops the lack and thus render this lack fully visible. For example, one respects one's father insofar as one accepts his assertion of authority at its word, without provoking him too much into effectively demonstrating his authority, being well aware that in this way, one might render visible father's imposture, i.e. the fact that his authority conceals a fundamental impotence. For this reason, cultures that insist on women wearing veils that cover them up, insist that they are doing this out of respect for women - for an Islamic 'fundamentalist', it is the western liberal culture that treats women in a disrespectful way, shamelessly exposing them as objects of sexual pleasure.[14]

It is against this background that one should approach the Kantian notion of *Achtung*, of respect for the Other Person who should never be treated only as a means. Things are here more unsettling than it may appear: let us take a criminal who cruelly and intentionally killed another person, how do we show proper respect for him? By condemning him and shooting him (since this way we treat him as a free reasonable person), while all the talk about the impact of social circumstances treats him 'disrespectfully', in other words not as a free responsible agent, but as a plaything of social mechanisms. Today's victimisation and 'understanding' are thus much less respectful of human dignity than the Kant-Hegelian notion of deserved punishment; Hegel takes this to its logical conclusion by claiming that the murderer himself, in his capacity of a rational free being, *wants* his punishment: in punishing him, we merely realise his true rational Will that he is unaware of. What the notion of respect thus involves is a split in the object of respect between the level of his symbolic ideal existence (a free being obeying universal laws) and the reality of his factual existence (a vile murderer): the only way to show respect for the other is to smash violently this reality of the factual existence on behalf of the symbolic ideal. On a somewhat different level, we encounter the same dilemma in the case of a person dying in debilitating and painful confusion, vomiting and regressing to childish and obscene rambling: when relatives opt for euthanasia to put an end to this painful spectacle, they do so not only to shorten the dying person's senseless pain, but also to retain his dignity, in other words to assure that he will be remembered by his relatives and friends as a dignified old person, not as a rambling idiot. Here we encounter the distinction between the Ego-Ideal and the Other *qua* real: do we really have the right to sacrifice the real Other for the sake of his Ego-Ideal, of the image of him retained for posterity? How can we be sure that the dying person did not find an intense *jouissance* in the 'undignified' drug-induced mortal delusions?

In Japanese culture, it is very crude and disrespectful to confront the other's gaze directly: averting the other's gaze, not looking him straight into the eyes, is considered not a sign of hypocrisy, but a sign of respect.[15]

14. Of course, the catch here is that woman's self-respect is defined in terms of her role within the patriarchal normative system of exchanges.

15. Therein resides the subversive effect of Ozu's films, which as a rule passes unobserved in the West: his films depict couples who, shown in standard American shots, directly return each other's gaze and look into each other's eyes - the emotional impact of this is much stronger in Japan than in Europe or the USA.

(Instead of veiling the object we are looking at, as in Islam, the veil is here as it were internalised, transposed onto the eye itself.) Perhaps this feature gives a clue as to what respect is: as we have already seen, to respect the Other means that one does not approach him too closely. So how does this work with Kant? What is worthy of respect in a person is, for Kant, his or her sublime dimension, i.e. his or her noumenal freedom, the fact that s/he is an ethical being. What, then, does respect consist of? In a first approach, one is tempted to say that, insofar as the Kantian Sublime stands for the failure of imagination to successfully schematise the noumenal dimension of Freedom, what makes a man worthy of respect is the very gap of castration that forever separates him as a 'real person' from his freedom as symbolic feature (a real person can never fully live up to his noumenal Duty). But is this the only possible reading? Isn't it also that, when we approach the Other Person too closely, we discover *not* that the acts that appeared to be ethical were effectively done for pathological reasons, but that his or her transcendental Freedom itself is that which is properly Monstrous. What respect veils is not the gap between Freedom and the pathological reality of a person, but the uncanny, monstrous obverse of transcendental Freedom itself.

V

Although, in contrast to Kant, the Sadean blasphemy does openly display the castration - not the executioner's, but the Other's, rendering the Other visible in his/her utter and shameful impotence - they both meet in the fundamental coldness of the subject who follows the unconditional injunction. Edward Said draws attention to Mozart's letters to his wife Constanze from 30 September of 1790, that is, from the time when he was composing *Cosi fan tutte*; after expressing his pleasure at the prospect of meeting her again soon, he goes on: 'If the people were to be able to see into my heart, I would have to be almost ashamed of myself ...' At this point, as Said perspicuously perceives, one would expect the confession of some dirty private secret (sexual fantasies of what he will do to his wife when they will finally meet); however, the letter goes on: 'everything is cold to me - cold like ice'.[16] It is here that Mozart enters the uncanny domain of *Kant avec Sade*, the domain in which sexuality loses its passionate, intense character and turns into its opposite, a 'mechanical' exercise in pleasure executed by cold distance, like the Kantian ethical subject doing his duty without any pathological commitment. Isn't this the underlying vision of *Cosi fan Tutte*: a universe in which subjects are determined not by their passionate engagements, but by a blind mechanism that regulates their passions? What compels us to bring *Cosi fan Tutte* close to the domain of *Kant avec Sade* is its very insistence on the *universal* dimension already indicated by its title: 'they are *all* doing it like this', determined by the same blind mechanism. In short, Alfonso the philosopher who organises

16. See Edward W. Said, 'Cosi fan tutte', in *Lettre international* Volume 39, Winter 1997, pp69-70.

and manipulates the game of changed identities in *Cosi*, is a version of the figure of the Sadean pedagogue educating his young disciples in the art of debauchery. It is thus oversimplified and inadequate to conceive this coldness as that of the 'instrumental reason'.

Kant and Sade have in common not only this coldness of the unconditional injunction: *Do your duty!* or *Enjoy*! that compels the subject to sacrifice his attachment to all contingent 'pathological' objects; it is interesting to note that they also share the same symptomatic gesture by means of which they shrink from the ultimate consequences of their theoretical edifice - in both cases, the term that allows this operation is that of nature: 'Nature is, in Sade as well as in Kant, the symptom of that which remains unthought in these two thinkers of the universal'.[17] That is to say, in both cases we are dealing with a certain structurally necessary ambiguity of this term. Kant first defines nature as the Whole of phenomena, of phenomenal reality, insofar as it is held together by (and subject to) universal laws; later, however, he also speaks of another, noumenal Nature as the kingdom of ethical goals, as the community of all rational ethical beings. Thus the very excess of Freedom over nature (the natural enchainment of causes and effects) is again naturalised. Sade, on the other hand, first conceives of nature as the indifferent system of matter subject to eternal change, inexorably following its course, submitted to no external Divine Master; however, in his claim that, when we find pleasure in torturing our fellow beings and destroying them, up to the interruption of the very natural cycle of reproduction, we effectively fulfil Nature's innermost request, he secretly introduces another form of nature, no longer the usual indifferent run of things 'beyond Good and Evil', but Nature which is already somehow subjectivised, turned into a transgressive/diabolic entity commanding us to pursue evil and to find pleasure in the destruction and sacrifice of every form of morality and compassion. Isn't this second nature, what Lacan referred to as the 'Supreme Being of Evilness', the Sadean counterpoint to (or reversal of) the Kantian Nature *qua* the community of suprasensible rational beings, the kingdom of ethical Goals? This ambiguity can also be stated in the following terms: what effectively brings pleasure to the Sadean hero? Is it the mere 'return to the innocence of nature', the unconstrained following of the laws of nature that also demand destruction, or is pleasure nonetheless inherently linked to the moral law it violates, so that what brings us pleasure is the very awareness that we are committing a blasphemy? This ambiguity between innocence and blasphemous corruption is irreducible. Another aspect of this same ambiguity is Sade's oscillation between *solipsism* of pleasure and the *intersubjective* logic of blasphemy: is the point merely that I must ignore the Other's dignity, reducing him to an instrument to satisfy my whims, so that the Other is not subjectivised but reduced to an impersonal tool, a kind of masturbatory resource for my solitary pleasure, or is it that I get pleasure out of the very awareness that I am humiliating the Other and causing him unbearable

17. Monique David-Menard, *op.cit.*, p64.

pain?[18] So, in both cases, in Kant as well as in Sade, the 'elementary' neutral notion of Nature as the indifferent mechanism that follows its course is supplemented by another, 'ethical' notion of Nature (the suprasensible kingdom of ethical goals; the diabolical commandment to pursue the evil path of destruction), and, in both cases, this second notion of nature masks a certain gesture of shrinking back, of avoiding the confrontation with the ultimate paradox of one's position: the uncanny abyss of freedom without any ontological guarantee in the Order of Being.

VI

The fundamental difference between Adorno and Horkheimer and Lacan resides in the fact that, for the first two, Sade is the truth of Kant in the sense that the Kantian ethical formalism implies the radical instrumentalisation of all contingent ('pathological') *content* - each and every other human being, each 'neighbour', is reduced to a potential object of manipulation in the service of the subject's survival - while for Lacan, *it is the sadist pervert himself who occupies the place of the object*, i.e. who assumes the position of the pure object-instrument of the Other's *jouissance*, displacing the division constitutive of subjectivity onto the other, onto his victim. In this respect, the sadist perversion is very close to obsessional neurosis, with the only (yet crucial) difference that the sadist pervert is active in order to generate the Other's *jouissance*, while the obsessional neurotic is active for precisely the opposite reason, i.e. in order to *prevent* the Other's enjoyment (*pour que ça ne bouge pas dans l'autre*).

This, however, is not the whole story. The decisive question is: is the Kantian moral Law translatable into the Freudian notion of superego or not? If the answer is yes, then 'Kant with Sade' effectively means that Sade is the truth of the Kantian ethics. If, however, the Kantian moral Law cannot be identified with the superego (since, as Lacan himself puts it in the last pages of *Seminar XI*, moral Law is equivalent to desire itself, while the superego precisely feeds on the subject's compromising his/her desire, i.e. the guilt sustained by the superego bears witness to the fact that the subject has somewhere betrayed or compromised his/her desire[19]), then Sade is not the entire truth of Kantian ethics, but a form of its perverted realisation. In short, far from being 'more radical than Kant', Sade articulates what happens when the subject *betrays* the true stringency of the Kantian ethics. This difference is crucial in its political consequences: insofar as the libidinal structure of 'totalitarian' regimes is perverse (the totalitarian subject assumes the position of the object-instrument of the Other's *jouissance*), 'Sade as the truth of Kant' would mean that Kantian ethics effectively harbours totalitarian potentials;[20] however, insofar as we conceive of Kantian ethics as precisely *prohibiting* the subject from assuming the position of the object-instrument of the Other's *jouissance*, i.e. to calling on him to assume full responsibility for what he proclaims as his Duty, then Kant is the

18. As Claude Lefort pointed out, see his 'Écrire à l'épreuve du politique', Calman Levy, Paris 1992, pp108-110, the same tension is discernible in the inconsistency of Sadean pedagogy: although Sade's goal is the asocial individual who merely exploits others as means for his pleasure, the only way to bring about such an individual in today's society 'degenerated' by religion is through a new pedagogy that expresses the will to corrupt innocent young girls by introducing them into the art of unconstrained pleasures. Sadean heroes thus nonetheless tend to form a new, 'authentic' community, an elitist closed circle of those initiated in the art of pleasures.

19. See Alenka Zupancic, *op.cit.*, as well as Bernard Baas, *Le desir pur*, Peeters, Louvain 1992.

20. A feature which, perhaps, points into this direction would be Kant's well-known thesis that Reason without intuition is empty, while Intuition without reason is blind: is not its political counterpart Robespierre's dictum according to which, Virtue without Terror is impotent, while Terror without Virtue is lethal, striking blindly?

anti-totalitarian *par excellence*.

The dream about Irma's injection that Freud used as the exemplary case to illustrate his procedure of analysing dreams is a dream about *responsibility* (Freud's own responsibility for the failure of his treatment of Irma) - this fact alone indicates that responsibility is a crucial Freudian notion. But how are we to conceive it? How are we to avoid the usual trap of the *mauvaise foi* of the Sartrean subject responsible for his existential project, i.e. of the existentialist motif of ontological guilt that pertains to the finite human existence as such, as well as the opposite trap of 'putting the blame on the Other' ('since the Unconscious is the discourse of the Other, I am not responsible for its formations, it is the big Other who speaks through me, I am merely its instrument')? Lacan himself pointed the way out of this deadlock by referring to Kant's philosophy as the crucial antecedent of the psychoanalythic ethics of the duty 'beyond the Good'. According to the standard pseudo-Hegelian critique, the Kantian universalist ethic of the categorical imperative fails to take into account the concrete historical situation in which the subject is embedded, and which provides the determinate content of the Good: what eludes Kantian formalism is the historically specified particular Substance of ethical life. However, this reproach can be countered by claiming that the unique strength of Kant's ethics resides in this very formal indeterminacy: moral Law does not tell me *what* my duty is, it merely tells me *that* I should accomplish my duty, that is, it is not possible to derive the concrete norms I have to follow in my specific situation from the moral Law itself - *which means that the subject himself has to assume the responsibility of 'translating' the abstract injunction of the moral Law into a series of concrete obligations*. In this precise sense, one is tempted to risk a parallel with Kant's *Critique of Judgement*: the concrete formulation of a determinate ethical obligation has the structure of aesthetic judgement, i.e. of a judgement by which, instead of simply applying a universal category to a particular object or of subsuming this object under an already given universal determination, I as it were *invent* its universal-necessary-obligatory dimension and thereby elevate this particular-contingent object (act) to the dignity of the ethical Thing. So there is always something sublime about pronouncing a judgement that defines our duty: in it, I 'elevate an object to the dignity of the Thing' (Lacan's definition of sublimation).

The full acceptance of this paradox also compels us to reject any reference to 'duty' as an excuse: 'I know this is heavy and can be painful, but what can I do, this is my duty ...' The standard motto of ethical rigor is 'There is no excuse for not accomplishing one's duty!'; although Kant's '*Du kannst, denn du sollst*! (You can, because you must!)' seems to offer a new version of this motto, he implicitly complements it with its much more uncanny inversion: 'There is no excuse for *accomplishing* one's duty!'[21] The reference to duty as the excuse to do our duty should be rejected as hypocritical; suffice it to recall the proverbial example of a severe sadistic

21. For a more detailed account of this key feature of Kant's ethics, see Chapter II of Slavoj Zizek, *The Indivisible Remainder*, Verso, London 1996.

teacher who subjects his pupils to merciless discipline and torture. Of course, his excuse to himself (and to others) is: 'I myself find it hard to exert such pressure on the poor kids, but what can I do – it's my duty!' The more pertinent example is that of a Stalinist politician who loves mankind, but nonetheless performs horrible purges and executions; his heart is breaking while he is doing it, but he cannot help it, it's his 'Duty towards the Progress of Humanity'. What we encounter here is the properly *perverse* attitude of adopting the position of the pure instrument of the big Other's Will: it's not my responsibility, it's not me who is effectively doing it, I am merely an instrument of the higher Historical Necessity. The obscene *jouissance* of this situation is generated by the fact that I conceive of myself as exculpated for what I am doing - isn't it nice to be able to inflict pain on others with the full awareness that I'm not responsible for it, that I merely fulfil the Other's Will - *this* is what Kantian ethics prohibits. This position of the sadist pervert provides the answer to the question: How can the subject be guilty when he merely realises an 'objective', externally imposed necessity? By subjectively assuming this 'objective necessity', i.e. by finding *enjoyment* in what is imposed on him.[22] So, at its most radical, Kantian ethics is *not* 'sadist', but precisely what prohibits assuming the position of a Sadean executioner.

22. See Alenka Zupancic, *Die Ethik des Realen. Kant mit Lacan*, Turia und Kant, Vienna 1995.

In a final twist, Lacan thus nonetheless undermines the thesis of 'Sade as the truth of Kant': it is no accident that the same seminar in which Lacan first deployed the inherent link between Kant and Sade also contains the detailed reading of *Antigone* in which Lacan delineates the contours of an ethical act that *does* successfully avoid the trap of the Sadean perversion as its hidden truth - in insisting on her unconditional demand for her brother's proper burial, Antigone does *not* obey a command that humiliates her, a command effectively uttered by a sadistic executioner. So the main effort of Lacan's seminar on the *Ethics of Psychoanalysis* is precisely to break up the vicious cycle of *Kant avec Sade*. How is this possible? Only if - in contrast to Kant - one asserts that *the faculty of desiring is not in itself 'pathological'*. In short, Lacan asserts the necessity of a 'critique of pure desire': in contrast to Kant, for whom our capacity to desire is thoroughly 'pathological' (since, as he repeatedly stresses, there is no *a priori* link between an empirical object and the pleasure this object generates in the subject), Lacan claims that there is a 'pure faculty of desire', since desire does have a non-pathological, a priori object-cause - this object, of course, is what Lacan calls *objet petit a*.

VII

In spite of the greater theoretical stringency of Lacan's *Kant avec Sade*, the fundamental lesson of *Dialectics of Enlightenment* is still more than relevant today: it directly bears on what the theorists of risk society and reflexive modernisation praise as the advent of a 'second Enlightenment'.

Apropos this second Enlightenment, with subjects delivered from the weight of Nature and/or Tradition, the question is to be raised again about their unconscious 'passionate attachments' - the so-called 'dark phenomena' (rising fundamentalisms, neoracisms, etc.) that accompany this 'second modernisation' can in no way be dismissed as simple regressive phenomena, as remainders of the past that will simply vanish when individuals fully assume the full freedom and responsibility imposed on them by the second modernisation. Proponents of the 'second Enlightenment' praise Kant - so the question arises again about *Kant avec Sade*. The achievement of Sade was to extend the utilitarian logic of instrumentalisation to the very intimate relations of sex: sex is no longer a phenomenon constrained to the private sphere exempted from the utilitarian cruelty of public professional life, it must also be made part of the utilitarian rules of equivalent exchange that structure what Hegel called civil society. With the so-called second modernisation, the attitude that was hitherto reserved for the public as opposed to private life (reflexivity, the right to choose one's way of life instead of accepting it as imposed by tradition, etc.) has also penetrated the most intimate private sphere of sexuality. No wonder that this step is paid for by the increase of 'sadist' sexual practices, by rituals that stage sexuality as the domain of contract and mutual exploitation.

The general conclusion to be drawn from the motif of *Kant avec Sade* is that those who advocate the subversive potential of perversions are sooner or later led to the denial of the Freudian unconscious, as was already the case for Michel Foucault himself. This denial is theoretically grounded in the fact that, for psychoanalysis, hysteria and psychosis - *not perversion* - are what offer the way to the Unconscious: the Unconscious is *not* accessible via the perversions. Following Freud, Lacan repeatedly insisted that perversion is always a socially constructive attitude, while hysteria is much more subversive and threatening to the predominant hegemony. It may seem that the situation is the opposite: don't perverts openly realise and practice what hysterics only secretly dream about? (This is how one usually understands Freud's thesis that perversion is the negative of neurosis.) However, this very fact confronts us with the paradox of the Freudian unconscious: the unconscious does *not* consist of the secret perverse scenarios we daydream about and (insofar as we remain hysterics) shirk from realising, while perverts heroically pass to the act and 'do it'. When we do this, when we realise ('act out') our secret perverse fantasies, everything is disclosed; yet the Unconscious is somehow missed - why? Because the Freudian Unconscious is *not* the secret fantasmatic content, but something that intervenes *in between*, in the process of the translation/transposition of the secret fantasmatic content into the text of the dream (or the hysterical symptom). The Unconscious is that which, precisely, is *obfuscated* by the fantasmatic scenarios the pervert is acting out: the pervert, with his/her certainty about what brings enjoyment, obfuscates the gap, the 'burning question', the stumbling block, that 'is' the core of the Unconscious. The pervert is thus the 'inherent transgressor' *par excellence*: s/he brings to light, stages, practices the secret fantasies that sustain the predominant public discourse, while the hysterical position precisely displays the doubt whether the secret perverse fantasies are 'really *that*'. In other words, hysteria is not simply the battleground between secret desires and symbolic prohibitions; it also and above all articulates the gnawing doubt whether secret desires really contain what they promise, i.e. whether our inability to enjoy really hinges only on symbolic prohibitions.

Lacan's heroines: Antigone and Sygne de Coûfontaine

Alenka Zupancic

Inhuman, cruel, inflexible, without fear or pity: these are some key-words that Jacques Lacan uses to describe the position of Sophocles' Antigone - for him, the ethical position *par excellence*. There are many commentators who focus on Antigone as an ethical figure, but what makes Lacan's reading quite unique is precisely the link he establishes between ethics and the 'inhuman' aspect of the heroine. This implies, of course, a certain theoretical stance which could be formulated as follows: at the core of ethics lies something essentially inhuman. Or even: there is no such thing as 'human ethics'. Exactly how are we to understand this?

Let us take up this question from a perspective which does not immediately involve Antigone, but which concerns simply the notion of ethics or, more precisely, a certain notion of ethics which might be called 'the ethics of the Real'.

The core of ethics is something which in and of itself is not 'ethical' (nor is it 'non-ethical'), i.e. it is something which does not belong to the register of ethics. In Lacanian theory, this 'something' is conceptualised by what he calls the Real. The fact that the core of ethics is itself not ethical is - while expressed in other terms - already the fundamental lesson of Kantian ethics: this ethics has for its starting point the subject's encounter with what Kant calls the unconditional (which is not in itself an ethical category). Kant's notion of the unconditional is quite close to the Lacanian notion of the Real insofar as it does not in any way concern the question of what may or may not be done and as such does not exclude the impossible. A second important point about Kantian ethics is that it displaces the notions of good and evil from the 'epicentre' of ethics and posits them as values which can only be determined afterwards, i.e. subsequent to the subject's encounter with the unconditional law. Kant evacuates, so to speak, the notion of the good from the order of causes (or fundamentals) of the ethical. The good - my own good, the good of my fellow man or the good of the community - can not be the cause (motive or ground) of an ethical action. Lacan's interpretation of catharsis and its function in Sophocles' *Antigone* owes much to this conception, as well as to Kant's effort to foreclose from the field of ethics that which he calls 'the pathological'. As Lacan, following Aristotle, defines catharsis, it is through the intervention of pity and fear that we are purged or purified of emotions such as pity and fear. In Lacanian terms, we are 'purified' of everything that belongs to the order of the imaginary: both the fear for our own good and the pity for our fellow man (our *semblable*). We know that Kant, in his *Groundwork of the Metaphysic of Morals*, insists on the fact that acting with a view to the well-being of others, out of sympathy for them, already means that we act with a view to our own well-being, thus making the action pathologically determined and non-ethical. This point of Kantian ethics was often criticised: the Kantian moral, the critics charge, is an alienating moral because it forces us to reject what is '*most truly ours*' and to subject ourselves to an abstract principle which takes into account neither love nor sympathy.[1] Some go as far as to say that it is repugnant to act exclusively *aus Pflicht*, just for the sake of duty - as Kant demands - for this seems to imply a complete alienation of the subject. Yet, what is most interesting in Kantian ethics is precisely that he recognises in this 'inhuman', 'strange' principle that which *is* 'most truly ours' and founds upon it the subject's autonomy and liberty. As for Lacan, he goes as far as to say: 'It is because ... the voice of the hero trembles before nothing, and especially not before the good of the other, ... that the subject learns a little more about the deepest level of himself than he knew before'.[2] Here, once again, we encounter, *on the deepest level of ourselves* - i.e. in what is 'most truly ours' - something strangely inhuman. One might object that this is nothing but a theoretical extravagance and that nobody can seriously expect the voice of an ethical subject not to tremble before the good of his or her fellow man. Wouldn't this kind of stance make 'Hitler's willing executioners' the greatest ethical heroes of the century? However this objection misses the whole point, for it is not in the least certain that the voice of 'Hitler's willing executioners' did not tremble before the good of their fellow men - one could say that it must have trembled quite a bit, since they needed to invent this '*unfellow man*', the Jew, in whom they could kill, destroy, exterminate that which they could not stand in the fellow men for whom they had the deepest human sympathy.

Lacan endeavours to conceptualise ethics outside of what he calls the 'service of goods'. This is why he formulates the question of ethics in terms of 'an absolute choice' which he defines as 'a choice that is motivated by no good'.[3] It is with these words that Lacan announces his commentary on *Antigone*.

We will focus our discussion on this level, on the level of an absolute choice which is, as we will argue, linked to the structure of the forced choice. This might seem paradoxical, or even contradictory, but it is nevertheless a fundamental feature of the ethics of the Real. There are two types of forced choice from which follow two different ethical figures: the first is personified by Antigone and the second by Sygne de Coufontaine, the heroine of Paul Claudel's play *The Hostage*.

The first type of forced choice is perhaps best formulated in the well known alternative 'Your money or your life'. If I choose the money, I lose both. If I choose life, I have life without money, namely, a life deprived of something.[4] The paradox of this type of forced choice originates in the fact that one of the two alternatives is at the same time the universal (and thus

1. We are borrowing the tone and the argument of these critics from Allison's presentation. Cf. Henry E. Allison, *Kant's Theory of Freedom*, Cambridge University Press, Cambridge, Massachusetts 1991, pp196-198.

2. Jacques Lacan, *The Ethics of Psychoanalysis*, trans. Dennis Porter, Routledge, New York & London 1992, p323. Our emphasis.

3. *Ibid.*, p240.

4. Cf. Jacques Lacan, *The Four Fundamental Concepts of Psychoanalysis*, trans. Alan Sheridan, Penguin Books, Harmondsworth & New York 1979, p212.

quasi neutral) ground of the choice itself: one of the two terms is at the same time part and whole, the object of the choice and that which supports and generates the choice. In the alternative: 'Your money or your life' the 'universal' term is, of course, life. 'Life' is not simply one of two alternative possibilities but is the indispensable condition of the choice itself. What good is money if you are dead? In other words, this alternative grants us no real choice. This minimal structure already allows us to deduce the ethical figure to which it is related. It could be defined as the ability *to choose where there is no choice*. This would mean, in the given case, to choose the money, but let us formulate the choice more generally.

What makes the impossible choice possible is the fact that the two terms are untied or untangled into three terms. This is to say, there is something which exceeds life, and it is precisely this something that is the ultimate point of identification for the subject who makes this 'impossible' choice. This is why we have the feeling that such a subject is 'larger than life'. What exactly is this third term, this thing which exceeds life and which functions as the ultimate support of the subject in question? It can appear, for instance, as a 'point of honour', but it is always something in which the subject recognises his/her own being - something which determines the subject beyond life and death.

In Sophocles' *Antigone*, the opening dialogue between Antigone and Ismene is situated in this dimension. The dialogue revolves around questions of decision, choice and its (im)possibility: around being and honour. Antigone has already made her choice, and she invites Ismene to make hers. Antigone's choice is presented to us through Ismene's hesitation and inability to break out of the mortifying alternative which is, in fact, no alternative.

> **Ismene**:
> I, for one, I'll beg the dead to forgive me -
> I'm forced, I have no choice - I must obey
> the ones who stand in power. Why rush to extremes?
> It's madness, madness.

To which Antigone replies, among other things:

> Do as you like, dishonour the laws
> the gods hold in honour.[5]

Or, a little before:

> No one will ever convict me for a traitor.[6]

Antigone has been often situated in the register of 'guarding'. This point was made, among others, by Hegel, as well as by Lacan: Antigone chooses to be the guardian of the divine law (Hegel), she chooses to be the guardian

5. Trans. Robert Fagles, *Sophocles: The Three Theban Plays*, Penguin Books Harmondsworth & New York 1982, p62-63.

6. *Ibid.*, p61.

of the family *Atè*, of the family being which is 'the being of the criminal as such' (Lacan). Yet, if we recognise Antigone's act as an act of choosing when there is no choice, this reveals still another dimension of her act. It is not only a matter of guarding, but also that of creating: creating a new possibility there where the options seemed to be exhausted. This also means that the subjective figure Antigone incarnates is not simply that of passive resistance, 'civil disobedience' or 'conscientious objector'. Antigone's act goes further than this: not only does she say *no* to Creon and is willing to pay for it with her life, her *no* also has the dimension of an act, and a violent one at that. It is a 'no' that engenders three corpses and a serious political crisis. Of course, an act of 'passive resistance' can be active and 'productive' in its consequences, a simple *no* can be an act. But the difference I am trying to establish here is that in Antigone's case, a certain violence is the essential component of her act. Antigone is not simply somebody who is confronted with a forced choice, she is also the one who, with the (impossible) choice she makes, *forces others to choose*, confronts *them* with a forced choice: first Ismene, than Creon and Haemon. Her dialogue with Ismene is quite striking in this regard. Antigone urges Ismene to decide, and she confronts her with a clear and sharp alternative:

> There you have it. You'll soon show what you are,
> worth your breeding, or a coward -
> for all your royal blood.[7]

7. *Ibid.*, p60.

Ismene makes the wrong choice (or rather, she refuses to recognise that there is a choice) and instead expresses her fear for Antigone. The latter bluntly replies:

> Don't fear for me. Set your own life in order.[8]

8. *Ibid.*, p63.

Antigone clearly sees her own choice as something which very much concerns the others and not solely as a private act, a solitary, 'isolated' sacrifice that she owes her brother and her gods.

As for Creon, it is clear that he recognises in Antigone's act and her attitude (the fact that she does not try to deny anything, but speaks proudly of it) a challenge and an invitation to make a choice, to reconsider his act of forbidding Polynices' funeral *in terms of a choice*, i.e. with full consciousness of the stakes involved. But he makes the mistake of taking it personally, i.e., as an offence to his masculine pride. Antigone invites him to *resubjectivise* himself as a master, but instead Creon tries to *reaffirm* himself as the master, which is not at all the same thing. He only sees in Antigone his rival: a woman who wants to be a man, a slave who wants to be master:

> **Creon**:
> ... And I've known spirited horses you can break

with a light bit - proud, rebellious horses.
There is no room for pride, not in a slave,
not with the lord and master standing by.

... I am not the man, not now: she is the man
if this victory goes to her and she goes free.[9]

9. *Ibid.*, p83.

In contrast to Ismene, who immediately understands the stakes of the choice and panics, Creon does not see at first where all this is heading - he panics only later, when Tiresias tells him, in the form of a prediction, what is at stake. Tiresias explains the real meaning of the choice Antigone imposed upon him, and that it was this choice in which he would necessarily, i.e. no matter what he would have chosen, lose his power. He could either lose it by his own decision (i.e. in a 'master's way') or by the force of circumstances. When Creon realises this, he wants to go back and choose the other option, but it is already too late.

And then there is Haemon who, after trying in vain to change his father's mind, also makes a choice - although he does not panic:

Then she will die ... but her death will kill another.[10]

10. *Ibid.*, p99.

From the moment Antigone makes her choice, nothing will ever be the same.

One of the central points of Lacan's commentary on Antigone is that he recognises in the heroine the figure of 'pure desire': 'desire in its pure state'. This point is often stressed, especially in relation to the famous formula *ne pas cèder sur son désir*, do not give way to your desire. But there is another, very curious phrase which appears in Lacan's commentary and which deserves our attention, namely 'the realisation of desire'. We could say that what makes Antigone Antigone is not simply that she does not give way to her desire, but, more precisely, that *she realises her desire*. But what does this mean?

> ... realising one's desire is necessarily always raised from the point of view of an absolute condition. It is precisely to the extent that the demand always under- or overshoots itself that, because it articulates itself through the signifier, it always demands something else; that in every satisfaction of a need, it insists on something else; that the satisfaction formulated spreads out and conforms to this gap; that desire is formed as something supporting this metonymy, namely, as something the demand means beyond whatever it is able to formulate. And that is why the question of the realisation of desire is necessarily formulated from the point of view of a Last Judgment.

Try to imagine what 'to have realised one's desire' might mean, if it is

> not to have realised it, so to speak, in the end. It is this trespassing of death on life that gives its dynamism to any question that attempts to find a formulation for the subject of the realisation of desire.[11]

11. Lacan, *The Ethics of Psychoanalysis*, *op. cit.*, p294.

It is clear that the realisation of desire does not mean the fulfilment of desire. It does not mean the realisation of what the subject desires. In Lacanian theory, there is no such thing as the desired object. There is the demanded object and then there is the object-cause of desire which, having no positive content, refers to what we get if we subtract the satisfaction that we find in a given object from the demand (we have) for this object. Essentially linked to this logic of subtraction which gives rise to a (possibly) endless metonymy, desire is nothing but that which introduces into the subject's universe an 'incommensurable' or 'infinite measure' (Lacan's terms). Desire is this 'infinite measure'. In this perspective, to realise one's desire means to realise, to 'measure' the incommensurable, infinite measure. This is why Lacan stresses that the question of the realisation of desire can only be formulated from the point of view of a Last Judgment, from the point of view of the End (the 'second death'). Once again, we must not miss the Kantian echo, for this is precisely the function of the two postulates of practical reason that Kant introduces in the dialectic of pure practical reason. Kant posits as the necessary object of the will determined by the moral law the *realisation of the highest Good*. This implies precisely the realisation of an infinite measure which could be paralleled with what Lacan calls the realisation of desire. For Kant, as for Lacan, what is at stake is not a realisation of some good - in this case the highest good. What is at stake is not a realisation of some object: the highest good is defined as complete fitness of the will to the moral law, and not as such and such (positive) object. In order for the realisation of the highest good to be possible, Kant has to introduce, first, the postulate of the immortality of the soul to open up a field beyond death (i.e. beyond the subject's relation to pathological objects) and thus make it possible for the subject to establish a relation to a second death, to the End, from the point of view of which, and from this point of view only, the question of the realisation of the highest good can be formulated. This point of view is what is introduced by the second postulate: the existence of God. Let us consider the passage in which Kant explains the function of these two postulates:

> On the basis of his previous progress from the worse to the morally better ... [man] may hope for a further uninterrupted continuance of this progress, however long his existence may last, even beyond his life [here we cross the limit of the 'first death']. But he cannot hope to be fully adequate to God's will ... This he can do only in the infinity of his duration which God alone can survey.[12]

12. *Critique of Practical Reason*, trans. Lewis White Beck, Macmillan Publishing Company, New York City, New York 1993, p130.

In other words, the postulate of immortality introduces the possibility of infinite progress. But this in itself does not yet make possible the realisation of the highest good. It is only the point of view of God, the point of view from which this infinite existence appears as a whole, as a totality, that finally makes possible the realisation in question. The frame that we are dealing with here is precisely the one discussed by Lacan: on the one hand, the field between the two deaths as the 'purgatory of desire', and, on the other hand, the point of view of the Last Judgment.

And this is also the frame, the basic structure, of *Antigone*: the heroine is situated between two deaths, 'walled up alive in a rocky vault',[13] going 'down to the halls of Death alive and breathing'.[14] As to the second point, that of the Last Judgment, it constitutes the core of Antigone's controversial complaint or lamentation, of the long speech in which she evokes, among other things, the fact that she will never know the conjugal bed, the bond of marriage, that she will never have any children ... We have here a kind of, if not Last, at least Infinite, Judgment in which the identity of the two elements is mediated by a central impossibility or incommensurability. The list of things that she will be deprived of by her precocious death, the list of things that never existed and never will exist (for her) has precisely the value of the infinite (or speculative) judgment realising the infinite measure. It has the same status as Hegel's famous dictum 'the spirit is a bone'. The violent feeling of absurd inadequacy to which this type of judgment gives rise, is probably what incited some commentators to cast doubt on the authenticity of these passages of *Antigone*. Indeed, it seems odd that after her brave resistance to Creon, with no after-thoughts, and while apparently detached from the concerns of common mortals, Antigone suddenly starts lamenting the fact that she is 'denied her part in the wedding songs', denied her part 'in the bridal-song, the bridal-bed, denied all joy of marriage, raising children ...'[15] It is quite true that this sounds somehow inadequate. But this is rather the whole point: it is through this lack of common measure that the incommensurable, infinite measure which is desire can be realised, i.e. 'measured'. Antigone's lamentation is absolutely essential to the text, and it does not mean that she suddenly became 'soft' and 'human'. It means, as Lacan justly remarked, that 'from Antigone's point of view life can only be approached, can only be lived or thought about, from the place of that limit where her life is already lost, where she is already on the other side.'[16] It is now time for us to turn to the other type of forced choice, the one which gives rise to a different ethical figure and poses the question of another kind of 'realisation of desire'.

13. Trans. Robert Fagles, *op. cit.*, p100.

14. *Ibid.*, p102.

15. *Ibid.*, p106.

16. Lacan, *The Ethics of Psychoanalysis*, p280.

This other forced choice could be formulated in terms of the alternative '*Freedom or death*!' Here, the situation is quite different, for it appears that we actually do have a choice: no matter what we choose, we'll have it all. And yet it soon becomes clear that this also is a forced choice, and of an even tougher sort than the previous one. There is no choice, since whatever term we choose, freedom or death, we'll have *both*. As Lacan puts it: '... in the conditions in which someone says to you, *freedom or death!*, the only proof of freedom that you can have in the conditions laid out before you is precisely to choose death, for there, you show that you have the freedom of choice.'[17] In other words, there is no escape from freedom: if you want freedom, you have to choose the other term, and if you say I'd rather die than be free, you've already chosen freedom. The configuration at stake in the second figure is the following one: the only way you can choose A is to choose its negation, the non-A; the only way the subject can stay true to his Cause is by betraying it, *by sacrificing to it the very thing which drives him/her to make this sacrifice*. This is the figure we encounter in Claudel's play *The Hostage*, on which Lacan comments extensively in his seminar *Le transfert*.

17. Lacan, *The Four Fundamental Concepts of Psychoanalysis, op. cit.*, p213.

The play takes place towards the end of Napoleonic rule, on the estate of the impoverished noble family of Coûfontaine in the French countryside.[18] After many years of assiduous endeavour, Sygne de Coufontaine, the last member of the family to remain there, has succeeded in bringing together what was left of the estate after the revolutionary turmoil. One night she receives an unexpected secret visit from her cousin Georges, heir of the family and a fervent Royalist, who emigrated to England. Sygne and Georges take a vow of eternal love which simultaneously expresses their profound attachment to the family land and title. The two lovers are united in the prospect of marrying and continuing the family tradition: they have dedicated and sacrificed everything, their youth and happiness to it; the family title and a small piece of land are all they have. However, new troubles are already looming on the horizon: Georges has returned to France on a very sensitive secret political mission - he has brought into their manor the Pope, who is on the run from Napoleon. The next morning Sygne is visited by Toussaint Turelure, Prefect of the region and a *nouveau riche*, a person she thoroughly despises: Turelure, son of her servant and wet nurse, has used the Revolution to promote his career - as a local Jacobin potentate, he ordered the execution of Sygne's parents in the presence of their children. This same Turelure, the arch-enemy of the family, now approaches Sygne with the following proposal: his spies have informed him of the presence of Georges and the Pope, and of course he has strict orders from Paris to arrest the two immediately. However he is ready to let them slip away if only Sygne will marry him and thus transfer to him the Coufontaine family title. Although Sygne proudly rejects the offer and dismisses Turelure, a long ensuing conversation with the local priest, confidant of the family, makes her change her mind. A year later, Turelure, now Sygne's husband and Prefect of Seine, conducts the negotiations for the surrender of Paris to the advancing Royalists; by means of his negotiating skills, he ensures for himself one of the most powerful positions in post-Napoleonic France. The chief negotiator for the returning King is none other than Georges; moreover, negotiations take place on the very day when a son is born to Sygne and Turelure. Unable to bear the fact that the corrupt and opportunistic Turelure has usurped the family title, Georges gets

18. We are borrowing here Slavoj Zizek's summary of the play from his *The Indivisible Remainder. An Essay on Schelling and Related Matters* Verso, London 1996, pp115-116.

involved in a violent fight with him. There is a shoot-out between the two men in the presence of Sygne; Georges is mortally wounded, while Sygne shields Turelure with her own body, intercepting Georges' bullet. In an alternative version of the scene which follows this shoot-out, Turelure, standing by the bed of the fatally wounded Sygne, desperately asks her to give a sign which would confer some meaning on her unexpected suicidal gesture of saving the life of her loathed husband - anything, even if she didn't do it for love of him but merely to save the family name from disgrace. The dying Sygne utters not a sound: she merely signals her rejection of a final reconciliation with her husband by means of a compulsive tic, a kind of convulsed twitching which repeatedly distorts her face. The last scene of the play: while Sygne is dying of her wound, Turelure bids a pathetic welcome to the King on behalf of a faithful France.

At the beginning of the play, Sygne and her cousin Georges are both in the subjective position of master. They have lived and live according to the maxim which Georges formulates as follows:

> Sadder than to lose one's life is to lose one's reason for living.[19]

19. Paul Claudel, *Three Plays; The Hostage, Crusts, The humiliation of the Father*, trans. John Heard, Luce, Boston, Massachusetts 1945, p118.

This, of course is a variation on Juvenal's famous verse 'Summum crede nefas animam praeferre pudori, et propter vitam vivendi perdere causas' - count it the greatest of all sins to prefer life to honour, and to lose, for the sake of living, all that makes life worth living. What we have here is the classical figure of desire, the same one we encountered in *Antigone*. In 'the reason for living' we can recognise what Lacan names the 'absolute condition' which constitutes the support of desire. When Turelure approaches her with his proposition, Sygne is ready to die in order to preserve this absolute condition which is formulated for her in terms of honour. But she changes her mind after her discussion with Badilon (the local priest and the confidant of the family) who makes her see, in a certain way, that her death would be an easy way out or, in other words, that *death is not an option*. For this is precisely what constitutes the terror of this configuration - it is situated, from the very start, 'beyond the first death' (the empirical death): it is 'the second death', the 'symbolic death', the annihilation of the heroine's being that is at stake.

The dialogue between Sygne and Badilon is a real masterpiece. The first important point is that the real terror Sygne is subjected to does not come from Turelure, her enemy, but rather from *her own people*. She dismisses Turelure without hesitation and is ready to die without much regret. In fact, Turelure's terror fades away when compared to the terror that the holy Father exerts on her (through the intermediary of Badilon). The second important point is that her possible decision of accepting Turelure's proposal and saving the Pope at the price of betraying everything she believes in, including God (whom the Pope represents on Earth), is situated beyond the logic of sacrifice. What makes her decision so difficult is that she is asked not to sacrifice herself for the Cause (something which she would do without hesitation), but to *betray*, to sacrifice this Cause itself, to give it up, to separate, to detach herself from it. She is asked to demonstrate her fidelity by an act of betrayal which is at the same time an act of no return. Badilon does not in the least try to help her to make the (right) decision. He does not try to persuade her that she would do a good deed by saving the Pope. They both know, for example, that by marrying Turelure, she would inevitably profane the holy sacrament of marriage. And Badilon does not try to persuade her that this evil would somehow be forgiven because it serves a good Cause. He says, on the contrary:

> It is not God's will that we should seek good by doing evil.[20]

20. *Ibid.*, p92.

When Sygne says that this act would mean to save the Pope at the price of her soul (here we are already on the doorstep of the 'second death'), he does not try to convince her of the contrary, but paints this decision in the darkest colours. He turns, so to speak, the knife in the wound: he says to Sygne that nobody, not even God Himself has the right to ask her to do this, that she will remain without sin if she refuses it and that she will inevitably sin if she accepts it ... The only incitement he allows himself is the one that we find in this crucial passage:

> **Sygne**: God gave me my life, and I am ready and anxious to give it back to Him. But the name is mine, and my woman's honour is mine, and mine alone!
> **Badilon**: Good is it to have something of one's own; for then have we something which we can give.[21]

21. *Ibid.*, pp54-55.

So, the most important question is how exactly does Badilon 'seduce' Sygne, how does he make her accept this horrible thing? By showing to her, opening 'before her, the abyss of this acceptance'.[22] He paints before her the abyss in which the most unheard-of thing is waiting for her: the loss, the 'sacrifice' of that in the name of which she has already sacrificed everything else. He makes her contemplate this abyss long enough for her to be caught by vertigo. And as it is well indicated in the dialogue, the whole affair takes place in the register of 'temptation'.

22. J. Lacan, *Le séminaire, livre VIII: Le transfert*, Seuil, Paris 1991, p322.

> **Sygne**: Father, do not tempt me beyond my powers!
> **Badilon**: It is not your strength, but rather your weakness that I am tempting.[23]

23. Paul Claudel, *op. cit.*, pp99-100.

Here we encounter another type of 'realisation of desire', something which Lacan calls *la réalisation abyssale* - abyssal realisation. As a first approximation we could say that the 'abyssal realisation' is only possible from the point of view of 'beyond the second death' (the point where not only the life, but the reason to live, the 'absolute condition'is at stake) - a point of view which opens up with modernity (in the sense of the contemporaneity). It is no coincidence that we find this same configuration in two of the greatest playwrights of this century, even though, 'ideologically', they seem to be as far from one another as possible: Brecht and Claudel. In Brecht's *The Measure Taken* it is precisely this same 'abyssal realisation' which is at stake. Lacan links this realisation to the Freudian concept of *Versagung*: *Versagung* implies, Lacan stresses, the breaking of a promise for which we have already given up everything.[24] Or, in other words, 'the subject is asked to accept with enjoyment the very injustice at which he is horrified'.[25] This is the crucial point which distinguishes the position of Sygne de Coufontaine from the position of Antigone:

24. Lacan, *Le transfert*, *op. cit.*, p353.

25. *Ibid.*, p355.

> The Word is no longer for us simply the law to which we are attached in order to carry the burden of the debt which constitutes our destiny. It opens for us a space of possibility and temptation from which to curse ourselves, not only as particular destiny, as life, but as the very path into which the Word leads us .... We are no longer just potentially guilty because of the symbolic debt ... [I]t is the debt itself in which we have our place that can be taken from us, and it is there that we can feel completely alienated from ourselves. The antique *Atè* has doubtless made us guilty of this debt, but to renounce it as we can do now means being burdened with an even greater misfortune: that destiny now amounts to nothing.[26]

26. *Ibid.*, p354.

In other words, the question that Antigone was confronted with was whether or not she would give way to her desire, i.e., betray the family *Atè*. The question that Sygne is confronted with is of a different nature. Sygne knows that if she refuses this act, she will betray her desire. But she also knows that if she accepts it, she will lose the very cause of her desire ('the reason for living'). Like Antigone she is perfectly able to act according to the maxim: 'Sadder than to lose one's life is to lose one's reason for living'. She is willing to give her life for her cause. This is the only thing that is left to her. And yet, as Badilon suggests, even this last remainder is one too many. If she has it, it is so that she can give it away - only at this point does it become clear whether or not one is really serious about one's charity. To give away everything that one has is rather easy, but to give away this remainder (what one *is*) is quite a different matter. And Badilon's strategy in his dialogue with Sygne consists in showing to her that this unheard-of thing which she abhors is nothing else but the ultimate consequence and horizon of her own cause, of her own honour, of her own desire.

What we are dealing with here may be termed the '*traversée du fantasme*' - going through the fantasy. Fantasy is the fundamental relation of the subject to her/his desire. The *a*, the support of the desire in his/her fantasy, is not visible in that which constitutes for the subject the image of his/her desire. More precisely, *a* is the support of the fantasy precisely in so far as it is excluded from it, invisible within its field of vision. We could say that for Sygne, this object which constitutes the support of her word and which, so to speak, opens the window onto her world, is honour. Honour is the object, the cause which absolutely cannot appear in the frame of this window as an object like the others, an object which could lend itself to exchange and substitution. And Sygne finds herself in a situation where, if she wants to save her fantasy and her desire, she has to sacrifice the very support of this fantasy, of this desire. When to her exclamation: 'God gave me my life, and I am ready and anxious to give it back to Him. But the name is mine, and my woman's honour is mine, and mine alone!', Badilon replies: 'Good is to have something of one's own; for then have we something which we can give', he makes the object-support of her fantasy appear in its frame and makes of it something one can give: he moves it from the register of being to the register of having. But for Sygne it was precisely because to 'give (away)' the honour was something absolutely inconceivable that she was able to give away, to sacrifice, everything else.

Let us now turn briefly to the end of the play, because it is there that we must situate the ethical value of Sygne's act. First we have this horrifyingly senseless, 'empty' suicidal gesture in which Sygne sacrifices herself for her loathed husband.[27] This scene is followed by another the function of which is to prevent any sense of closure. Here we come, once again, to the 'absolute choice' defined by Lacan as 'a choice that is motivated by no good'. Sygne didn't do it to save the family's honour, nor did she do it for her newborn son whom she refuses to see. She also refuses to do what is necessary for her redemption and salvation - she refuses to forgive Turelure and to abandon herself to God. If she had elected to abandon herself to God, she would have restored the function of Destiny or, rather, Providence, and the play would have ended on a sublime note. Instead, it ends with this twitching flesh - a compulsive tic which distorts the face of the heroine. If one can speak of Antigone's sublime beauty, this aesthetic reference is no longer valuable for Claudel's heroine.[28]

27. For a more detailed commentary of this scene see Slavoj Zizek, *The Indivisible Remainder*, *op. cit.*, pp117-8.

28. Cf. J. Lacan, *Le transfert*, *op. cit.*, p324.

This brings us to the final point of our argument. The first thing that can be deduced from our discussion of the two ethical heroines is that the 'ethics of the real' is not the ethics of the finite, of finitude. The right answer to the religious promise of immortality is not the pathos of the finite; the basis of ethics cannot be an imperative which commands us to endorse our finitude and renounce 'higher', 'impossible' aspirations. Not simply because this would mean giving in to necessity - the stakes are more radical: the infinite is not impossible to attain, rather, it is impossible for us to escape it completely. The end of the promise of a life after death (i.e. of an infinite outside this world) doesn't imply that we are henceforth 'enclosed', confined within this finitude. It implies, on the contrary, that the infinite is ceaselessly parasitic upon the finite. The absence of the beyond, the lack of any exception to the finite 'infinitises' the finite. To use the formula of Jean-Claude Milner, 'the infinite is what says no to the exception to the finite'.[29] The problem of the infinite is not how to attain it, but rather how to get rid of its stain which pursues us. The Lacanian name for this parasitism is enjoyment (*jouissance*).

29. Jean-Claude Milner, *L'Oeuvre claire*, Seuil, Paris 1995, p66.

How, then, is the infinite parasitic upon the finite, our existence as 'finite beings'? As a matter of fact, there are two modes of parasitism, each of them resulting in a different figure of the infinite: first, there is the infinite of desire which one might describe as 'bad infinity' (linked to the logics of non-accomplishment), and then there is the infinite of *jouissance* or drive (linked to the logics of the real and of realisation). We can shift the ethics in the passage from one to the other. However, this passage can itself take two different paths. The paradigm of the first is indicated in the figure of Antigone and brings out the co-ordinates of 'classical ethics'. The paradigm of the second is given to us in the figure of Sygne de Coufontaine and constitutes what we might call 'modern ethics'.

The infinite which Sygne 'realises' is not the same as that in Antigone's case. Antigone realises the infinite in a negative form, she realises it as absence. The infinite is evoked in the 'all' that Antigone sacrifices it for. The realisation of desire is accomplished in three steps:

- In life, there is one thing which one cannot give away ('the absolute condition').
- For this thing one is ready to give away everything, one's 'all' (even life).
- One realises the absolute condition by sacrificing, in one single gesture, the 'all' of what one is ready to sacrifice.

Here, we can see, first, how the 'all' is constituted in a reference to an exception. This is also the constitution of the subject of desire as a divided subject (divided between the absolute condition of desire and the whole series that opens up by exempting this absolute condition). In this context, to realise one's desire means to find a way of making a 'whole' out of everything that one is ready to sacrifice in order to preserve the absolute condition. In other words, one has to find a way of closing (i.e. ending) the potentially infinite series, so as to distinguish the only infinite that counts, the infinite of the unconditional, of the absolute condition. This is quite manifest in Antigone's lamentation in which she covers the distance that separates the moment when she is speaking from the moment when this *all* or *whole* will be accomplished. She is lamenting everything she will lose by her precocious death. On a closer examination we have to notice, however, that what is at stake is not the loss of what she has (or had). She is lamenting the loss of that which she doesn't have and which she could (perhaps) have had, had she continued to live. She starts unwinding virtually the rest of her life, and this remainder is created and accomplished only in this gesture of sacrificing it; she creates it by sacrificing it. Antigone realises this virtual remainder through its loss, i.e. by establishing it as lost. This gesture puts an end to the metonymy of desire by realising, straight away, the infinite potential of this metonymy. As in the case of the sublime, the 'true' infinite (the infinite of the unconditional) is evoked here in the violence done to our imagination by the representation of the totality of a series (of conditions). We don't see the infinite, we only see the effect it has on the figure of Antigone who functions as its screen. This explains the sublime splendour of her figure which is the result of the Thing that she hides and announces at the same time.

The 'abyssal realisation' that one encounters in the case of Sygne de Coufontaine is not of the same order. It, also, is accomplished in three steps, yet the conjectures of these three steps are different:

- In life, there is one thing which one cannot give away ('the absolute condition').
- For this thing one is ready to give away all (but this 'all' tolerates no exceptions).
- The only way of realising the absolute condition is to sacrifice it as an exception (i.e. to sacrifice its character as an exception).

Here we are dealing with a kind of short-circuit which, instead of evoking the infinite by realising the whole of the finite, suspends the infinite as an exception and thus renders the finite not-all, i.e. contaminates it with the infinite. The infinite is visible here in a different way than in the case of Antigone: not as an absence which illuminates the figure of the heroine with a sublime splendour, but rather as some embarrassing and 'out of place' presence, manifesting itself in the distortions, in the torsions of a body which is not made in the measure of the infinite (of the *jouissance*) which inhabits it. In the last part of the play we see the heroine (though, one could ask whether the term 'heroine' is still appropriate in this case) agitated by a nervous twitch which constitutes a very distressing and poignant image of the infinite that is parasitic upon the finite.

The Atè of Antigone; Lacan, Heidegger and Sexual Difference

Cecilia Sjöholm

THE BEAUTY OF ANTIGONE

Jacques Lacan's engagement with tragedy concerns a question as simple as it is intriguing: what is the beauty of Antigone? Occupying a central place in a seminar entitled *The Ethics of Psychoanalysis*, the question may seem odd. Sophocles does not describe Antigone in terms of beauty. What we find in her dialogue with Ismene is the wish of *kalos thanein*. To 'die with honour' is the proper translation, but we could read: 'die beautifully'. Lacan's admiration of Antigone's beauty is in fact a fascination with her death. Showing how not to betray one's desire, her uncompromising relentlessness makes her a heroine of the ethics of psychoanalysis. In order not to replace one fantasmatic screen with another, psychoanalysis should not promise a good or even a better life. The aim, rather, is to make the subject assume a position as cause of his or her own desire, killing both the illusion of an ultimate end and of an authentic origin. In this respect, the existential dimensions of his thinking seem close to such a thinker as Heidegger. A crucial aspect is added, however: ethics is a function of a symbolic 'death' that has already taken place, not of our being towards death as a projective form of temporality, or the otherness of nature. As in Heidegger, it carries the inherent possibility of a transgression, crime or extreme action violating its own foundations in it, but the violation does not concern humankind in the face of external forces. It concerns the law enforcing castration, and the desire of the ethical subject. Such an ethics inscribes the relation to our fellow being under the same law as sexual difference. If the challenge of an ethics for a secularised twentieth century consists in the encounter with our desire, then the negotiation of sexual difference is an integral part of it. This is where Heidegger and Lacan diverge; Heidegger interpreting Antigone's fate according to the general definiton of *Dasein* or man. Lacan, with a gesture as strange as it is provoking, insists on making her extraethical. He gives us two reasons.

Firstly, Antigone's death as an ethical heroine has a particular poignancy because she is a woman. Struck by the 'beauty' of her suicidal act, Lacan evokes a phenomenon pointed to by many feminist philosophers and literary historians - Elisabeth Bronfen, Adriana Cavarero and Luce Irigaray to mention a few - the male struggle with death in the history of philosophy and literature employs a complex strategy to cover the worrying fact of sexual difference and femininity. Secondly, she dies because she is haunted by *ate*, the family curse. Following the fate of her father Oedipus she transgresses the law through an act of incestuous desire. But in Antigone's case, her desire, is directed towards a dead body.

The first point concerns ethics and the traumatic inscription of difference. Woman is a *Vorstellungs-Repräsentanz* for death, Irigaray writes, using the Freudian term for how a trauma comes to be represented. A castrated woman is a representation 'of the death drives that cannot (or theoretically could not) be perceived without horror, that the eye (of) consciousness refuses to recognise'.[1] The phenomenon constitutes a powerful subtext in Western philosophy up to Freud. In the case of Lacan, fear of death, or castration, is no longer symbolised by the mutilation of bodily organs as in Freud. The rejection of heterogeneity and difference is in fact a symptom of a death that, in a manner of speaking, already has taken place. Castration becomes the symbolic mark of a constitutive lack and feminine desire its manifestation. Such a definition of finitude, naturally, gives a horrifying aspect to femininity which is immediately connected to the second point and the desperation and bereavement of Antigone.

1. Luce Irigaray, *Speculum of the Other Woman*, trans. G. Gill, Cornell University Press, Ithaca, New York [1974] 1985, p55.

The second point concerns the particularity of Antigone's desire. Bearing the *atè* of her family name, as the daughter of Oedipus, her desire is 'pure'; says Lacan; a designation which is difficult to understand in the wake of the perversion which she also represents.[2] Leading back to the void that determined the course of the play in the first place, her action becomes exemplary, both of death drive and desire. Antigone's walk towards death is a symbol for heroic action in a nihilistic perspective – it is undertaken without concern for any rewards to follow. This is a crucial point. Even if such a vision of feminine heroism appears questionable and overstated, the fact remains that it challenges, for instance, Heidegger's more general view of the action, where the issue of sexual difference is forgotten, hidden or sublated.

2. Jacques Lacan, *The Ethics of Psychoanalysis*, trans. D. Porter, Routledge, London [1986] 1992, p282.

The question of sexual difference in *Antigone* is originally posed by Hegel. However critical he may be in the *Ethics*-seminar, Lacan's indebtedness to Hegel is vast in many crucial aspects. Setting the tone for the discussion from the beginning of the nineteenth century onwards and foreshadowing the paradigm of psychoanalysis, *Phänomenologie des Geistes* shows that desire is bound up with sexual difference in the ethical community. In the profound discord between male and female two orders collide which are both justified, each achieving its goal only at the cost of the other.[3] Placing woman on the side of intuition, nature and the unconscious may seem to denigrate her. But there is one function in which a woman can act and be recognised by patriarchal society: a sister is equal to her brother in a way that a wife or a daughter can never be in relation to her husband or father. The relation between siblings is supposedly 'pure' in terms of sexual and hierarchical components proper. But Antigone also defends the place of 'natural' desire in the ethical community – that is, of sexual desire.[4]

3. G. W. F. Hegel, *Lectures on Aesthetics*, volume II, trans. T. M. Knox, Clarendon Press, Oxford [1835] 1975, p1196.

4. G. W. F. Hegel, *Phenomenology of Spirit*, trans. A.V. Miller, Oxford University Press, Oxford [1807] 1977, p456-459.

Inspired by the Hegelian quest for a 'pure' Antigone, Lacan sets the scene for a reading of *Antigone* where moral, political and feminist issues are swept aside in order to bring the reader back to the evasive origin of the tragic conflict. The theme is not a conflict between two orders of discourse, but truth itself.[5] Ethics in the Lacanian sense has to go beyond calculation or the search for recognition. Brother and sister, again, constitute a particular case in this respect. They are nearly but not quite separate, transcending the aporia of similarity and difference in their desire. But if Antigone's actions cease to concern the burial as a family task and start to express a desire turned towards the dead brother himself, then the aporia opens up to the full. It no longer concerns the justifiability of Creon's or Antigone's claims to justice, but Antigone's impossible desire for her dead brother Polynices.

5. Lacan, 1992, *op. cit.*, pp 236, 248, 265.

'Pure' desire means getting rid of soft, human objects, establishing a limit beyond which we could not possibly go.[6] This limit is the primary preoccupation for Lacan, and this is also where Antigone takes us in her obsession with her dead brother. Naturally, it can only be shown through a work of art. Tragedy's play with absence and appearances, coverings and uncoverings, reveals its function. Working through such concepts as the beautiful, the good and the true the Platonic legacy is unveiled; tragedy shows us that these concepts could never coincide with saturation or fulfilment. What moves us in art is a function of displacement. That which is rejected, denegated, abjected or appears non-sensical finds a form. It becomes beautiful because it displaces horror, good because it is a mask for evil, and true because it touches an empty space. The *atè* of Antigone, which causes her death, also coincides with the radiance of her beauty.[7]

6. Bernard Baas, *Le désir pur*, Peeters, Louvain 1992; and Alenka Zupancic, *Die Ethik des Realen*, Turia und Kant, Wien 1995, pp35-44.

7. Lacan, *op, cit.*, 1992 p281.

The secret behind the tragic experience evoked by *Antigone* is ultimately revealed by her beauty. She takes us beyond a metaphysical or religious conception of good and evil, the point at which we have to look elsewhere for an ethical foundation. Lacan displaces the ground for an ethics from calculative thinking to the experience of the beautiful. 'The effect of beauty' points to something which we desire but cannot interiorise or integrate. By analogy, we cannot interiorise the human objects of our desire. The limit which separates us from them is also the limit of our desire. Looking closer at *Antigone*, we find that sexual difference is intrinsically involved in the fixation of this limit. Finding Antigone beautiful and pure in the face of death, Lacan elevates her into a 'Thing' of courtly love, beyond the contamination she actually represents in Sophocles' text. His own gaze at the female heroine is filtered through the fantasmatic, and his reading is full of the very symptoms, projections and distortions that he himself analyses, and that we associate with a patriarchal view of women. But Lacan's reading is not just a patriarchal negation-elevation of a feminine other. We are dealing with a double perspective: the motives behind Antigone's decisions on the one hand and the fear and fascination she inspires in us, the viewers, on the other. Lacan's questions are never made external to the involvement with the text itself or extrapolated from it. Inspired by

Heidegger's existential archeology, Lacan provides us a with a new take on what it means to live without a metaphysical framework. But rather than sublating sexual difference into a more general view of human agency, he proceeds the other way: we have to go through the illusions and the beauty that all take part in the fantasmatic play of sexuality, as well as the screens of narcissistic gratification. Otherwise we cannot possibly conceive of the true function of the beauty effect and unravel the void behind it.

HYMN TO MAN

An eager admirer and translator of Heidegger, Lacan may well have known both of the latter's published *Antigone*-reading from 1935 and the one from 1942 from other sources. Since there is no documented evidence, all speculation on details is fruitless but a global comparison of ideas indicates crucial similarities and differences. Tragedy in this perspective has nothing to do with conflicts between characters, nor with dialectics. For both, tragedy is a poetic creation or re-creation of an absence that touches upon a moment of orginal loss, the 'Thing' that gives a dignity of 'non-foundational foundations' to politics and ethics beyond *praxis*.[8] Turning our attention towards the controversial readings of the second stasimon in the play, we see that there are important similarities between Heidegger and Lacan not only in the details of the analysis but in the overall insistence on moving away from dialectics and placing the conflictual orders on a common source or ground. For Heidegger, reading tragedy is a way of keeping the question of the *polis* open. The 'poetisation' of the political is a return to the 'pre-political' in the same way that Lacan's seminar is a search for a 'pure' formula for ethics.[9] The question is whether these domains are also 'pre-sexual'. Where Antigone is beautiful or inhuman for Lacan, she is *unheimlich* for Heidegger. Bearing Freud in mind, it seems as if a strange reversal has taken place between the psychoanalyst and the philosopher in this regard, the psychoanalyst avoiding a Freudian interpretation of fear of castration and the philosopher evoking it despite himself.[10] Both clearly point to the tragedy's sexual undertone, even if it remains unexplicated in Heidegger.

'Hymn to man', the second stasimon, gives the key. Not clearly pointing out the object of the wrath of the gods, or the guilt requiring a final bloodshed or *catharsis* through somebody's downfall, the chorus turns the audience's eyes towards both Antigone and Creon. Man, the chorus sings, is the most remarkable of all beings, to *deinon*: 'Wonders are many, and none more wonderful than man' (334). As everyone who has followed the debate on tragedy will know, this line, *polla ta deina*, is impossible to transpose into another language. It can also mean 'terrible, horrifying', which is Hölderlin's choice: 'Ungeheuer'.[11] Heidegger, in his own version of Hölderlin's translation, changes it into 'Unheimlich'.[12]

Like Heidegger, Lacan has his own reasons for bending the philological

8. Philippe Lacoue-Labarthe, *Lacan avec les philosophes*, Collège International de la philosophie, Albin Michel, Paris 1993, pp33-4.

9. Martin Heidegger, *Hölderlin's Hymne der Ister, Gesamtausgabe* Vol 53, Vittorio Klostermann, Frankfurt, p102.

10. Sigmund Freud, 'The "Uncanny"', *Standard Edition*, XVII, p231.

11. Friedrich Hölderlin, *Antigonae, Sämtliche Werke*, Frankfurter Ausgabe, Roter Stern, Frankfurt [1804] 1988, p299.

12. GA 53, p70-71.

tradition. If Heidegger wants to unravel the question of being, Lacan wants to reveal the structure of desire in making a number of interpretative claims that may be outrageous for the classicist , but manage to capture aspects of the text that more prudent scholars may fail to see. The chorus celebrates the formidable ways of man, only in the face of death does he find himself *aporos*, without solution. Death is the only phenomenon which he cannot conquer, 'but he has devised escapes from baffling illnesses.' Turning the meaning around 'in Prévert's style' the negation comes to allude to man's facing the future not his resources: man never faces his future without being resourceless. He *always* lacks the means. That is why he is *aporos* to his very nature, infinitely cunning in his capacity to get into trouble: 'He always manages to cause things to come crashing down on his head'.[13] He has not just learnt to escape strange illnesses, he has learnt to escape *into* them. His 'clever constructions' are not just cures, they are the *maladies* themselves. A parallel aporetic construction returns in the last strophe:

13. Lacan, 1992, *op. cit.*, p275.

> ...Respecting the laws of the
> land and the right of oaths sworn by the gods, he is a man of a lofty city; cityless is he who recklessly devotes himself to evil. Never may he be a guest at my hearth or a sharer of my thoughts, who does these things.[14]

14. Trans. Andrew Brown, Aris & Phillips, Warminster 1986.

The laws of the land are the 'cthonic laws' also referring to the feminine divine laws of Demeter and Persephone, symbolising the rights of the dead. The chorus, pointing to the ambiguity of the law, implicitly points to both Creon and Antigone as 'cityless' lawbreakers in their determination to stick to just one side. Lacan has another interpretation. The passage, he says, is not about obeying laws, it is about mixing them up.[15] Antigone, therefore, becomes the object of the passage. Creon fails in his judgement. Antigone, however, is *deinon*, which we could rephrase in the following way: she confuses the *rights of the dead* with the *law of death,* that is, with the death drive. Her being instrumental for the elevation of the brother's singularity seems to collapse at the point where she clearly goes one step beyond the piety of her sisterly duty: that is why Hegel could not be right about her gesture as aimed towards recognition. There is a perverted desire for death involved in Antigone's actions.

15. Lacan,1992, *op. cit.*, p276.

Heidegger comes to similar conclusions, but for different reasons. In *Einführung in die Metaphysik*, he gives special attention to the same places in the text as Lacan, making the word *deinon* resound with ambiguity. Man is cast out through an original act of violence, of which he himself is both the maker and the object: he is both violent and *unheimlich*, uncanny and homeless, violently forcing nature under him and widening the gap between the overpowering and the overpowered. *Uncanny* refers to *Dasein's* own violent character rather than fear of mutilation, as in Freud. For Freud, it gives rise to anxiety. For Heidegger it is released through anxiety. In both cases, however, it points to an original loss or lack.[16] *Dasein* will always be cast under the overruling order he tries to overcome, tragedy resulting in a disaster which '... governs and waits in the conflict between violence and the overpowering'. [17] Human existence *is* tragic since human beings, as the most *deinon*, will bring disasters upon themselves through their aptitude to respond with violence to their own constitutional exposure. Man comes to 'nothingness', he is *aporos*, in spite of the fact that he can go everywhere, is *pantoporos*, thereby revealing the ontological foundations of his *Dasein.*[18] In many ways this view is similar to the idea of desire as the other side of the death drive in Lacan. Man strives towards the limit of his being. Clever schemes and constructions, the capacity of thinking and creating, both respond to and produce violence. Being, in turn, shows itself as disruptive, threatening, uncanny. *Dasein* as a product of originary violence provides us with an image close to Lacan's idea of the castrated subject - with the difference that the split, for Lacan, concerns not the ontological foundations of our being but desire. From a Lacanian perspective, Heidegger's interpretation of the tragedy brings out the sheer brutality which lies at the core of its sexual connotations, but without making it explicit.

16. Michael Düe, *Ontologie und Psychoanalyse*, Athenäum, Frankfurt am Main 1986, pp83-86, 105-6.

17. Martin Heidegger, GA Vol 40, Vittorio Klostermann, Frankfurt am Main, p124; Trans. R. Manheim, *An Introduction to Metaphysics*, Yale University Press, New Haven, Connecticut 1959, p163.

18. *Ibid.*, p116.

In 1942, Heidegger's reflections in *Hölderlin's Hymne 'der Ister'* provide us with a more elaborate interpretation. It is steeped in a rhetoric of blood and soil; carrying anxious (and perhaps defensive) references to an authentic Germanic form being and to 'Nationalsozialismus' but we will forego the debated implications of this anxiety or dubiousness which have a complicated relation to the text's philosophical intentions and instead turn our attention to the figure of Antigone. Transferring the attention from the first strophe of the chorus to the last, the most conspicuous difference from the reading of 1935 is that Being is revealed in and as the human community rather than through the overpowering forces of nature. The key to *deinon*, in this reading, is no longer given by the first lines of the chorus but the last ones: (s)he is *deinon* who exposes the community to the contingency of its own laws. 'Never may he be a guest at my hearth or a sharer of my thoughts, who does these things', the Thebean elders say, providing Heidegger with the next key-word in his reading: *estia* or hearth. Antigone's uncanniness is revelatory of the limit of home or hearth. Exposing the boundaries of the community, she shatters the illusion of belonging.

Who is expelled from the hearth and rejected as a fellow being? Antigone's wish to *kalos thanein*, of a 'beautiful' death, is where her essence protrudes: she, herself, will not only suffer *deinon* but also incarnate it.[19] Her willingness to die for her brother and to follow the divine laws make visible the unnameable extremes of existence relating human beings to Being itself: death and blood, 'blood' connoting not only family ties but also passion. Heidegger does not identify these natural bonds with our relation to being, but they are indicative of its function .[20] Antigone herself

19. GA 53, p128-9.

20. *Ibid.*, p147.

is uncanny, shut out from the hearth for showing the gaps in its foundation but at the same time making it visible as such. Heidegger's understanding of Sophocles' tragedy as a poem about the disruptions and disclosures of being stands and falls with the identification of Antigone as *deinon*, the uncanny disclosure of the split in the *polis*. She incarnates 'the purest kind of poetry in herself'.[21]

21. *Ibid.*, p149.

Heidegger makes Antigone into a *Vorstellungs-Repräsentanz* for a traumatic and violent origin. Rather than linking it to the more impersonal effects of *atè*, Antigone's death becomes the necessary sacrifice for the sake of the community's possibility of an authentic relation to its (lack of) origins. It saves the 'pre-political' foundations of the community. The divine or natural laws seem to require such a sacrifice. But the notion of male/female discordant orders and the feminine as representative of divine law is not mentioned in this passage; sexual difference is subordinated to the conflict between beings and Being in the construction of community's bonds.[22] Heidegger's reading, therefore, becomes exemplary of the kind of phenomena Irigaray has pointed to: Antigone's role in the tragic conflict becomes projected as death, reduced to a necessary sacrifice. In other words, the 'uncanniness' seems to refer to an unspoken link between 'femininity' and death which secretly influences Heidegger's whole analysis. The question of sexual difference is never stated. But the poetic beauty that Heidegger reads into Antigone clearly covers something much more brutal which is intimately linked to her clinging to the divine laws and her reverence for blood ties.

22. *Ibid.*, p147.

THE DESIRE OF ANTIGONE

The key word associated with Antigone in Lacan's reading is *atè*. His original contribution to the long line of *Antigone*-interpretations derives from this crucial observation. Antigone's *atè*, often translated as 'madness' but rather indicating the drive behind her fate, leads the way towards the limit of desire. Opposing Antigone's *atè* to Creon's *hamartia*, the contingent mistakes and wrongful calculations which eventually cause his downfall, the *Ethics*-seminar shows that *atè* designates, 'the limit that human life can only briefly cross'.[23] This is the very limit Antigone seeks: not just death, but the annihilation of desire, a return to the point of its inscription. The same word returns in the French word *atroce* (or *atrocious*) in the sense of 'inhuman'. The play describes her this way, in her uncanny transformation into a wailing, birdlike creature at the side of her brother's body, giving up ' ... a piercing cry, the shrill note of a bird, as it cries/ when it sees, in its empty nest, the bed bereft of nestlings.' (425)

23. *Ibid.*, p262.

Her sight when she is arrested is *deinon*, says the chorus, like an animal or a ghost. The 'madness' of Antigone the sister is the desperation of a bereaved, loving mother, echoing the fate of Iocaste. This alone, however, is not enough to make her *deinon*. The uncanniness of Antigone is a consequence of her placing herself in an inhuman sphere, her refusal to compromise and her disregard of human goods. How dare you transgress my law, Creon asks, and Antigone answers that his edict does not come from Zeus or from *dike*. Her motive may seem to rely on divine law alone. Lacan's correction of this impression is crucial: Antigone believes *dike*, justice, to belong to the nether world, to dwell 'with the gods below'. If Creon fatally mistakes human law for divine it is the other way around with Antigone. The goal of her action originates in the nether world itself, a sphere ultimately governed by death.

In Attic tragedy, *atè* is part of the ethical vocabulary concerned with the relation between necessity and freedom.[24] Sophocles lets the word ring of both destruction and madness, the Homeric sense of 'infatuation' soaking into 'more objective' manifestations. In Sophocles' own text, *atè* is the haunting from one generation to another. If human beings are *deinon* in their capacity to overpower the forces of nature, the overpowering force of *atè* appears even more terrifying. *Atè* is the very limit of the forces of man, where he loses his power. Man's capacity only manifests itself against an ultimate defeat which derives from the dead contaminating the living: 'sorrows falling on dead men's sorrows'. The chorus deplores that the last root in the house of Oedipus is cut down by the bloody knife from the nether world: 'by folly of speech and a Fury in the mind.' (600) These lines may refer to Antigone, or perhaps the fate she herself laments: she will never have any children, she is promised to Hades. But they may also refer to Creon, who will be left without descendants. In the text *atè* belongs *neither* to Antigone nor Creon. It is, the chorus, tells us, the limit we should never pass. 'What human transgression can challenge your power?' (605) they ask Zeus. Every insolence in the face of his power, 'does not come/ upon men's lives in its greatest force without disaster'. The last line reads *ektos atas*: nobody escapes *atè*. The uncanny nuances of the word derive from its indeterminacy: neither outside nor inside, neither object nor subject. Sophocles uses the word with particular sophistication in exploiting this indeterminacy. *Atè* is both a ruinous power descending from the gods, acting independantly of the tragic characters, and a madness caused by the gods and internalised by the doomed hero or heroine as a god 'leading his mind to disaster'. (625)[25] It may be introjected as madness or associated with an outside appearing to turn against the subject: *tuche*. Antigone's *atè* is somewhere in between these two perspectives. It pushes her towards ruin but the origins of her destruction belong neither to the subject nor the world.

The *atè* of tragedy has the function of inscription, not divine fate. It can only be determined *après-coup* through acts trying to oppose the destiny that they, in the course of events, turn out to fulfill. When the gods prohibit Laios from having a son, the crime against the prohibition is inscribed in the lawgiving itself. *Atè* is the contamination spreading from a transgression of the fundamental laws of the community. These laws, such as the law

24. R.E. Doyle, *Atè, Its Use and Meaning*, Fordham University Press, New York, pp1-6.

25. *Ibid.*, p106.

against incest in the story of Oedipus, will always be founded upon the myth, or actuality, of an original crime. Put in another way: there is no law which does not carry the injunction of its own transgression within it. Creon's barring the dead from the living may be intended to save the city from contamination, but instead brings out the excessive forces proper to the dynamics of tragedy. The prohibition against touching the dead brother's body only enforces the incestuous overtones of Antigone's desire. The limit of *atè*, engenders the wish to embrace the forbidden things that lie beyond it.[26] When Antigone goes beyond *atè* towards a reunion with the dead brother, she only pursues a path that was staked out for her to begin with.

At the bottom of *atè*, there is a founding crime. Contrary to what we may believe, the founding crime is not the incest of Oedipus but the desire of Oedipus' (and Antigone's) mother, the incest of Iocaste. 'The desire of the mother is the origin of everything', according to Lacan, challenging the idea that Oedipus is the hidden focus of the tale.[27] Her initial transgression, carrying the house of the labdacids towards extinction, is mirrored in Antigone's extreme attachment to her brother. She could have another husband, another child, but her brother is irreplacable, she laments. These 'scandalous' words, considered as doubtful in terms of authorship, are nothing but a 'dialectical calculation', Goethe complained.[28] In other words, the incestuous overtones are only too obvious. Iocaste's children come from the 'bloody root' of the labdacidean curse, according to Aeschylus' version of the story in *Seven against Thebes*.[29] Antigone's action can be interpreted as an expression of a particular bond to the mother. She reveres the genealogy of the mother and the maternal heritage.[30] But the reason she can never have a new brother ultimately stems from the fact that she is descending from a monstrous union between mother and son. Her appeal to divine rights is not only a righteous plea for justice; it is also a desperate sign of her death drive. Blurring the lines of demarcation between deathwish and love, she challenges the very structure of desire. Nobody lives *ektos atas*, outside of *atè*, says the chorus. Lacan takes the connotation of limit literally: no mortal lives *outside* of ate. *Atè* is the very limit beyond which we cannot live: it coincides with the limit of desire.

The limit of *atè*, or desire, cannot be reduced to a barrier against incest. It also points to a void which we have to negotiate: there is no guarantee that our desire is directed towards any ultimate end or meaning. On the other hand, this nihilistic vision demands that we 'follow our desire', go all the way in order to recognise the void behind its inscription. Unlike Creon, who aspires to know the good and do good for the community, Antigone is clearly a metaphor for the existential position of the subject as such in this regard. The aim of psychoanalysis is not to do 'good' but to turn us away from a fantasmatic position as victim or toy of an invisible Other, such as destiny, into a position where we recognise and assume our desire.[31] This is Antigone's heroic gesture in going all the way towards the

26. Slavoj Zizek, *Tarrying With the Negative*, Routledge, London 1993, pp115-16.

27. Lacan,1992, *op. cit.*, p283.

28. J. P. Eckermann, *Gespräche mit Goethe*, Carl Hanser Verlag, München 1986, pp542-546.

29. Gerald F. Else, *The Madness of Antigone, Abhandlungen der Heidelberger Akademie der Wissenschaften*, Carl Winter Universitätsverlag, Heidelberg 1976, p17.

30. Irigaray, 1985, *op. cit.*, p219. See also *Le Temps de la différence*, Minuit, Paris 1987, pp86, 112.

31. For an illuminating discussion of a male versus a female position in this regard, see Bruce Fink, *The Lacanian Subject*, Princeton University Press, Chichester 1995, p115. See also Ellie Ragland, *Essays on the Pleasures of Death*, Routledge, London 1995, p168.

limit of 'atè'. It does entail her death. But it also uncovers the true face of freedom, the fact that there is no Other of the Other, no Supreme Good, no relief or metaphysical justification to be found as the goal of our actions. The law is contingent, and therefore cruel. There is no justice in its web. It is symptomatic of Lacan's way of thinking that it takes the 'beauty' and 'purity' of a bereaved female heroine to point it out to us. The idea of Antigone's action as 'pure desire' may seem to rely on a fantasm in itself.[32] But Lacan both constructs the screen and takes us beyond it in a triple layering of mirrors involving the male psychoanalyst, the female heroine and the reader. The effect brings out the radical nihilism of Antigone's action. It is a nihilism that could only be effected by a woman. Unlike Creon she does not fool herself into doing either good or bad, she does what she has to, even if her desire is directed towards the void. In her exposure to the contingencies of patriarchal law, the feminine subject is a more revealing model of subjectivity than the male.

32. Patrick Guyomard, *La Jouissance du tragique*, Aubier, Paris 1992, p66, pp44-5, 127-8.

TWO DEATHS

For Lacan, there is not one death but *two*, placing the subject in between. Death can only be thought through the same cutting signifier which produces sexual difference as well as the 'beauty effect', the split between ourselves and our objects of desire.[33] All that exists lives only 'in the lack of being'.[34] Living in the lack of being means, as Jean-Luc Nancy has put it, to lack nothing. There is nothing to be 'lacked' since being manifests itself as lack, or void.[35] The second death is a function of the lack of nothing experienced as unbearable pain or pleasure: *jouissance* or enjoyment. It is the ultimate *transgression*, a nihilistic embracing of nothingness.

33. Lacan, 1992, *op. cit.*, p281.

34. *Ibid*, p292.

35. Jean-Luc Nancy, *Lacan avec les philosophes*, p204.

In the *Ethics*-seminar, the relation between ethics, sexual difference and the question of femininity is still an issue that remains to be fully explored. In the *Encore*-seminar from 1975, Lacan comes back to it in a way that may help us understand the notion of the two deaths. Here, he tells us that the Other is the other sex and since there is no Other of the Other; no connection between the two sexes. There is, in other words, nothing to assert any ground for desire at all.[36] Truth, from that perspective, comes to reside in the sheer fact that there is no sexual relation: there is no way to relate to being beyond fantasy, masquerade, the pretension that one has what one has not got. Feminine enjoyment, or *jouissance*, famously illustrated by Bernini's statue of an ecstatic St Theresa, confirms the missing existence of the phallus. The ironic gesture in the choice of a saint as a symbol of feminine sexuality implies, of course, that enjoyment is made possible because there is nothing beyond the castrating signifier. What we lack is nothing, there is no God beyond our faulty existence, even if we invent one and act as if there was, as little as the enjoyment of a woman lacking the phallus would rely on it.[37]

36. Lacan, 1975, *op. cit.*, p40; 1992, *op.cit.*, p75.

37. Jacques Lacan, *Encore*, Seuil, Paris 1975, pp70-7, trans Jacqueline Rose, *Feminine Sexuality*, Macmillan, London 1982, pp147-8.

Returning to the *Ethics*-seminar, we find a castrated woman as a symbol for the ethical subject. Between two deaths, she is unable to participate in life. She is cold as ice, Creon complains to his son, to embrace her would be like embracing a stone. She wants to marry someone in Hades! (640-660) Antigone's beauty correponds to her pain. Her descent into the zone between two deaths is nothing but a consequence of her distress. She has been dead for a long time, she tells her sister, even before she made the final choice. (559) She is driven by something other than a belief in what is right and she disregards any kind of compensation or good resulting from her action. Getting rid of the illusory layers of a final purpose, Antigone affirms the unique value of her brother's being, without reference to any content, to whatever good or evil Polynices may have done.[38] Marked by *ate* Antigone acts 'in conformity with her desire' because she has, literally, nothing to lose. For Lacan, this is the secret behind the beauty and the uncanniness of Antigone. It may seem odd that he links her fate to ethics, as if death is the only solution. She is not, however, the symbol of a death to come, but of a death that has already taken place. There are important differences in his perspective if we compare it with Heidegger. Rather than projecting her spookiness as 'pure poetry', Lacan makes her uncanny precisely beacause she is a woman and because this places her at the limits to begin with; this is what makes her act possible.

38. *Ibid.*, p279.

BROTHERS AND SISTERS

The famous lack of analysis of sexual difference in Heidegger's writing on the whole is modified by a reading of Georg Trakl's poetry in *Unterwegs zur Sprache*. *Geschlecht*, the German word for sex, also connotes filiation and humankind in the universal sense. Trakl, in his poems about the atrocities of the First World War, writes about the future possibility of '*Ein Geschlecht*' collecting the discordant notions of the term into one.[39] The word '*Geschlecht*' becomes softened by a poetic reference to unity but it is a word of discord in itself: 'The curse of the decomposing *Geschlecht* consists in the fact that this ancient *Geschlecht* has been dispersed in the discord of the *Geschlechter* ... That *Geschlecht* is "foreign" and it follows the stranger'.[40] Sexual difference is a sign of the falling apart of humankind. Jacques Derrida accordingly, in a famous essay on the presumed non-sexual character of *Dasein*, remarks that it is not to be regarded as pre-sexual, but that it is conducting us towards a dispersive and multiple notion of difference as such.[41]

It is interesting to note that Heidegger is concerned with brothers and sisters when he touches upon the issue of sexual difference in the two cases we are dealing with here. As we have noted, the brother-sister relation evokes intricate questions concerning the relation similarity/ difference, and challenges the notion of 'pure' desire *v* incest. The stranger, in the quote above, has a redemptive function. Both in Sophocles' text and in the poems of Trakl the sign of redemptive femininity for Heidegger is a

39. GA 12, p74.

40. *Ibid*, p46, trans. David Krell, *Intimations of Mortality*, Penn State University Press, University Park 1986, p167.

41. Jacques Derrida, *Psyché*, Flammarion, Paris 1987, pp401-3, 414.

dead sister, incestuously attached to her brother. In the poems of Trakl, the dead sister belongs to the dusky haze of the youngsters, not yet falling apart as *Geschlechter*. Death for Trakl, he says, is not a sign of decomposure, but of taking leave of the decomposing function of *Geschlecht* itself.[42] That is, death is a remedy for the brutal fact of sexual difference. The dead sister relieves humankind from the discord of sexual difference in a logic reminiscent of the subtext in *Antigone*. In the reading of the play, the stranger is a woman exposing the community by transgressing the limits of the *polis*. Her death, as in the reading of Trakl, becomes a gesture tied up with a redemptive function, compensating for the decomposure that threatens the bonds of the community. Death is nothing like as tragic or violent as sexual difference itself.

42. GA 12, p58.

For both Heidegger and Lacan, Antigone brings us closer to the sphere of the ethical and the 'pre-political' respectively, as the limit of the community. Not only does she belong to the fringe or margin, she *shapes* its limits in the process of their respective interpretations. Her difference gives us the very measure of the field of the 'pre-political' and the ethical: the *polis* or whirl for Heidegger, the zone between two deaths for Lacan. In Heidegger the violent impact of her difference as a woman in the community is not made explicit, but her death is clearly a consequence of it.

For Lacan, in turn, anything we could possibly say about Antigone is a product of the projections, creations and fantasmatic viewpoints we create as sexuated beings. Any view that we take on ethics, any notion of politics we construct, will point to a limit where we finally come upon the question of sexual difference. For Heidegger it is the linguistic exposure of being towards nothingness which constitutes the bonds of the community. In other words: the ek-static and projective relation to death. For Lacan, language or the symbolic order implies the dimension of death as *a function* of sexual difference, exposed through the radical status of feminine sexuality. For Heidegger, there is nothing outside of *Dasein*'s projective points, whereas for Lacan, we have the Real beyond the symbolic, which is where the question of ethics is posed. If Heidegger makes sexual difference a secondary issue, and considers death to be the limit that also creates the tragic conflict, then Lacan makes sexual difference into that limit.

Tragedy begins at the limit of desire. Desire, rather than mankind's exposure to death, forms the ground of our tragic condition.

BEHEADING THE DEAD: RITES OF HABEAS CORPUS IN SHAKESPEARE'S *MEASURE FOR MEASURE*

Jane Beverly Malmo

INTRODUCTION: PARDONING VIOLENCE

If the task of a critique of violence is to represent the relation of violence to law and justice,[1] Shakespeare's *Measure for Measure* performs this task capitally. Not one blow is struck in the play, and yet the machinations of Duke Vincentio reveal as much about the violence of the law as any atrocity of blood staged on the scaffold.

In the dramatic performance of public executions, law has always emerged as the figure of total control. The sovereign's first right and his subjects' last rites coincide at the gallows. It is precisely by exercising such violence over life and death that the law reaffirms itself. 'But in this violence', Walter Benjamin has insisted, 'something rotten in law is revealed'.[2] At the heart of the law lies a traumatic kernel of violence that both founds and preserves the law; and it triggers the need for a symbolic apparatus to disguise this violence, while dealing it out in lethal legal doses.

States rise on fallen heads; they thrive on downcast eyes. Slaughter, punishment, surveillance and repression guarantee the sovereign's rule. But legal history records the forgetting of such law-founding and law-preserving violence. The rule-governed institutions of law have supposedly domesticated the mythical violence that founds the law's unconscious. But as Benjamin's 'Critique of Violence' reveals, the violence at work in myth continues to spell the law. Only the scene has changed, from the gods' halls to the judges' chambers, where the arbitrary force in myth gives way to arbitration in the law, the oracle is announced as legal argument, and the curse pronounced as judicial sentence. Meanwhile, the rottenness of the death penalty yields to a more insidious, subtle rottenness, in which violence is concealed. The root of legal violence spreads underground, dispersed in the 'all pervasive, ghostly presence of the police',[3] or embedded in the abstract codes and regulations that metaphysically found the law. As Tom McCall has recently emphasised, even something as amicable as a contract conceals its own legal violence: 'Coiled up in the contract, ready to strike, is the power that guarantees the contract in the first place. The legal contract is thus the tradition's land mine of forgotten, internalised violence'.[4]

The same can be said for the pardon, which functioned so brilliantly in the staging of political power by James I. From 1600, an entire social order was constructed around the threat and commutation of capital punishment. Alongside the prerogative of violence ran the prerogative of

1. Walter Benjamin, 'Critique of Violence', trans. Edmund Jephcott, in *Reflections*, Schocken, New York 1979, p277.

2. *Ibid*, p286.

3. *Ibid*, p287.

4. Tom McCall, 'Momentary Violence', in *Walter Benjamin: Theoretical Questions*, David S. Ferris (ed), Stanford University Press, Stanford 1996, p206. Throughout these introductory remarks, I am indebted to the coherent, provocative insights of McCall's reading of Benjamin's 'Critique of Violence'.

mercy, allowing the monarch to stage a strategic retreat from the scaffold's grim display.[5] Never relinquishing his right to impose death, the monarch nonetheless demonstrated that mercy reserved for the last hour generates a mystery more compelling than any spectacle of the old theatre of blood.

None of the cunning of this strategic retreat is lost on Shakespeare's Duke of Vienna, who adds his own twist to the new variation on the sovereign's standard plot. Looking on from under a Friar's hood, Shakespeare's Duke rules by inciting desire in his subjects and luring them to their downfall; then he terrifies them with a dispatch to prison or a summons to death, only to find an 'apt remission' in himself that substitutes, at the last moment, weddings for beheadings. To set Angelo up for a fall, and then to skulk about in dark corners watching it happen, re-enacts as intensified parody the elements of his former fourteen-year reign. By inaction or complicity, the Duke had helped to stage a scene of corrupt sensuality in which he himself did not participate, but which allowed him to condemn the sins of others. In actuality, however, the Duke himself now exploits sexual desire as a mode of entrapment, playing upon Angelo's desire for Isabella, and Mariana's desire for Angelo. He capitalises on sexuality just as Pompey does, proving with devastating effect at the end, that 'Mercy . . . would prove itself a bawd',[6] to insure the right subjection.

In the closing scene, the Duke pardons everyone from Barnadine, a confessed killer, to Isabella, an entrapped perjurer. But for good reasons the Duke refuses to pardon Lucio, because behind the alleged distortions in Lucio's slanders about the Duke lies a potent truth: the Duke takes a voyeuristic pleasure in the sins of others; and he not only enjoys exposing those who have sinned, he also enjoys exposing himself as the one who has *seen*. Furthermore, the Duke's taunting of Mariana, his condemnation of Angelo, and his lies to Isabella about her brother's death are all prologues to his sweeping reprieves. Therefore, he and everyone else must eventually know that the Duke's show of strict justice tempered by mercy is all a hoax. He exploits the Friar's habit and the judicial process to pursue another agenda, through which he can tighten the screws of terror before dispensing pardons. As Harry Berger has recently emphasised:

> The Duke's strategy of licensing his subjects' licentiousness . . . seems mildly suspicious, until read alongside the chilling advice of Brutus about the proper conduct of an assassin-to-be: 'Let our hearts, as subtle masters do,/ Stir up their servants to an act of rage,/ And after seem to chide 'em' (*Julius Caesar*, 2.1.175-77).[7]

'Thoughts are no subjects', Isabella protests (5.1.451), which might help to explain as resistance the awkward absence of any expression of gratitude for the Duke's flurry of pardons and commands to marry. But a more likely explanation turns on the Duke's strategy of mortifying his subjects in order to exercise and thereby reaffirm his own redeeming power. When six men

5. J. A. Sharpe reports that while 'there was a draconian legal code with ample provision for the death penalty, an overwhelming majority of those theoretically at risk of the noose evaded it'. *Crime in Seventeenth-Century England*, Cambridge University Press, Cambridge 1983, p148.

6. William Shakespeare, *Measure for Measure*, J.W. Lever (ed), *The Arden Shakespeare*, Routledge, London 1965, 3.1.149. All subsequent quotations will be taken from this edition and will appear parenthetically in the main text.

7. Harry Berger, Jr., *Making Trifles of Terrors: Redistributing Complicities in Shakespeare*, Stanford University Press, Stanford, California 1997, p365.

and women suffer in silence the Duke's ungentle rain of mercy, Shakespeare proves how efficiently clemency internalises coercion. No skin or bone is broken; spirit is.

In the absconding Duke, who spies upon his subjects from behind a mask of mercy, observing without being observed, Richard Wilson finds 'the remote architect of the Benthamian prison, who defers the sentence of death in order to exercise a greater dominion over the life of his subjects'.[8] Having made an unprecedented intrusion into the privacy of his subjects, the Duke then ushers them off the stage, two by two, to embark on their well-disciplined reproductive lives. As the curtain falls on this docile procession, a grim reality attaches to an early remark by Escalus: 'Mercy is not itself, that oft looks so' (2.1.280).

8. Richard Wilson, *Will Power: Essays on Shakespearean Authority* Wayne State University Press, Detroit 1993, p125.

YOU ONLY DIE TWICE: THE LAW'S TAUTOLOGY

The *tour de force* staged in *Measure for Measure* puts yet another twist on the law's turn of the screw. A peculiarly subversive plotter, the Duke refuses to bring legitimate force to bear upon his wayward subjects and thereby replaces the sovereign act with a different kind of acting. Because so much of the Duke's strategy is revealed to be hoax, and because he ultimately reinstates the lax order that Angelo had temporarily stiffened, the sovereign act turns out to be only an act. The resulting intrigue gives rise, in turn, to a different kind of plotting, an imbroglio that is nonetheless revealed to be very highly organised. The Duke finds himself to be the instrument of a compulsively repeating law of substitution.

Recall the fundamental plot. Apparently chagrined by the corruption that his permissive rule has licensed, the Duke rationalises away his responsibility for reimposing order:

> Sith 'twas my fault to give the people scope
> 'Twould be my tyranny to strike and gall them
> For what I bid them do. (1.3.35-37)

The nasty job of reigning in his subjects the Duke imposes on the reluctant Angelo, who puts on with unprecedented vigour all the 'terror' with which his new office comes dressed. Determined to clean up the 'stews' of Vienna, Angelo sharpens the teeth of an old biting statute that calls for the death of any man who 'gets a woman with child' without being married to her. When Claudio, in love with his betrothed, Juliet, and intending to marry her, falls within the statute's bite, the plot lurches forward into its redemptive, libidinal economy, which turns explicitly upon a series of substituted bodies and body parts.

Claudio's head must fall to take the place of Juliet's broken maidenhead; Isabella must yield to Angelo the 'treasure of her body' in order to save her brother's life. This crisis provokes the intervention of the Duke, who operates undercover as a Friar; resorting to the old 'bed trick', the Duke arranges for Angelo to receive Mariana, his former betrothed, in place of Isabella, and later he arranges for Angelo to receive Barnadine's head in place of Claudio's. But neither plot nor law can function without the summoned body. When the condemned prisoner Barnadine refuses to be executed to fit the Duke's 'persuasion', divine providence and the playwright step in: the pirate Ragozine is suddenly found dead in the prison, and his subsequent decapitation provides the *caput in machina* needed to fool Angelo and bring the Duke's plot to a head.

When carefully tracked, the progression of bodily substitutes reveals a movement of rhetorical figures from metaphor to simile to tautological identity. Under Angelo's regime of strict liability, the letter of the law is blind to distinguishing differences. In his scales of justice, Claudio's head is equivalent to Juliet's maidenhead; and Isabella's maidenhead can redeem Claudio's head. *Head for maidenhead; maidenhead for head*: this is the tyranny of metaphor, which declares, 'This is *that!*' by fiat.

With the Duke's return as the disguised Friar, comparable worth turns on similarity: Mariana's maidenhead can pass for Isabella's; Barnadine's head can pass for Claudio's. *Maidenhead for maidenhead; head for head*: the reign of simile is less arbitrary, but requires that craft be applied against vice. Mariana must be veiled under cover of cloth and night, and her voice muted in whisper. Barnadine, who looks nothing like Claudio, is to have his head shaved and his beard tied back; his head will thereby pass as Claudio's because 'death's a great disguiser' (4.2.174).

Finally, pressed to reveal himself to the Provost, the Duke orders that Ragozine's head be dispatched to Angelo, as a substitute for Barnadine's head, when the drunken prisoner refuses to answer the summons to the block. No resort to disguise is necessary, since Ragozine was 'a man of Claudio's years; his beard and head/ Just of his color' (4.3.71-72). *Head for head for head*: this turn toward tautological identity is ushered in when the still-hooded Duke procures the Provost's complicity in the 'head trick': 'You will think you have made no offence if the Duke avouch the justice of your dealing?' When the Provost asks, 'But what likelihood is in that?', the Duke assures him, 'Not a resemblance, but a certainty' (4.2.184-87).

In the final trial scene, the drive toward tautological identity continues. Thanks to Isabella's pardon of Angelo, 'another prisoner/ Who should have died when Claudio lost his head/ As like almost to Claudio as himself' can be saved and can be revealed, by unhooding, to be Claudio himself. Likewise, thanks to Lucio's unpardonable unhooding of the disguised Duke, Friar Vincentio turns out to resemble the Duke of Dark Corners as much as Claudio resembles himself. Thus, before the curtain falls, all the major characters in the play undergo some form of disguise or dissimulation, and all are exposed or 'unmuffl'd', so that even the greatest unlikelihood - once unhooded - turns out to be likely.

Given the play's round of substitutions - from bed trick to head trick to dead trick - a relation begins to emerge between the decapitation of Ragozine's corpse and the authority of the law. The blow of the axe does not kill Ragozine, who had already died of fever; the blow takes his head, not his life. This is a brilliant stroke by which Shakespeare reveals both the violence at the heart of the Duke's law and the gesture that disavows it. What could be more tautological than Ragozine dying twice, first by fever, then by the axe? Beheading the dead enacts with a peculiar performative force the law's tautological authority.

It is for this reason that the move from metaphorical substitutions to ones based on simile and tautological identity is so important to the law of the play. If the law refuses to acknowledge the violence that founds it and keeps it in place, what other guarantee of its authority can the law invoke? 'Blood thou art blood', Angelo declares; 'Grace is grace', Lucio remarks; 'Truth is truth', Isabella pronounces. To these tautologies the Duke would add, 'The law is the law'. In the wake of the disavowal of the law's violence, tautology steps in as the ultimate cover-up.

Behind such tautological declarations lies no other legitimising authority than the brute force of the declarant. Rhetorically, tautology already stands on shaky ground. On one hand, tautology sets forth a seemingly stable, unalterable truth; but on the other hand, it sets out two mirror images that collapse into each other. What pretends to be self-affirming turns out to be self-effacing, even self-cancelling. The most dazzling instance of the self-cancelling effects of the Duke's tautological rule comes in the play's closing lines. Exercising his royal prerogative to pardon, the Duke instructs Angelo as to the nature of the Provost's complicity in the ducal plot:

> Forgive him, Angelo, that brought you home
> The head of Ragozine's for Claudio's.
> The offense pardons itself. (5.1.529-31)

'*The offense pardons itself*': Thus the Duke announces his credo, as he sets out to perpetuate his charade as the executive who does not execute.

THE LAW'S DESIRE TO HAVE THE BODY

The sudden chance to 'satisfy the deputy with the visage/ Of Ragozine, more like to Claudio' (4.3.74-75), brings the round of bodily substitutions to a close where the similarity of human features meets the radical otherness of death. 'O,'tis an accident that heaven provides', exclaims the Duke (4.3.76). But more than accident is at play when Shakespeare has a pirate provide the 'loose end' needed to tie up the plot. Twice directed to quickly dispatch the head to Angelo, the Provost exits, only to make a brief reappearance: 'Here is the head', he assures the Duke, 'I'll carry it myself'. And the Duke exclaims, '*Convenient is it*!' (4.3.101-02).

'Convenient' means 'fitting, commensurate, congruent with,' and

9. Marcus Rediker, *Between the Devil and the Deep Blue Sea: Merchant Seamen, Pirates, and the Anglo-American Maritime World, 1700-1750*, Cambridge University Press, Cambridge 1987, p286.

10. See Christopher Hill's quotations from the 1638 publication, *A True Relation of the Lives and Deaths of the two most Famous English Pyrates, Purser and Clinton* in *Liberty Against the Law*, Penguin, London, 1996, p. 117.

11. A specimen of the writ in effect at Shakespeare's time appears in J.H. Baker,

indeed, Ragozine 'fits' the beard and hair of Claudio far better than the retrograde Barnadine does. 'Convenient' also means 'befitting, appropriate' or 'due'. It befits a play about the 'measure' of the law that a pirate marks the law's limits by operating outside it. Pirates were beyond the reach of the law, sailing on the so-called high seas, outside the jurisdiction of any one nation. More significantly, 'pirates constructed a culture of masterless men', part of a tenacious tradition that linked medieval peasants and seventeenth-century radicals such as the Levellers.[9] According to one popular account, a group of common seamen formed a pirate crew, after reflecting on 'what baseness it was in them to be no better than servants ... who had the ability to command'. They flourished until Queen Elizabeth 'thought rather by her clemency to reclaim them' and offered a pardon. Holding that they were 'free commanders', the buccaneers rejected the offer. As a result, they were proclaimed traitors, captured and ultimately executed.[10] No doubt the trait that made them traitors was their scorn for mercy.

Most significantly, Ragozine's head fits the Duke's convenience because 'convenient' also means 'bringing together', from the Latin, *convenire*, to meet or to convene. Indeed, without the head of Ragozine, the rites of habeas corpus essential to the Duke's court could not be performed.

With the summons of habeas corpus, the law expresses its desire to have the body. The law and the body come together on a given day, in a given court, pursuant to the king's command to the sheriff.[11] Without the presence of the defendant's body, court could not convene: no body, no trial, no *corpus juris*. More urgently, without the presence of the defendant's body, there could be no display of sovereign power. The writ of habeas corpus set the stage for the performance of the monarch's special power to enact clemency. Able to pardon in the face of guilt, the king stood above the law. He thus wanted and needed the body of the accused to demonstrate his status above and beyond statute.[12]

This status troubled Parliament, and the subsequent history of habeas corpus shows the writ changing from an instrument of the sovereign's pardon into the exercise of legal procedure - from an exception to the rule of law, to the rule of the law's routine. What comes to count most is the consistency of the law; the regularity of its practice becomes the measure of the law's legitimate rule.

More importantly, with respect to the round of substitutions in *Measure for Measure*, the writ of habeas corpus gradually opened up the space for substitution and delay. Bail allowed the accused to offer a sum of money or title to property as a replacement, or place holder, for his body in detention. Meanwhile, investigation placed increasing emphasis on getting the depositions of witnesses. Such recorded testimony could be used at trial should the witness become unavailable. Thus, witnesses made depositions and defendants made deposits, conserving actual bodies through written and monetary surrogates.[13]

Introduction to English Legal History, 3rd ed., Butterworths, London 1990, pp626-27. For a view of the complexities and ironies attending the Great Writ's history, see Edward Jenks, 'The Story of the Habeas Corpus, in *Select Essays in Anglo-American Legal History*, Little Brown, Boston, Massachusetts 1908, Volume 2, pp531-48.

12. For these observations about the history and significance of the writ of habeas corpus, I have drawn liberally upon the work of Anselm Haverkamp and Cornelia Vismann. See their provocative essay, 'Habeas Corpus: The Law's Desire to Have the Body', in *Violence, Identity and Self-Determination*, Stanford University Press, Stanford, California 1997, pp223-35.

13. For Haverkamp and Vismann the gradual acceptance of substitutions for the body marks an intriguing movement in the law, from concern with the actual body to concern with more abstract things, especially legalism itself, *op. cit.*, pp228-29. As Edward Jenks notes, 'It is somewhat disconcerting to find that this high prerogative document is not an Original Writ at all, but a mere interlocutory mandate or judicial precept, which occurs in the course of other proceedings', *op. cit.*, p532.

The point still to be emphasised is that without the body, or its substitutes, there could be no sovereign act or action of the law. But as the Duke in *Measure for Measure* exemplifies, the law's desire for the body was not to have the law executed, and with it, the body of the summoned criminal. Such an execution would demonstrate too openly, too intolerably that the force of the law lay in its display of force. Instead, the body becomes desired as a means of keeping attention focused on the business of the law.[14] As a result, the writ comes to mark the stages of the legal process through which the summoned body moved, according to the repetitive and therefore reliable routine of the law's *procedure*. In short, the hallmark of the writ is process, not substance; 'convenience', not right.

14. This movement - what some would call 'progress' - from execution to pardon to legal due process - reflects what Haverkamp and Vismann call 'the law's desire to have the body cited rather than executed', *op. cit.*, p225.

THE BODY OF THE LAW

Pardons, piracy, habeas corpus: these historical landmarks are important for a richer, more disturbing reading of *Measure for Measure* as a critique of violence. According to Walter Benjamin, institutions and positions of power exist as so many mobilisations and consolidations of singular acts of violence. 'Power is an agency with the capacity to repeat similar, singular acts over time', Tom McCall observes, 'it is force as a repetition compulsion'.[15] It is hard to deny that there is something compulsive about the law of substitution in *Measure for Measure*. If the Duke's aim is to reinstate a fair legal order, why does he not simply remove Angelo from office as soon as he learns of Claudio's arrest or the base proposal to Isabella? Something else, something not necessarily related to the public good, seems to be driving the Duke through a complicated series of plots and counterplots, whose end result is to return the Duke and the 'stews' of Vienna to the same place from which they started. The law's desire to have the body has apparently shifted onto another level, giving rise to a repetition compulsion of its own.

15. McCall, *op.cit.*, p192.

Freud recognised such repetition in the famous child's game of *fort-da*, in which the child seeks to endure the mother's absence by staging the recall of the lost or absent object. But the child can recall the object only by first making the same object disappear. This staging locks the child into the structure of symbolic representation, but more crucially, it allows the child to achieve his or her aim only on the condition that he or she continually repeat the very moment sought to be avoided. A similar, perverse mechanism can be illustrated by the law's due and overdone process, in which what is sought - the body - and what is sought to be avoided - its permanent absence through execution - continually change places.

This process of uncanny and self-defeating repetition Freud came to oppose to eros, relating it to his theory of the drives and their paradoxical vicissitudes. At the heart of this theory is Freud's insistence that a drive is only a drive because of its utter indifference to what path it might take. This trait, Freud first observes, 'is found in erotic cathexis, where a peculiar indifference in regard to the object displays itself'. Then he shifts to a social example:

> Not long ago, Rank published some good examples of the way in which neurotic acts of revenge can be directed against the wrong people. Such behaviour on the part of the unconscious reminds one of the comic story of the three village tailors, one of whom had to be hanged because the only village blacksmith had committed a capital offence. Punishment must be exacted even if it does not fall upon the guilty.[16]

Likewise, Ragozine must be beheaded for Claudio's crime, even though he is not guilty of it and, with a further Shakespearean twist of the screw, even though he cannot suffer the death sentence imposed. If we take Freud's account of crime and punishment - that the law embodies the very crime it punishes and that it may strike at random even where no crime exists - then the law starts to look uncannily like that principle of blind repetition that characterises the death drive itself.[17] In Freud's work, the death drive comes increasingly to stand for that demonic and contradictory repetition - a drive indifferent to its object - which ultimately becomes subordinated to the mechanism of the drive itself. And it is precisely this mechanism that comes to claim the head of Ragozine.

16. Sigmund Freud, 'The Ego and the Id', in *The Standard Edition of the Complete Psychological Works of Sigmund Freud*, vol. 19, trans and (ed) James Strachey, Hogarth Press, London 1961, p45.

17. Jacqueline Rose, *Why War? Psychoanalysis, Politics, and the Return to Melanie Klein*, Blackwell, Oxford 1993, p112.

In Act One, shortly after the Duke's hasty departure from Vienna, we overhear him deny an offstage suggestion that he has come to Friar Thomas for help in arranging a lover's tryst:

> No. Holy father, throw away that thought;
> Believe not that the dribbling dart of love
> Can pierce a complete bosom. (1.3.1-3)

Like the 'precise' Angelo, who 'scarce confesses/ That his blood flows' (1.3.50-1), the Duke would put himself above the pleasure principle only to find himself way beyond it, where the denial of desire gives way to a drive that is indifferent to its object. *Measure for Measure's* off-stage mutilation of the dead is obscene not only because it is unseen, but also because it bears witness to the law's perversion: perverted rites of habeas corpus bring the Duke's plot to a disturbingly literal head, attaining their object in the head *of* a nobody and a head *with* no body. With the beheading of the dead, the law's desire to have the body gives way to a drive to have *any* body, and ultimately, to have an object that is no body at all.

How does the head of Ragozine come to figure the body of the law and thus the body of the play? The substituted head is both a figure, a death's mask, and the condition under which the law of substitution can proceed. More precisely, Ragozine's head comes to mark that procedure through which compulsive repetition both delays and disguises the death that the law's violence deals. Thus, with the beheading of Ragozine, already dead before summoned to the block, *Measure for Measure* stages the spectacle of the law performing the disavowal of its own performative force.

REMEMBERING RAGOZINE

This spectacle of disavowal is deceptively flat. The lack of affect associated with the death of the 'notorious pirate' makes his submission to 'cruel fever' a casual event, no more than a providential 'accident' that is 'part of the routine, "natural" landscape and lifescape of the poor'.[18] Ragozine's death is no accident, of course. It is the predictable result of a known cause. Jails in Shakespeare's England were packed and foul. Lengthy incarceration often translated a prison term into a death sentence.[19] The so-called prison deaths mostly resulted from 'gaol fever', what we now call typhus. Such a 'cruel fever' was Ragozine's first executioner.

His second executioner was probably Pompey, the convicted bawd who is paroled into a work release program as the apprentice to Abhorson, the Duke's official hangman. An apt irony attends this execution, since it would please Abhorson to initiate his sarcastic new aide into the mysteries of their profession by assigning him the low, fail-proof task of beheading a corpse. But such speculation is inapt, since we have so little basis for imagining the details of Ragozine's life or his double death. He is a real 'nobody' in the play. He never speaks, he never appears; his name cannot be found among the *Dramatis Personae*. He dies and is unburied; that is almost all we know about him. No one - either in the play or in the considerable scholarship about the play - comments on the peculiar nature of Ragozine's death and transfiguration.

This glancing dispatch of a character so minor that he does not even rate a listing in the cast is the very form of what Francis Barker calls the occlusion of violence in Shakespearean drama. 'When violence is shown, it is occluded, and the occlusion is more than a mere lack of ostentation'.[20] It is the casual, almost opaque incidents such as Ragozine's decapitation that disguise and disavow the systematic violence of the law. Violence is represented as providential, accidental, something 'convenient', just as the Duke's coercive reign of mercy is dramatised as a comedy of pardons.

The exchange between the Provost and the Duke - 'Here is the head./ Convenient is it' - marks an uncanny moment in the play precisely because of its brisk, offheadedness. Slipping unnoticed into the text of the play, the exchange guards a guilty secret, which the play would keep, as to the apotropaic figure of Ragozine's head.

Metaphor substitutes one thing for another not so much to reach the second as to escape from the first.[21] As heightened, frightened metaphor, the apotropaic figure works in the same way: it repels the uncanny by attracting and absorbing it within itself. In the gesture of the fetishist, who manages to appropriate a hidden secret without acknowledging it, the apotropaic figure also emerges: the fetish substitutes a tolerable image for an intolerable one.

18. Francis Barker, *The Culture of Violence*, University of Chicago Press, Chicago, Illinois 1996, p192.

19. J. S. Cockburn, *Calendar of Assize Records: Home Circuit Indictments, Elizabeth I and James I, Introduction*, HMSO, London 1985, p36.

20. Barker, *op. cit.*, p194.

21. Giorgio Agamben, *Stanzas: Words and Phantasm in Western Culture*, Ronald Martinez, trans., Minnesota University Press, London 1993, pp32, 34. fn 4 (quoting, without citing, Ortega y Gasset).

Ragozine's head most obviously figures as an apotropaic fetish because it substitutes the tolerable image of his decapitation for the intolerable image of Claudio's or even Barnadine's. Less obviously, Ragozine's head figures as a fetish in another way. Coined from the Portuguese *feticio*, fetish does not derive, as commonly believed, from the Latin root of *fatum*, meaning 'enchanted thing'. Instead, it comes from the Latin *facticius*, meaning 'artificial', which in turn derives from the same root as *facere*, whose archaic sense was 'to make a sacrifice'.[22] Essential to any sacrifice is a system of exchange. The fundamental formula comes from the ancient brahmanic ritual: 'Here is the butter. Where are the gifts?'[23] Where the law is concerned, both in Shakespeare's England and the Duke's Vienna, butter will not do. The law exacts its due through the exchange of one body for another, according to the new rites of habeas corpus and the ancient rights of the victim's kin.

22. *Ibid*, p35.

23. Jean-Luc Nancy, 'The Unsacrificeable', *Yale French Studies* Volume 79, 1991, p36.

In *Measure for Measure*, bodies are exchanged on two fronts. In the lawless suburbs of bawds and brothels, bodies are exchanged *for* money; but in the law-full court of the Duke, bodies are exchanged *as* money. Thus the head of Ragozine can pass for the head of Claudio just as two coins of the same denomination can pass for each other. Redemption under the Duke's rule is commercial only. It stands for the denial of the redemption sought through sacrifice and a refusal of the loss that sacrifice entails. In substituting the head of Ragozine for Claudio's, the Duke makes the fundamental gesture of the pervert: 'I know very well that the law demands punishment for transgression, a sacrifice to redeem a stolen life or thing, so I will hand over the head of Ragozine. But all the same, I can avoid paying any real penalty, I can refuse to make the sacrifice demanded, since Ragozine is already dead'.

What emerges from the Duke's reign of mercy is an ethics of perversion that would substitute a transgressive but impotent law for the 'precise' letter of the law, the symbolic law of the Dead Father. From a Lacanian perspective, the apparent contradiction in perversion's disavowal can be described as follows: 'I know full well that my father has not forced me to give up my mother and the pleasure I take in her presence, whether in the flesh or in fantasy; but I am going to stage such a forced giving up with someone who will stand in for him and exact that pound of flesh required for symbolic castration; I'll make someone else pronounce the law, and then I'll disobey it'.[24] Such a logic helps to explain how the Duke can enjoy testing the suspected nature of his appointed vicar while at the same time claiming to be tightening up the law's administration through the most reliable means at hand. Caught in the law's repetitive circuit of substitutions, the Duke takes on the pervert's tyrannical psychic economy, which fixes him in 'an imperative, blind pattern of action in which he ceaselessly tries to demonstrate that his law, not the law of the other, is the sole law of desire'.[25] The Duke clearly relishes the two-step, self-cancelling routine of his law, whereby he first incites his subjects to sin, and then he mortifies them through public exposure, so that his pardons can deliver 'heavenly comforts

24. Bruce Fink, *A Clinical Introduction to Lacanian Psychoanalysis: Theory and Technique*, Harvard University Press, Cambridge, Massachusetts1997, p170.

25 Joel Dor, *The Clinical Lacan*. Susan Fairchild, trans., Jason Aronson, London 1997, p43.

of despair/ When it is least expected'.(4.3.109-10) The Duke seems to be saying to his subjects, 'Look what I have done for you'; but by the end of the play, we hear something else emerging from his sly, self-congratulatory tone: 'Look what I have done *to* you'.[26]

26. For ample evidence in support of this point, see Berger, *op. cit.*, pp391-404, especially p395.

When the enunciation of the law gives obvious pleasure to the judge, a smear of *jouissance* slips across what is supposed to be the clear, expressionless visage of the law. Justice is supposed to be imposed by a detached, disinterested agent who applies the rules uniformly. Such a view of justice and the just judge comes from the symbolic Father: 'This symbolic Father, insofar as he signifies the Law, is clearly the dead Father'.[27] Through his orgy of coercion and clemency, the Duke of the Dark Corners refuses to play dead.

27. Jacques Lacan, *Ecrits. A Selection*, A. Sheridan, trans., Norton, New York 1977, p199.

Such perversion could be accepted as mildly troubling comedy were it not for Ragozine. An ethics of perversion will always have as its unavowed aim a challenge to the symbolic order, which includes not only the law, but also the orders of naming and memory. It is from this realm of the name and its meaning that Ragozine is excluded when he suffers the second death of his beheading. This second death is beyond the two deaths that he suffered physically, first by fever, then by axe. The second death of significance here is the one suffered by Ragozine when his head is presented as bearing the visage of Claudio. Stripped of his name and identity, Ragozine is murdered symbolically when his death is given over to another man.

As a result, Ragozine's head ultimately functions as an apotropaic figure because it substitutes the tolerable image of his severed head for the intolerable image of his headless corpse. The head sets forth the unique features of the face that guarantee 'Ragozine' as a proper name, a 'rigid designator' that applies to his body, his being, and no other. Thus Antigone confirms the precious individuality still incarnated in the body of Polynices by addressing him as *Kasigneton kara*, 'beloved head, beloved face of my brother'. But how are we to address what remains of Ragozine?

The headless corpse confronts us with the traumatic real of brute corporeality - the broken torso of a symbol, ripped away from any network of associative meaning. Excluded from the symbolic order of naming and remembrance, the dismembered remains of Ragozine stay un-remembered, unmourned. Haunted by this headless corpse, *Measure for Measure* stages the difference between a redemptive revolution that would bestow meaning on the host of no-bodies, such as Ragozine, who lie forgotten under the state capitols, and the onslaught of totalitarian rule, where even the dead will again be lost and suffer a second death: in Walter Benjamin's memorable words, 'even the dead will not be safe from the enemy if he wins'.[28]

28. Walter Benjamin, 'Theses on the Philosophy of History', in *Illuminations*, Harry Zorn, trans., Schocken, New York 1978, p255.

Shakespeare sets his Duke at a particular historical crossroads where, through cunning use of the pardon in place of the axe, ritualised sovereignty begins to give way to internalised repression, and substantive legal rights begin to yield to bureaucratic legal process. Beneath this crossroads, Shakespeare has buried a headless corpse, to remind us that even when the sovereign disavows the violence of the law, a body must be there to pay the price.

THE VIOLENCE OF IRRESPONSIBILITY; ENIGMAS OF MEDICAL ETHICS

Marinos Diamantides

Common law's understanding of the encounter between patients and doctors and other therapists is marked by emphasis on patient autonomy and consent.[1] The ways in which the judiciary construct the meaning and scope of patients' consent is of great importance in the practice and theory of medical law. But an unproblematic emphasis on the autonomous patient obscures how - if at all - the idea of consent guarantees the fundamental human rights of patients with no consciousness or with severe mental disabilities. In this regard I have dealt elsewhere with the problem of responsibility for decisions to discontinue treatment from patients who are comatose and so unable to reject or consent to such decisions.[2] English law does not have a way to depict and qualify the tragic and individuated responsibility of those who engage in such one-way actions. Instead it seeks to justify them by reference to an 'implied' consent by the comatose to such therapeutic actions as are deemed to 'objectively' serve their 'best interests'. *Absurdly*, such justifications are accompanied by the admission that a-conscious patients have no interests whatsoever.[3]

Here, I am focusing on patients whose consciousness is not extinguished but severely debilitated. The tragic responsibility of doctors, relatives and, often, judges to act unilaterally upon such patients is obscured if we remain in the realm of ideal doctor-patient reciprocity in the division of therapeutic labour. This is what happens at present in law where the emphasis is put on so-called tests of patients' 'competency'; that is tests which establish whether a patient is/is not capable of consenting or rejecting medical intervention.

For most of this century lawyers did not need such tests for patients' 'competency' was derived from their juridical 'status' (in turn, this was informed by medical/psychiatric assessments). Thus, minors and mentally disturbed adults were automatically incompetent. However, we now accept that a patient's capacity to reject/consent to treatment must be presumed as 'of right', that is irrespective of immaturity or mental impairment. Yet, there are many instances in which those who assume the care of such patients wish to rebuff this presumption. In this respect several tests have been proposed for establishing whether a patient can exercise the right to refuse treatment. These included the 'reasonable outcome' test whereby a court reviews the 'reasonableness' of the most likely outcome of the patient's choice. This test has been rejected by liberal lawyers as being potentially too 'subjectivist'. Further there is the 'evidencing a choice'

1. It is only through obtaining a 'free and informed consent' that a doctor engaging in intrusive therapeutic actions escapes criminal and civil liability.

2. 'Ethics in law: Still life or Nature Morte? - A vision of Judgement as Vegetating', *Law and Critique*, Vol.VI no. 2, 1995.

3. This absurdity characterises American law too. For example, a New York court ruled that although Mr Saikewicz had been a sectioned person throughout his conscious life his falling into a coma created an obligation to his ward to substitute his judgement for the patient's. That is, the ward had to find out and honour Mr Saikewicz's will prior to his falling into a coma, namely when he was thought too 'mad' to care for himself. That a person's will is legally overuled whilst he is conscious but becomes significant when he has lost consciousness is an absurdity in the heart of the court's judgment, or an absence of judgment.

test whereby patients must show that in refusing treatment they have made a proper 'choice', i.e. weighed the pros and cons. This, too has been rejected as too arbitrary. Why, after all, cannot a patient refuse treatment without having considered at all the implications of no-treatment?

Both these tests have, now, supposedly been superseded by a third one whereby all patients need to show, before being allowed to refuse treatment, that they 'understand' the nature and purpose of the medical treatment which is proposed to them. This more 'liberal' view is now officially embraced by the British state.[4] I argue, however, that this 'objective' test pays lip service to the idea that patients' autonomy ought to 'transcend' their circumstances and not depend upon the 'rationality' of their choice or even the existence of a genuine choice. The relevant legal literature recognises this to a certain extent, pointing to an ambiguity in law on whether the new test requires a patient to be generally capable of understanding or merely to show 'actual understanding' in the event. In the former sense the new test is nothing but a concealed version of the old status criterion. The preferred interpretation is that the patient ought to be expected to show no more than *actual* understanding of their treatment.

Nevertheless, it can always be argued that even if the more liberal interpretation (i.e. actual understanding) was somehow entrenched, this would not prevent the judiciary from qualifying the 'reasonableness' of a patient's refusal (where the patient evidences a choice) nor oblige them to recognise the patient's right to refuse treatment with no proper choice. There is justifiable concern that any legal test for 'competency' inevitably obscures the many considerations that weigh on judges' minds before allowing a patient to refuse treatment. Already in the 1970s, when the new approach began to emerge, the radical academic view was that the recourse to law by those who care for mentally vulnerable persons in order to provide an 'objective' test of competency was comparable to the search for the Holy Grail.[5]

In short, the debate over the degree and timing of 'understanding' that patients are expected to have before being deemed capable of exercising their autonomy is misleading. The real issue is how the responsibility of carers for their subjective reactions to the welfare of the mentally vulnerable is concealed behind malleable competency 'tests'. Case law verifies this view. For example even where a minor suffering from anorexia shows that she 'actually understands' the nature of the proposed treatment (force-feeding), the court presumed that it is a feature of anorexia that the subject can no longer understand the importance of food.[6] In another example an adult mentally handicapped woman was deemed incompetent to refuse and was sterilised 'in her best interests ...' The test of 'actual understanding' of the purpose of treatment was not employed albeit the woman was said to have the mental age of a six-year-old, i.e. an age where a girl can 'understand' the difference between 'having babies' and not.[7]

4. Law Commission Consultation Papers 'Mentally Incapacitated and Decision-Making: A New Jurisdiction', no 128, 1993, paras 3.19-3.35 .

5. 'The search for a single test of competency is a search for a Holy Grail. Unless it is recognised that there is no magical definition of competency to make decisions about treatment, the search for an acceptable test will never end.' Roth, Meisel and Lidz, 'Tests of Competency to Consent to Treatment; *Am J Psychiatry* Vol. 134, 1977, p279.

6. *Re W (a minor) [1992] 4 All ER 627.*

7. *Re F (a mental patient: sterilisation) [1990] 2 AC 1.*

Here I propose that the problem with the consent of the mentally vulnerable be disassociated from tests which purport to establish whether a patient *is* competent. I agree that they must always be treated as if autonomous; for it is only through such a presupposition that the absolute nature of their person is recognised and their unique being is 'elevated' above the circumstances of their weakened, confused or non-existent consciousness. But it is important not to forget that this absolute uniqueness is not so much 'recognised' as unilaterally *imputed*.

When a patient's consciousness is diminished or missing, his/her unicity does not depend on certain 'basic' biological functions of patients without which it would be permissible to treat the comatose as already dead; nor, respectively, does this unicity depend upon the ability of the patient to manifest signs of a weak but nevertheless still 'working' consciousness, the presence of which obliges us to treat them as a 'fully autonomous' person. In consequence, what carers 'ought to do' with respect to the medical treatment of such persons should not be inferred from the patient's objective and/or subjective interests. By contrast, the treatment of such persons should be judged on whether it responds to the idea of the other patient as a unique being *beyond* their objective/subjective circumstances.

How is it at all possible that a doctor or judge can respond to a duty to face the mental sufferer as unique despite the fact that his/her consciousness recedes and so the manifestation of individual difference gives way to anonymity? How can diminished consciousness not leave the patient a mere object for medical manipulation? Alternatively, how can the diminishing of self in a patient not open the way for the onlooker to substitute this actual self-less subjectivity with a projected view of 'self'? An answer may be sought in the idea of the 'face-to-face' relationship which is at the centre of Levinas' thought. In his 1967 Lecture on 'Substitution' Levinas analyses touching not as the palpation of a graspable object but as aimless caress; furthermore language is interpreted not as reciprocal traffic of information but as a 'blind' desire for contact with the other being. The desire for proximity with a unique other is irreducible to consciousness and thematisation. It is a relationship with the other who is not just inordinate with respect to a theme but who is incommensurable with it. The other's singularity is not that of the particular as opposed to the generalised. The other's individual difference is possible because of the prior, irreducible uniqueness which I desire. In short , the loss of individual difference in a human being does not do away with its *epiphany* as unique before the neighbour.

Further, proximity is explained as an anarchical relationship with a singularity, without the mediation of any principle or ideality. The face-to-face is not identical with the - supposedly - inoffensive relationship based on knowledge and representation where everything and everyone is equivalent. Rather, there is violence from both ends of proximity. The other summons me as more unique than the difference I can recognise. In consequence, I am affected by the unique other *obsessively*. This obsession takes the form of an insatiable desire for compassion for the other, a desire to address that 'aspect' of the other which exceeds their manifested individuality. This obsessive approach of the other, however, must not be understood as a form of spontaneity, but as still a response to the other as otherwise than what they appear and, therefore, as a form of unilateral or one-way action which nevertheless requires responsibility.

In the particular instance of the law with which I am concerned here, the enquiry must begin at the level of the *face-to-face* ethical relation that obtains between, the one (doctor, relative, judge) who must decide whether a patient must undergo medical treatment and the patient as absolute other and subject of inalienable rights, that is, as a unique being 'in the abstract'. The uniqueness of such an abstract being must be understood as the product of a 'violent' compassion which extracts the patient from all reference, including the reference to the subjective/objective manifestations of its existence and the juridical notion of 'competency'. Indeed the human rights of the mentally vulnerable must exist independently of their actual circumstances and also from all entitlement '... all tradition, all jurisprudence, all granting of privileges, awards or titles, all consecration by a will abusively claiming the name of reason '.[8]

Levinas distinguishes between two kinds of 'violence' in relation to the abstraction of the other person as if unique.[9] On the one hand, there is the inescapable 'violence' of the desire to approach the other human as other to its circumstances. It is this singular force which makes possible the later recognition of the other as a subject of *a priori* human rights. Compassion stands as a strange *authority*, older and higher than any other which at once binds and frees one to do so; it does not so much authorise anything, but obliges one to act *as if* this was authorised, thus implicating oneself in a responsibility for such violence. In short, it is authority-qua-responsibility for this violence which justifies the respect for the abstract rights of the other.

Thus to begin an encounter with the ill by recognising rights which are independent of conferral and deprivation entails a 'violent tearing loose' of the patient, first from the determining order of nature in which his/her existence is caught and, second, from the social structure in which his/her person is involved. The 'suspension of all reference' is a necessary price for expressing the alterity or absoluteness of every person. It is a paradox that such violent responsibility should also secure the freedom of the absolute person - that which is incomparable, non-exchangeable and 'unique' beyond the individuality of multiple individuals, such as patients of the 'same kind'.

In any case the imputation of *a priori* rights to the other cannot be authorised by anything else other than the subjective compulsion to face

8. Emmanuel Levinas 'The Rights of Man and the Rights of the Other' in *Outside the Subject*, Translated by M. B. Smith, Athlone Press, London 1993 p117.

9. *Ibid*.

the other as other to their circumstances. Under this rubric, the determination to recognise autonomy even in the most horror-implicated patients can be thematised as the result of an obsessive, 'insatiable desire for compassion' for the sufferer as other to the objectively/subjectively suffering patient. The object of compassion is not the concrete patient but an impatient and abstract sufferer who demands to be treated uniquely. The idea of abstract 'sufferer' who attracts unilateral compassion is ultimately compatible with the idea of an abstract other who is imputed with inalienable rights.

On the other hand, apart from the inherent violence in the respect of rights, Levinas points and alerts us to a different, 'irredeemable' violence that *surrounds* the respect for rights. It consists of acts of compassion and respect for the abstract other (as unknowable unique sufferer and subject of rights) where the responsibility for the force by which this other is abstracted is hidden behind false authorities. In so far as the recognition of rights for the mentally vulnerable is linked to 'truth' either about their status or about their ability 'to understand' there is a deficit of judicial responsibility. Without personal responsibility for the unilateral act by which the mental patient is faced as other so that s/he can be abstracted as an absolute rights-holder, the principles of patient autonomy and self-determination (which consent is meant to express) lose all sense and appear absurd and arbitrary. However, the judges' utterly individuated, unshareable personal responsibility in their proximity to patients can reverse this situation. Through assuming responsibility as their only authorisation, a judge can uphold the incompetent patient's autonomy (or, more precisely, can impute autonomy to the patient) and shift the accusation of absurdity from the principles of law to the intrinsic absurdity of the patient's situation. After all, human suffering is and must be recognised as totally *absurd*.

THE REQUIREMENT OF DISINTERESTEDNESS

The recognition of rights in another being requires a 'disinterestedness' towards its existential qualities. Let me explain by using Levinas' categories of undifferentiated existence, anonymous existent and, finally, eponymous being.[10] When consciousness is suppressed under the burden of one's existence, in the sleep that follows a hard day's work but also in states which we call 'diminished consciousness', we cannot talk of 'one' as anyone in particular. The one who is embraced by sleep 'is there' - although s/he does not actively exist. Of course as long as biology allows, the heart still beats, the lungs still inhale and there is still neurological activity, we may still talk of a particular 'existent', separated from anonymous, undifferentiated 'existence' by its own effort and perseverance.

10. See E. Levinas, *De l'existence à l'Existant*, Vrin, Paris 1947.

But the compassion and concomitant responsibility of the carer does not increase or decrease in accordance with the other's existential activity. In fact responsibility presupposes that we approach the other as if unique irrespective of the activity of organic perseverance or the absence of it. Responsibility for the other's unique being is independent of our fluctuating interest in the other's relative activity and passivity. It is responsibility for a being *suspended* between sleep and awakening or a being *exposed* to the alternatives of activity and passivity. The other 'says': come to me in my sleep, or in my illness where only my body's effort still separates me from anonymous existence and, despite all my exposure, approach me gently, as if I was the only being that mattered. When one's consciousness is dormant or weak, if one's neighbour does not succumb to the impulse to approach one as unique in the abstract, one's eponymous and singular being might be obscured by one's anonymous existence and treated accordingly. This is the essence of our complaint against those who 'kick' us out of bed. Alternatively, individuated being is equally obscured if one's conscious activity is falsely equated with one's existential struggle in persevering 'against all odds' or in enduring suffering.

In cases of insanity and depression it is important not to subject our respect for the sufferer's individuated being and our concern for the concomitant demand they express to their capacity or incapacity either to 'endure' or to render intelligible their suffering. For then the other's demand to be recognised as a unique being is falsely equated to their existential ability to persevere or endure. Such false equation ultimately collapses a mentally disturbed being into its illness and gives false license to irresponsible and abusive attitudes against it such as *pity* and *disgust*. When the imputation of rights to mentally ill persons does not explicitly refer to the inescapable compassion that precedes and motivates it, it becomes a form of just such abuse.

Coming back to the legal notion of 'competency' to reject/consent to medical treatment, no matter which competency test a court employs, the issue of judicial respect for the patient's uniqueness is inseparable from their responsibility for 'abstracting' a unique being and subject of rights independently of its existential qualities. This responsibility must not be obscured by judgments on patient competency which purport to be authorised by reference to the 'truth' of the patient's general status and/or their state of mind. If this negative condition does not obtain, one is entitled to criticise the authors of such decisions not for the inescapable violence of compassion (which is inherent in the idea that rights exist in a being despite its physical and psychological horror) but for the different, deliberate kind of violence of pity or disgust. The existence of such pity and/or disgust indicates that the disinterestedness in the patient's own existential effort that both compassion and respect require, has given way to either interest or indifference in such effort.

JUSTICE FOR THE SUFFERER

For Levinas justice is done to the sufferer only when the absurdity and the unknowablility of their suffering is recognised and given a sense *only* in the carer's responsibility. He goes as far as to affirm absurd and unknowable human suffering as:

> ... [the] ... knot of human subjectivity to the extent of being elevated to a superior ethical principle - the only incontestable one- until it governs the spirits and practical disciplines of vast human groupings.[11]

11. Emmanuel Levinas, 'La Souffrance Inutile' in *Entre nous - Essais sur le penser - à - l'autre*, Figures-Grasset, Paris 1991, p111.

Just like the abstract notion of the 'subject of human rights', the abstract notion of the unknowable 'sufferer' also tears the other apart from the determining order of nature and the social structure in which s/he is involved. This is because 'suffering' is not to be identified with a sensory content - such as measurable pain - nor with an idea that the mind can master. 'Suffering' is at once unique and untotalisable: consciousness cannot 'assimilate' it - that is, comprehend it - and will cannot master it. What is distinctive about the abstract notion of unique 'sufferer' as opposed to the more concrete but generalisable theme of 'patient? The difference of 'sufferer' does not lie in some sort of sensorial 'excess' or 'too much' - pertaining only to patients in extreme pain - pain which may be endurable or eventually overcome. Rather the notion of 'sufferer' is helpful in depicting the pre-existential condition of the human being as primarily an abstractly unique subject, not 'in itself' but in its exposure to its neighbour's 'blind' compassion.

For these reasons the idea of anarchic compassion for the patient as suffering 'unknowably' must qualify the notion of respect for patients' rights. The violence of recognising autonomy and self-determination in those who can barely speak, breathe or move is redeemable only if the carer assumes responsibility for the anarchy of their compassion to face the other as other to their condition. To conceal this anarchy by appealing to the knowledge of the extent to which the other's suffering impedes the exercise of their rights is an offensive bestowal of false sense to a relationship with someone who is as much exposed to their sufferings as to our compassion and attempts to offer relief.

Justice to the sufferer requires individuated compassion, benevolence and empathy all of which are described by Levinas as individuated human 'vocations' disposing, in a political society, '... of a kind of extra-territoriality ... lucidity not limited to yielding before the formalism of universality' and not limited by natural determinism.[12] Without these vocations in place the protection of sufferers' absolute rights is amenable to deviations and mockery imposed in the name of 'necessity' or pragmatism, with the same indifference towards the other human that nature displays. From such an 'extra-territorial' point of view the unique 'sufferer', to whom compassion is not spared, is extracted from any eidetic kind of suffering as well as from any formal category of relief.

12. E. Levinas 1993, *op. cit.*, p123.

The compassion for the suffering other of which Levinas speaks is always a violent process. It responds to a higher duty to recognise in the abstract a unique person in the suffering other, independently of how weak or strong they may be in terms of energy and social status. In a juridical sense we are responsible for our acts of compassion, although we are not responsible for the other human's misery. This scheme makes compassion appear secondary and exceptional, confusing it with the guilt that follows our inaction before the inevitable. For Levinas, however, both responsibilities exist simultaneously. I am responsible for the other's obscure suffering which is not commensurate with consciousness and which therefore *demands* unauthorised compassion from me. It is a 'guiltless' responsibility for suffering one has not caused and for compassion which does not qualify but constitutes my engagement with the sufferer.

Without the courage of its responsibility, without bad conscience, compassion slips into abusive pity or disgust, excusing itself behind false truths and authorities. Compassion may even be substituted entirely for an attitude of indifference where there is no judgement for the suffering of the other and no responsibility on the part of the neighbour - as in the Book of Job. Where the relationship is mainly based on equalising knowledge (e.g. in the application by a judge of human rights law) the lack of responsibility for one's compassion (or the partial, economical admission of compassion) renders the application of rules and principles absurd.

YETTER: AN INSTANCE OF JUDICIAL CONCEALMENT OF COMPASSIONATE 'RELIEF'

Such absurdity characterises each of the two American cases which pioneered the new 'competency test' in the 1970s: *Yetter* and *Northern*.[13] The sixty-year-old Ms Yetter had spent the longest part of her life in an institution suffering from 'schizophrenia chronic undifferentiated'. When a routine physical examination indicated the possible presence of a carcinoma in her breasts, the doctors recommended that a surgical biopsy be performed together with any additional corrective surgery that would be indicated by the pathology of the biopsy. Ms Yetter opposed the treatment. When the matter reached the court, the judges heard her objecting to the operation mainly because she was convinced that biopsy would have 'similar' results to those suffered by her aunt (who had her ovaries removed). 'Thereby' the biopsy would 'interfere with her genital system, affecting her ability to have babies'. Also, she was convinced that biopsy would necessarily lead to mastectomy and that would 'prohibit a movie career' which she was anticipating.

13. Re *Maida Yetter* (1973) 96 D & C 2d 619 (CP Northampton County PA) &, *State of Tennesseee v Northern* (1978) 563 SW 2d 197 (Tenn CT App).

The judges decided that in law the schizophrenic Ms Yetter was not incompetent to refuse life-saving treatment. I have said earlier that the recognition of inalienable rights to the other human entails a paradoxical form of violence whereby we achieve their extraction from all reference so as to mark them with an absolute identity of uniqueness. Thus, it can be said that the court's decision in *Yetter* is an instance of judicial 'disinterestedness' in Ms Yetter's existential circumstances which made possible their offer of compassionate relief to this patient as abstract 'sufferer' and subject of a-priori rights.

However, the judges also went out of their way to stress that at the hearing Ms Yetter had appeared 'alert, interested and obviously meticulous about her personal appearance'. Thus framed, the decision only seemingly incorporates the principle that the patient's right to refuse treatment exists independently of her mental illness and the outcome of her choice. For it appears that the court did not say that it allowed Ms Yetter to decide independently of her actual mental disability. According to the judges, her refusal of the biopsy was made in 'a moment of psychological lucidity' - something which was not confirmed by forensic psychiatrists.

Further, it was important that her 'meticulous appearance' was consistent with her desires to 'become a movie star'. For lawyers this is important both from the point of view of continuity of personality and of coherence in the various desires a subject articulates. Therein lies an assumption that the identity of the patient survives their suffering intact, if they show themselves to be the same person before and after their illness.

Further, the fact that the court admitted the specialist's evidence that death could follow if no treatment was given, and that it felt obliged to reiterate that suicide is no longer illegal, suggests that the judges did in fact consider the consequences of the patient's choice. In short this case was framed in such a manner so that the 'new' test of competency based on understanding only seemingly superseded the less desirable tests based on 'reasonableness' of choice and 'evidencing a choice'. In fact the new test can be seen as incorporating these other tests. In this case the unreasonableness of the patient's desires and the deadly consequences of her rejection did not stop the judges from granting autonomy on the basis that Ms Yetter had clearly made a choice.

In essence this decision shows that despite Ms Yetter's schizophrenia, the judges *felt* obliged to recognise her as a unique subject of a right to refuse treatment independently of her psychological and physiological impairments. The judges did not so much evince a moment in which the patient had 'clear understanding' as they invited her to perform a show of understanding. The suffering that they witnessed was absurd. There was no better way to recognise this suffering and to extract Ms Yetter's person from all this absurdity, than to give her a moment in court in which she could *act* that she understood. It was not that her performance in court showed understanding; rather, the performance was construed as 'understanding'. In this sense the true 'moment of lucidity' did not concern Ms Yetter but the judges. It was a moment in which all that mattered was their responsibility for the sufferer 'here and now', disconnected from her past and future. They were concerned for her suffering 'right now' and not for her future biological preservation or perishing or for the survival of her identity as someone who had wanted, in the past, to become a movie star. It was with such force that the right of Ms Yetter to refuse treatment would indeed be disconnected from all her circumstances.

But the judges' false insistence that Ms Yetter had experienced a 'moment of lucidity' conceals their compassion. It was as if Ms Yetter was capable of approaching the judges already as a unique being and, from the supposed vantage point of momentary lucidity, to enact her self as someone who 'has always desired to be a movie-star' (in the past) and who 'is free to commit suicide' (in the future). The judicial emphasis on the patient's 'momentary lucidity' implies - falsely - that there is a distance between the patient as abstract subject of rights and the patient as sufferer subject to the horror of illness. Moreover, it implies that this is a distance that the patient must cover herself.

Also, with all the emphasis the judges placed on the schizophrenic woman's 'meticulous appearance', it becomes nearly impossible to trace in their judgement the extent to which the horror and absurdity of human suffering had weighed on their decision. The artificial disconnecting of Ms Yetter's refusal of treatment from her naturally-inflicted suffering, underestimates the effects of such suffering on her and presents her as someone who could conveniently endure her affliction - if only 'momentarily' - and who could imagine compensations for her endurance - by not losing her breasts she could still imagine becoming a movie star. In this way the judges seemed to have invested her suffering with a meaning that is almost a *theodicy* and imply that the crucial decision could be reached by the patient herself on the basis of this meaning. Before the famous phrase 'Arise and walk' Jesus had not condemned suffering as absurd but had correlated it to the sins that supposedly had brought it about. In *Yetter*, too, it was as if what was condemned was Ms Yetter's inability, before and after her 'moment of lucidity', to assimilate her suffering into an experience she could reflect on and understand.

Yetter can be understood as a case of irresponsible compassion, that is compassion which was legitimised by reference to false truths. The judges disobeyed their own law: that is, the test they wished to formulate in order to recognise a patient's right to refuse treatment, independent of her circumstances. This disobedience coincides with a reluctance to take responsibility for their disinterestedness and compassion. Instead the test which they devised presents them as, in principle, interested in Ms Yetter's schizophrenia but 'entitled' to be indifferent towards her illness 'for a moment'. But although 'disinterestedness' is something one can take personal responsibility for (how else can the subject of diminished consciousness be treated as if unique?), the selective interest in another's existential trouble must be justified by recourse to false 'truths'. Here, the false truth was that Ms Yetter had risen above her condition through her own efforts. In *Yetter* the judges turned away from the nakedness and exposure of a present, singular sufferer who was also a subject of rights under the disguise of deluded schizophrenic. Instead, their starting point was her status as schizophrenic from which they claimed a miraculous, momentary exception. Further, as the judges' emphasis on Ms Yetter's presence as 'alert, interested and obviously meticulous about her personal appearance' indicates, they conceived of a subject which, supposedly, could on its own invest or divest its persona of incompetence. It is for this reason that - contrary to the essence of their new test - *Yetter*'s judges did look at the nature of her past desires and the future consequences of her decision.

This situation is unacceptable. The framing of this decision denies that Ms Yetter was a sufferer, that is, someone who exists but has trouble being unique without help by others. Since the recognition of her right to refuse treatment was linked to her supposed ability to be herself - if only for a moment - it is as if the court was presuming her miraculous ability to come forth as a human being on her own: it is a case of 'Arise and walk'. However, although it can be argued that each human has a constitutional 'obligation' to exist (or, to stay with the Christian theme, to 'arise') there is no obligation to *be* ('... and walk' - but walk where? towards whom?). 'Being' is not like waking up to morning light in order to face life: it requires a different light which is no less than the responsibility of other people. The individualisation of an existence which seems to be slipping into the obscurity of a clouded mind on the part of its neighbour requires a certain violence on the part of the latter. Every human being carries alone the burden of its existence, it perseveres and endures. But, the different burden of being *unique* weighs on the neighbour's shoulders.

'IF YOU DON'T PERSEVERE YOU HAVE NO RIGHTS'

The inability of the judges to disconnect the issue of patient's rights to refuse treatment from the requirement that the patient must 'make a choice' is further highlighted by a comparison of this case with a similar and subsequent one. Seventy two- year-old Ms Northern had no specific mental disability other than a tendency to forgetfulness sometimes associated with old age. She was admitted to a hospital by her neighbours with a case of severe gangrene. She refused life-saving surgery (amputation) but without any reasons being offered. Being sane, one would expect that her refusal of treatment would be recognised in law. This, after all, would have been the case even under the old, less liberal 'status criterion'.

However, in court, she was found to be incompetent to refuse the treatment. The court noted that 'she looks at [her feet] and insists that nothing is wrong with them' although they were 'evidently rotting and smelly'. Had she agreed that her feet were smelly and blackened, she would still be allowed to reject medical treatment and the court would not have judged the rationality of such refusal. Most importantly, however, the court also contrasted her with the case of Ms Yetter and noted that Ms Northern, apart from refusing to admit that anything was wrong, had virtually nothing else to say to the court and gave no reasons for refusing medical treatment.

Let me return briefly to the phenomenology of suffering, in which 'suffering' is so abstract and incomprehensible that it does not offer itself for the description of what would be the 'object' of intentionality and will. Illness pacifies the human beyond belief, overwhelming experience and consciousness. Suffering is foreign to consciousness, inside consciousness. There can be no moment of 'understanding' suffering. The inability to perceive and represent suffering is not evidence of a 'failure' by perception and consciousness for which the sufferer is to be blamed. Thus Levinas does not claim a martyr's sense that suffering is an existential opportunity for self-transcendence. As far as the sufferer's self is concerned, suffering is useless. However, the sufferer's passivity turns into a neighbour's compassion. Levinas rejects intellectualism according to which one's suffering cannot signify in another but only through the limited categories employed by the mind. Instead Levinas insists that one's passively expressed suffering, as pure 'epiphany' revealed by the face, ought to cause in the witness an obsessive compassion which traverses their consciousness 'countercurrentwise', and is inscribed in the face as something foreign to it, as disequilibrium or delirium.[14] The silently ill, the comatose and those who respond to their suffering with anger or self-abandonment, cannot become mere objects in the eyes of the rest of us because, through the inevitability of violent compassion, we must still hypostasize them as unique recipients of our responsibility. They are subjects in a unique sense, perhaps absurdly so, as 'pure exposure', vulnerability and nakedness. The ethical subjectivity of the ill is secured by the fact that despite their sickness their face 'still speaks' with a voice which is supplication as well as demand. The uniqueness of the vulnerable other is not jeopardised by the absence of articulated desire and by the imminence of death as long as we feel obliged to seize it as unique. Medical responsibility for every unique sufferer goes a lot further than merely doing what is possible to cure a body or appease an ego; judicial responsibility, too, extends further than merely respecting formal patient autonomy. Both these professions are underlined by vocational compassion and a desire to approach those who are at the brink of becoming anonymous, and treat them as unique. In the absence of God, this is also a desire to condemn the absurdity of naturally inflicted suffering. Yet, because of the absence of God, this desire to extract the sufferer from both nature and the social order must be accompanied by a sense of infinite responsibility and bad conscience.

14. See E. Levinas, *Otherwise than Being, or Beyond Essence*, Transl. Alphonso Lingis, Martinus Nijhoff, The Hague 1981, p101.

Ms Northern was deemed incompetent to refuse treatment for a more fundamental reason than that she 'looks at her feet and insists that nothing is wrong with them'. Unlike Ms Yetter, Ms Northern had not only rejected the 'objectivity' of the medical diagnosis; moreover, she had declined the opportunity to pass a subjective judgement on her afflictions and failed to give any reasons why non-treatment would have been better than treatment.

Ms Northern had expressed her suffering silently, passively, without subsuming it under any considerations and calculus of treatment benefits versus the benefits of no treatment. She showed that she could not take responsibility for the horrific, absurd and utterly unjustifiable suffering that nature had inflicted on her. It was entirely left to the judges to assume this responsibility and act.

Northern shows the ethical limitations of the new, more liberal competency test. This test, based upon patient 'understanding' allowed the judges in *Yetter* to invite that patient to at least act as if she 'understood'. But in *Northern* even this was not possible. It appears, therefore, that there is still a critical 'choice' that the patient is still expected to evidence before being allowed to refuse treatment. What is critical is no longer the reasonableness of the choice between treatment and alternatives, illness and health, life and death. Under the new liberal test for competency these aspects are now a matter of complete indifference. But this is not yet meeting the standard that the patients' rights exist independently of everything. In fact the court in *Northern* appears to have made the right to refuse treatment subject to an existential requirement: patients must take a *pro-active attitude* towards their suffering. They must speak 'of it' - whether reasonably or not. But this is no less than obliging sufferers to cover their horrific nakedness, vulnerability or destitution.

JOB

In the *Book of Job* the suffering of illness is repeatedly depicted in all its absurdity, arbitrariness and unjustifiability. But in the beginning, Job's comforters insist on engaging him in a dialogue geared towards bestowing his sufferings with the meaning of a theodicy. They excuse themselves - 'if we assay to commune with thee, wilt thou be grieved? But who can withhold himself from speaking?' (4:2) - and, then, persecute him so that he may remember possible reasons why he suffers and anticipate future compensations. They do not care for the present Job who says: 'I cry out of wrong, but I am not heard: I cry out aloud, but *there is* no judgment.'(19:7) Job's comforting neighbours demand from him a 'constructive' attitude. They want him to pretend that there is judgment to be made about his suffering. In other words, the comforters refuse to supply Job's suffering with the meaning of their responsibility. Job is self-exposed as a being about to collapse and give up - which, in the biblical context, amounted to losing face before God by 'cursing the day he was born'. This is something the 'comforters' would not face.

Today's equivalent of losing face before God is given by Levinas in his idea of 'existence without existent': the human, on its own, perseveres in its existence thus becoming, by his/her own effort, a separate existent. But the uniqueness of the human being does not result directly from this effort, nor through the recognition of this effort by others. The uniqueness of being is expressed in the *hesitation* between slipping into anonymous existence and becoming a separable existent; between surrendering to Orpheus' obscure embrace in the evening and waking up to smell the coffee. Our disinterestedness towards these two poles frees us to face the *unique* being that lies between the two poles in its hesitation, in its tiredness, where the exhaustion with 'having to live' is not yet incorporated into the will to be left alone or cease to exist. There is a price to be paid for our freedom to face the suffering other as unique irrespective of the degree to which s/he slips into diminished consciousness and, conversely, independently of the degree to which their consciousness still perseveres. This is our responsibility for our compassion. A responsibility with no excuse and no blame, including blame for one's compassion, which might also be called a persecution. This responsibility for the other's vulnerability and nakedness must not be inverted as if it were dependent on the degree to which the other either still 'hangs in there' or, alternatively, 'has already given up'. For then our compassion becomes abusive pity or disgust; then, the suffering other is asked to cancel their hesitation, their tiredness, on penalty of being called lazy, and being abandoned. This is what happened in the *Northern* case where the judges, disgusted with the patient's rotting feet and pitying her passivity, ordered the amputation.

Job's visitors come to him intrusively, compelled by compassion - under no authority but their own responsibility. Bad consciousness and irrevocable responsibility is the price to pay for calling out Job's unique person just as he seemed to be losing it. It is a paradoxical form of violence which extends to the modern determination to recognise a right to refuse treatment to patients independently of their absurd circumstances. But when, as in the case of Job's comforters, the guiltless responsibility for the ineluctable violence of compassion is refuted, then guilt for the deliberate violence of another sort is substituted instead. Job's comforters abused him by repudiating his anger just as the judges of Ms Northern abused her by repudiating her silence. Job complained 'I am as one mocked of his neighbour'(12:4). And, as if anticipating Ms Northern, Job's anger gives way to silence:

> Oh that my grief were thoroughly weighed, and my calamity laid in the balances together! (6.2) For now it would be heavier than the sand of the sea: therefore my words are swallowed up.(6.3)

Stages of Formation

Martin Murray

Elisabeth Roudinesco, *Jacques Lacan*, translated by Barbara Bray, Polity Press, Cambridge 1997, 574pp; £25 cloth.

The French psychoanalyst Jacques Lacan's best-known paper 'The Mirror Phase as Formative of the Function of the I' (first version 1936, revised version 1949) claims to describe a moment or state that is crucial to the formation of the human self. In receiving an image of itself in reflection, Lacan argues, the human infant first sees itself as a unified being. This situation is ideal and figural as well as actual, and stands for accession to identity in general. It is also at least as deceptive as it is veracious. What seems identical is grasped by way of reflection, which can only take place in something else: a mirror, or more exactly an image. Whether it is internal or external this image must be minimally alterior; otherwise the self would only, and tautologically, know itself as what it already knows itself as. The self's epistemological and ethical condition, though not impossible, is problematic. It sees itself in terms of what it in some sense isn't, which means it might not know itself as well as it thinks it does. Its truth, got through what it is not, always might be false.

Elisabeth Roudinesco's *Jacques Lacan* shows how Lacan's life both might be judged by and might have given rise to his theories. In doing so it provides an admirable account of a body of work that is alternately obscure and brilliant, and of a man who was capable of both integrity and duplicity. Yet it is neither simply exegetic nor psychobiographical, and contains astute commentary on, and scrupulous descriptions of, political and historical dimensions of Lacan's life. This much might be expected of Roudinesco, who is also the author of an excellent, comprehensive history of French psychoanalysis.[1]

Roudinesco reveals that from the outset Lacan was subject to the egoistic division, and concomitant egotistical self-assertion, or phantasised eradication of that division, that his own work was to chart so insistently. He was both a melancholy and a precocious child. Born into a family of petite-bourgeoise semi-provincial Catholic vinegar merchants, he soon rebelled against the mediocrity and conformism of his upbringing. This rebellion, which in some respects only ended with his death, betrayed a thorough ambivalence. Lacan became both more and less bourgeoise, particularly as an adolescent and young man. He affected haute-bourgeoise manners and the dress of a dandy, and even flirted with the chauvinistic philosophy of Charles Maurras. However, he was also drawn to the anarchism of dada and to surrealism in its first, revolutionary, phase which

1. Elisabeth Roudinesco, *La Bataille de cent ans: histoire de la psychanalyse en France vol 1*, Ramsay, Paris 1982; *La Bataille de cent ans: histoire de la psychanalyse en France vol 2*, Editions du Seuil, Paris 1986; vol. 2 trs. Jeffrey Mehlman as *Jacques Lacan and Co. A History of Psychoanalysis in France 1925-1985*, Free Association Books, London 1990.

was ambiguously Freudian and Marxist. He could be said to have cultivated the 'aristocratic radicalism' sometimes attributed to Nietzsche, who was one of his boyhood heroes.

The young Lacan eventually became a medic. The choice was only made after some deliberation, and with reluctance to give up other career options, particularly academic philosophy. Perhaps because of his philosophical interests, Lacan took up psychiatry during the 1920s. The profession brought him into contact with a number of eminent teachers, notably Clérambault, whose work in a science which was in neither decline nor infancy was both traditional and radical. Clérambault began to pay close attention to psychical as well as organic dimensions of illness. This involved elucidating relations between symptoms that implied that they had some meaning for the subject who suffered them. Most influentially, Clérambault showed that erotomanic subjects, who were deluded that they were the object of another's excessive affection and aggression, had become so as the consequence of a desire. In many such cases, he argued, an inadmissible sexual urge is transformed into something acceptable by way of projection and paranoia. The (usually female) erotomaniac sees her desire in another (so that she can disown it) and as aggression (so that it can be seen as something other than desire).

During the 1930s and 1940s Lacan both absorbed and developed these and other radical psychiatric ideas, and did so with an intellectual boldness, breadth and complexity that was to lead his forebears, including Clérambault, to judge them non-psychiatric and invalid. Lacan's innovations were often couched in the language of, and were heavily influenced by, modern Germanic philosophy, psychology and psychoanalysis. Lacan's generation of French intellectuals used such ideas to challenge both the stuffy, chauvinistic, Cartesian rationalism of the academy and the naive or dogmatic scientism of the training hospital.

Hence Lacan stressed the non-constitutionalism of Clérambault's work, claiming that symptoms have meaning *for* the subject, rather than in terms of any objectively identifiable physical state, or biological cause. In doing so he was advancing a type of argument made first by Brentano and later, as phenomenology, by Husserl. However, Lacan's 'phenomenology', like all of his adoptions of others' ideas, is not 'pure.' For both Brentano and Husserl the idea, and thus meaning, is presented lucidly for, and also by, the subject in consciousness. For Lacan the meaning of the symptom for the subject is first of all obscure, and can only be elucidated by way of what is not conscious. Now this non-consciousness, which bears important information about a personal *history,* has a number of different characteristics and dimensions. It resists conscious apprehension by the subject except in a distorted and disturbing form, and thus resembles the unconscious as described by Freud. However, the material borne by the state of non-consciousness described by Lacan, unlike the sort described by Freud, is not only or primarily infantile and familial, but is to do with a broader environment and personal history (including, for example, work relations), although it is no easier to assimilate to consciousness for all that. The meaning of the subject is to be sought in what is inside, outside, and prior to, and hence other than, its presently conscious state. It is therefore only through the *other* that the subject can make any sense of itself. As suggested earlier, this necessary alterity of subjectivity is irreducible. Because, in this state of affairs, the (self)same is only got at otherwise, its recognition is dialectical. Because the alterity which allows (self-)recognition is irreducible, such recognition is never absolutely certain, or positive.

Lacan's early method thus amounts, to use Adorno's phrase, to a kind of negative dialectic. In doing so it takes its inspiration from the teaching of the Russian emigré philosopher Alexandre Kojève whose seminars Lacan attended in Paris in the 1930s along with Merleau-Ponty, Bataille, Queneau and others. Kojève's work was crucially important in the transportation of modern German philosophy into France. He took dialecticism and historicism from Hegel, anti-idealism from Marx, anti-positivism from Heidegger and offered them all to Lacan. Never one to think that enough is enough, Lacan added the Freudianism just mentioned, and adopted a written and spoken style which was a bizarre mixture of baroque academicism and surrealism that would go on to both seduce and infuriate his increasingly large public.

Roudinesco writes lucidly and informatively about this important, often ignored, first part of Lacan's career. She rightly understands the peculiarly modern intellectual position he adopted in it, of a dialectician who did not believe in synthesis. She also finds a thesis in his personal life manifest as both integrity and conflict. Lacan was both a loyal and a duplicitous husband, a generous and a parsimonious father and a passionate and paranoid friend. When his first marriage, to Marie-Louise Blondin, broke down their three children were not told that he had taken up with another woman until two of them chanced on the couple in the street. The other woman, whom Lacan later wed, was Sylvia Bataille, an actress and political activist whose intelligence and fervour matched his own and who was the ex-wife of Georges Bataille, who was one of Lacan's friends. They lived in separate but adjoining apartments and conducted a relationship of ostensible civility, though it involved affairs. Lacan had close friendships with many people, most of them members of the Parisian intelligentsia. Some, like Merleau-Ponty and Lévi-Strauss, liked and respected Lacan but were bemused by his ideas. Others, who were generally less well-known and more involved with psychoanalytic theory and practice, admired and even worshipped him. Lacan alternately, and quite passionately, loved and mistrusted them all.

Lacan produced his best known, most influential work between 1949 and 1960. During this period he developed his earlier ideas in terms of three themes: language, the subject and the unconscious. Like many French intellectuals of the 1950s he became fascinated by the work of the early twentieth-century Swiss linguist Ferdinand de Saussure, whose two great contributions to linguistic science are the notion of linguistic arbitrariness and the notion of linguistic value. The notion of linguistic arbitrariness involves an assertion that manifest linguistic elements (more particularly signifier and sign) bear no necessary relation to the linguistic or real elements (more particularly signified and referent) to which they ostensibly refer (this amounts to saying, for example, that the term 'hatred' or the term 'cat' might be used to invoke something other than what they currently or apparently do). The notion of linguistic value follows from this. Linguistic elements can't be determined by way of fixed concepts or things but they *can* be discerned by way of their relations to and differences from each other ('hatred' is understood in comparison with 'love', 'cat' in comparison with 'dog'). These 'values' make up a structure, which is the objective structure of language. Lacan maintained some aspects of Saussure's argument and altered others. More precisely, he stressed the notion of arbitrariness by declaring the 'autonomy of the signifier' (accentuating Saussure's anti-empiricism), prioritised differential, and hence negative linguistic functions over 'positive relations' (countering Saussure's tendency towards positivism) and sought to do so in a spirit of 'conjectural' scientism (both continuing and questioning Saussure's objectivism). The subject, in this setup, only recognises itself by way of the linguistic structure or order that precedes and instructs its formation, which Lacan calls that of 'the signifier'. Because the signifier only ever appears negatively, that is by way of other signifiers that it is not, and because each of these also only appears otherwise, the subjectivity informed by the signifier only appears negatively and otherwise too. The subject thus only accedes to meaning in an anticipatory or deferred, and hence always incomplete, way. What informs the subject is irreducibly 'ex-centric' to it, frustrates any possibility of its integration or recognition of itself in consciousness, and is hence unconscious.

Roudinesco's exposition of Lacan's work during this period is competent but somewhat unenthusiastic. Perhaps she is simply tired of it, having dealt with it so thoroughly elsewhere. A similar fate seems to have befallen important institutional disputes Lacan and some of his colleagues were involved in, notably those between dissident French psychoanalytic institutions and the International Psychoanalytic Association. Rather than detailing these disputes, Roudinesco refers the reader to her earlier historical work. That this work demonstrated the historical, political and personal significance of these disputes so brilliantly might have been an argument for reiterating them in, as much as leaving them out of, the current text.

Roudinesco's description of the final phase of Lacan's intellectual life, which ran from about 1960 to his death in 1981, is even more uninterested than the one she gives of his mid-century work. His later intellectual interests - Kierkegaard, Wittgenstein, Joyce, logic, topology, and mathematics - are sometimes treated cursorily, ironically or not at all. Roudinesco seems suspicious of the influence of Lacan's son-in law, the logician Jacques Alain Miller, on Lacan during this period and on his legacy subsequently. Although this suspicion blunts her appreciation of some of Lacan's later ideas, which are too easily dismissed as incomprehensible, it is supported by detailed, typically astute accounts of recent Lacanian institutional wrangles.

Roudinesco also includes some fascinating personal and historical material regarding Lacan's involvement in political and intellectual upheavals in Paris from the mid-1960s to the mid-1970s. All in all, she provides perhaps the best, and certainly the most detailed, account of Lacan's life and work to date.

Starting Something

Mark Bevir

Edward Said, *Beginnings: Intention and Method*, Granta, London 1997, 416pp; £12.99 paperback.

How do I begin this review? Now that I have done so, how does my beginning plot the rest of this review? Said's elegant exploration of such issues was published in the US in 1975 and is now published in the UK for the first time. A beginning, he tells us, is to be defined in contrast to an origin. Origins are divine, mythical, ideal presences - Yeats' 'self-born mockers of man's enterprise.' Beginnings are secular, human, constantly re-examined. An origin is a stable source that both guarantees and explains what it leads to, as, for many thinkers, God made the world, authors created their work, and our reason underlay our action. A beginning is a tentative, provisional step made without the assurance provided by a claim to the authority of an origin. Said explores the nature of beginnings by drawing on history, philosophy, and critical theory as well as literature: indeed, *Beginnings* played a role in the shift in literary criticism from explicating the inner workings of texts in their historical, social and political contexts. Said's focus, however, is literary modernism as it developed from 1875 to 1930.

In Said's view, the novel was the principal attempt to give beginnings an authoritative role during the eighteenth and nineteenth centuries. Narrative fiction reflected the desire to mime the biological processes of life and death. The classic novel sought to authorise itself by reflecting the linear movement from parents to children. Hence the popularity of autobiographical and biographical forms as in *Robinson Crusoe* and *Tom Jones*. Literary modernism arose out of a crisis in this dynastic notion of beginning and origin. No matter how far back one pursues a genealogy, one only ever reaches another person - another child with parents. The biological idea of beginning leads, therefore, not to an origin, but to an endless regress. It was to avoid this regress that many classic novels had as their leading protagonists orphans, outcasts, solitary figures, or parvenus. Modernists, often acutely aware of the crisis of the genealogical mode of authorisation, turned to the non-linear ties of complementarity and adjacency. They rejected the idea of reaching an origin by tracing back from beginning to beginning. In modernist writing, the origin, whether as the author of a text, or God as the maker of the world, or the unconscious as the basis of subjectivity; the origin in all its forms becomes an opaque object that we can approach only through the inadequate tool of language. Conrad's darkness never before us but sensible about us, Kafka's trial which is always planned but never takes place, these are typical modernist metaphors for our relation to original, ideal presences. Modernism retains mythical or utopian evocations of an origin, but the origin remains inaccessible, hidden from view.

The hidden nature of the origin creates the perpetual fact of error. We have no authoritative source by which to validate our impressions, beliefs, narratives. Thus, all knowledge remains at best provisional, something we have constantly to re-examine and re-explore. Henry James' *What Maisie Knew* and Conrad's *The Heart of Darkness* attempt to reconstruct an event that is presumed to have happened: neither author nor reader witnesses the event, which remains opaque even after the novel has striven to bring it into view. Authors do not even have knowledge of themselves, so they sometimes treat themselves as objects of interpretation. Here again Conrad is exemplary, with his narrator, Marlow, reflecting on both his distance from his subject and his entanglement with the tale he narrates. Finally, writing itself becomes deeply problematic, for the author has no basis from which to begin. 'My task appears to me,' Conrad wrote, 'as sensible as lifting the world without that fulcrum which even that conceited ass, Archimedes, admitted to be necessary'. No wonder modern writers are often figures of suffering, plagued by self-doubt, the anxiety of being derivative, and the burden of production.

Said examines also the form of criticism appropriate to literary modernism. Although he identifies the French structuralists as the most insightful contemporary theorists, it is by returning to the beginning made by Vico that he describes his own position. Whereas the stucturalists believe we must forsake origins and beginnings, Said wants to hang on to a modernist notion of beginning. He argues, correctly I believe, that modernism is not solely an elegiac, negative movement, but also a positive affirmation of new artistic forms that are open to the world in new ways. A modernist beginning respects the obligation to recognise that we write in a given context but cannot appeal to an origin to authorise its context. A modernist beginning recognises the need for sympathetic imagination to intend a text, which then needs to be ceaselessly re-examined.

To conclude Said highlights some problematics for which he hopes his study will act as a beginning. Among them is the question of the cultural domination of one domain over another. Later, Said himself wrote an enormously influential study of this problematic in *Orientalism*. For anyone interested in the development of one of the major scholars of our time, therefore, *Beginnings* is a vital text - even a beginning. But perhaps the beginning here should be Said's previous study of Conrad, or even some earlier event. No, we cannot privilege any particular beginning of this kind; after all, the modernists have shown us how forlorn, how endlessly recursive, is the quest for a linear or biological quest for an origin. I had to begin this review by overcoming flux in an act of wilful intent. I had to do so for that is the fate of a modern consciousness.

Booknotes

Daniel Miller, *A Theory of Shopping*, Polity Press, Cambridge 1998, 180pp; £11.95 paperback; £39.50 cloth.

Miller's theory derives from two sources: ethnography (79 shoppers in North London); and theories of sacrifice and consumption (Georges Bataille). Miller's insight is 'that shopping is a regular act that turns expenditure into a devotional ritual that constantly reaffirms some transcendent force, and thereby becomes a primary means by which the transcendent is constituted.'

Shopping is made up of three moments. The first is that of popular discourse where shopping is thought of as selfish consumption. This is placed theoretically as the 'vision of excess.' However, the shopper transforms herself in the act of provision shopping by doing two things: saving money in order to consume more and buying for the members of the household. At the theoretical level, Miller calls this 'thrift' and 'devotion.' He collapses the theory of sacrifice upon the ritual of shopping. The shopper (the woman invariably) engages in classic sacrificial consumption. The shopping is distinguished from the 'treat' which is for pure expenditure, for her, while the shopping is for the idealised images of the members of the household, for example healthy food, suitable clothes. The household becomes the ritual's transcendent value. The shopper has sublated her desires into that of the household. Her objects are, contrary to feminist concerns with domestic labour, devotional. The shopper, the ritual provider, understands her sacrifice as an act of love. Hence the logic of shopping 'is not one of economics ... but of objectification.'

Miller's Hegelian assumptions are provocative and testing. That Bataille's notion of pure expenditure was itself primarily directed at Hegel's 'restricted economy' means that there is much to mull over and debate. That feminist research is developing theories of emotional work means that these ideas of devotion are helpful. In short, an exhilarating book.

Norman Crowther

Timothy Brennan, *At Home in the World: Cosmopolitanism Now*, Harvard University Press, Cambridge, Mass. and London 1997, 369pp; £14.50 paperback, £26.50 cloth.

This wide-ranging book unearths and challenges the spectral tenets of cosmopolitanism as articulated through the thesis of globalisation. In a highly entertaining and thorough dissection of the 'new' cosmopolitanism, Brennan argues that it is indeed not new, but founded on existing Western-oriented values, beliefs and structures. Brennan traces this movement across a varied but totalled terrain to note a theory of cosmopolitanism expressed within academia, the media and political and economic discourses and institutions. Through this analysis, Brennan uncovers an uncritical celebration of postmodernity and perceptions of differentiation, for example, cultural syncretism and cultural specificity, that fail to note the discourses of Western hegemony informing and sustaining these discussions.

This iniquitous counter-narrative is unveiled in a variety of ways. Synthesising W.E.B. Du Bois' Marxism and activism as intellectual biography with a reading of his *Color and Democracy: Colonies and Peace* (1945), Brennan points to the discourses of cosmopolitanism engaging the political without incorporating a concerted politics. An example being how the 'post-colonial' is embracing without critiquing the existing relations between 'North' and 'South' or within the three worlds. Cosmopolitanism's defence of the third world, through arguments such as the retention of culturally specific practices and values - as well as preserving certain socioeconomic and political interests of the industrially advanced world - is revealed as fuelling exoticised representations of the 'other' while measuring them against the metastandards of cosmopolitanism. Using Francis Fukuyama's 'end of history' thesis, Brennan suggests that dissent against internationalism (Americanism) becomes re-articulated as ethnic or sectarian dissension, preserving the triumphal (moral) hegemony of liberal democracy and free markets.

At Home in the World is ostensibly an American-centric book, intending to be introspective and self-critical. An important dilemma of self-reflexivity, however, is the extent to which one can expect to be insightful about oneself. In his discussion of C.L.R. James' *American Civilization* (1993) and its concern with happiness as an expression of an elusive 'socialist desire', Brennan states that, 'the America project is in many ways a more thorough and sustained example of James' applied cultural theory than *Beyond a Boundary*.' The privileging of, the arguably pedestrian, *American Civilization* over a nominally quasi-autobiographical, social and cultural critique of the experience of colonialism internalises a variety of American exceptionalism.

Brett St Louis

1 **Peter Wollen** on fashion and orientalism / **Denise Riley** on 'women' and feminism / **Dick Hebdige**'s sociology of the sublime / **Laura Marcus** on autobiographies / **John Tagg** should art historians know their place? / **Franco Bianchini** on the GLC's cultural policies / **Homi K Bhabha**, **Stephen Feuchtwang** and **Barbara Harlow** on Fanon

2 **Mary Kelly, Elizabeth Cowie** and **Norman Bryson** on Kelly's Interim / **Greil Marcus** on subversive entertainment / **Georgina Born** on modern music culture / **Geoffrey Nowell-Smith** on popular culture / **Ien Ang** on 'progressive television' / **Alan Sinfield** on modernism and English Studies in the Cold War / **Tony Bennett** on Eagleton.

3 *TRAVELLING THEORY* – **Julia Kristeva** on the melancholic imaginary / **David Edgar** on carnival and drama / **Kobena Mercer** black hair – style politics / **Jacques Ranciere** on journeys into new worlds / **Peter Hulme**'s Caribbean diary / **Bill Schwarz** on travelling stars / **Ginette Vincendeau** on chanteuses realistes / **Steve Connor** on Springsteen / **Christopher Norris** on Gasché's Derrida.

4 *CULTURAL TECHNOLOGIES*
Out of print

5 *IDENTITIES*
Out of print

6 *THE BLUES* – **Jacqueline Rose** on Margaret Thatcher and Ruth Ellis / **James Donald** how English is it? / **Benita Parry** on Kipling's imperialism / **John Silver** on Carpentier / **Mitra Tabrizian** and **Andy Golding**'s blues / **Barbara Creed** on *Blue Velvet* / **Joseph Bristow** on masculinity / **Graham Murdock** on Moretti's *Bildungsroman* / **Edmond Wright** on post Humptydumptyism.

7 *MODERNISM/MASOCHISM* – **Victor Burgin**'s Tokyo / **Linda Williams** on feminine masochism and feminist criticism / **John Tagg** on criticism, photography and technological change / **Geoff Bennington** l'arroseur arrose(e) / **Emilia Steuerman** on Habermas vs Lyotard / **Paul Crowther** on the Kantian sublime, the avant-garde and the postmodern / **Mark Cousins** on Levi Strauss on Mauss / **Iain Chambers** being 'British' / **Adrian Forty** on lofts and gardens / **Lisa Tickner** on Griselda Pollock.

8 *TECHNO-ECOLOGIES* – **Peter Wollen** cinema: Americanism and the robot / **John Keane** on the liberty of the press / **S.P. Mohanty** on the philosophical basis of political criticism / **David Kazanjian** and **Anahid Kassabian** naming the Armenian genocide / **Paul Théberge** the 'sound' of music / **David Tomas** the technophilic body / **Felix Guattari** the three ecologies / **Margaret Whitford** on Sartre.

9 *ON ENJOYMENT* – **Slavoj Zizek** the undergrowth of enjoyment / **Peter Osborne** aesthetic autonomy and the crisis of theory / **Rachel Bowlby** the judgement of Paris (and the choice of Kristeva) / **Joseph Bristow** being gay: politics, identity, pleasure / **Gail Ching-Liang Low** white skins black masks / **Christine Holmlund** I Love Luce / **Line Grenier** from diversity to indifference / **Mark Cousins** is chastity a perversion? / **Simon Critchley** review of Christopher Norris.

10 *RADICAL DIFFERENCE* – **McKenzie Wark** on the Beijing demonstrations / **Paul Hirst** on relativism / **Cindy Patton** African AIDS / **Anna Marie Smith** Section 28 / **Tracey Moffatt** something more / **Susan Willis** Afro-American culture and commodity culture / **Hazel V. Carby** on C.L.R.James / **David Lloyd** on materialist aesthetics / **Peter Redman** Aids and cultural politics.

11 *SUBJECTS IN SPACE* – **Dick Hebdige** subjects in space / **Iain Chambers** on the Sony Walkman / **Meaghan Morris** on Sydney Tower / **Sam Appleby** on Crawley New Town / **Raphael Samuel** on brick / **Peter D. Osborne** on Milton Friedman's smile / **Victor Burgin** on Breton's Nadja / **Donatella Mazzoleni** on the city and the imaginary / **Ann Game** on Bondi Beach / **Nicholas Green** on monuments and memorials.

12 *NATION, MIGRATION AND HISTORY* – **David Morley** and **Kevin Robins** no place like Heimat / **Renata Salecl** national identity and socialist moral majority / **McKenzie Wark** Europe's masked ball /

Peter Wollen tourist art / **Victor Burgin** paranoiac space / **Elizabeth Grosz** Judaism and exile / **Mitra Tabrizian** surveillance / **Gail Ching-Liang Low** narratives of empire / **Peter Middleton** vanishing affects.

13 *NO APOCALYPSE YET?* – **Angela McRobbie** new times in cultural studies / **Slavoj Zizek** the king is a thing / **Geoffrey Nowell-Smith** broadcasting: national cultures – international business / **Paul Du Gay** enterprise culture and the ideology of excellence / **Colin Mercer** neverending stories: the problem of reading in cultural studies / **Peter Nicholls** consumer poetics: a French episode / **Lyndsey Stonebridge** the subject of the father: from ethics to love / **Jenny Taylor** dreams of a common language: science, gender and culture / **Joseph Bristow** life stories: Carolyn Steedman's history writing.

14 *ON DEMOCRACY* – **Chantal Mouffe** pluralism and modern democracy: around Carl Schmitt / **Renata Salecl** democracy and violence / **Joan Copjec** the *Unvermögende* other: hysteria and democracy in America / **Mladen Dolar** the legacy of the Enlightenment: Foucault and Lacan / **Slavoj Zizek** act as the limit of distributive justice / **Zdravko Kobe** death of the political / **Bill Schwarz** exorcising the general: Gabriel Garciá Márquez *Clandestine in Chile* / **Patrick Parrinder** Leeds, intellectuals and the avant -garde.

15 *JUST LOOKING* – **Kevin Robins** the postmodern city / **Charlotte Brunsdon** satellite dishes and taste / **McKenzie Wark** from Fordism to Sonyism / **Sarah Kember** the geometry of chaos / **Gill Frith** the female reader / **Christopher Norris** deconstruction versus postmodernism.

16 *COMPETING GLANCES* **Out of print**

17 *A QUESTION OF 'HOME'* – **Ariel Dorfmann** present / **Doreen Massey** a place called home / **Tzvetan Todorov** bilingualism, dialogism and schizophrenia / **Jamie Owen Daniel** on Adorno and the language of home / **Aine O'Brien** homeward bound / **Celia Applegate** the question of Heimat in the Weimar Republic / **Jeffrey M. Peck** rac(e)ing the nation / **Helen Fehervatu** homeland – November 1989 / **Jenny Bourne Taylor** re-locations from Bradford to Brighton / **Bill Schwarz** on Paul Scott / **Theodor W. Adorno** refuge lot the homeless / **Mary Ellen Hombs** on America's homeless / **Mananna Torgovnick** Slasher stories / **Irena Klepfisz** *Fradel schtok*

18 *HYBRIDITY* – **Christopher Norris** old themes for new times / **John Frow** the concept of the popular / **Annie Coombes** inventing the 'postcolonial' / **Simon Frith** Adam Smith and music / **Andreas Bjørnerud** outing Barthes / **Rod Giblett** philosophy (and sociology) in the wetlands.

19 *PERVERSITY* **Out of print**

20 *WALTER BENJAMIN* **Out of print**

21 *POST-COLONIAL INSECURITIES*– **Benita Parry** speech and silence in fictions of J.M. Coetzee / **Kenneth Parker** J.M. Coetzee: 'white writing' / **Jon Stratton** beast of the apocalypse / **McKenzie Wark** engulfed by the vector / **Kevin Robins** politics of silence / **John Borneman** continental divide in German subjectivity / **Anne Beezer** women and 'adventure travel' tourism / **Marcia Pointon** Ian Botham at the National Portrait Gallery.

22 *POSTCOMMUNISM* – **Vitaly Komar and Alex Melamid** monumental propaganda / **Michael Holquist** cultural criticism for Russian studies / **Ted Levin** reimagining central Asia / **Mark Slobin** sight-reading St. Petersburg / **Svetlana Boym** 'Back in the USSR' to 'Bye-Bye Amerika' / **Mikhhail Yampolsky** Chekhov / Sokurov / **Katerina Clark** Russian Intellectuals post perestroika / **Nancy Condee and Vladimir Padunov** Pair-a-dice lost.

23 *LACAN AND LOVE* – **Joan Copjec** the invention of crying / **Renata Salecl** love: providence or despair / **Juliet Flower MacCannell** love outside the limits of the law / **Mladen Dolar** la femme-machine / **Alenka Zupancic** what's love got to do with *id*? / **Miran Bozovic** on Lacan and Spinoza/**Jane**

Malmo on Milton's *Samson Agonistes* / **Slavoj Zizek** on Otto Weininger.

24 *ON NOT SPEAKING CHINESE* – **Ien Ang** on not speaking Chinese / **Ghassan Hage** locating multiculturalism's other / **Rob Wilson** Hawaii and cultural production in the American Pacific / **C.J.W.-L. Wee** Kipling and the 'colonial condition' at home / **Julia Emberley** simulated politics / **Iain Chambers** the judgement of the angels / **Neil Roughley** on the phenomenology of *Camera Lucida* / **Gillian Swanson** on national character in the Profumo Affair / **Johan Fornas** on authenticity in rock, rap and techno music.

25 *MICHEL FOUCAULT: J'ACCUSE* – **David Macey** *J'Accuse* / **John Rajchman** Foucault ten years affer / **Kate Soper** forget Foucault? / **Alan D. Schrift** reconfiguring the subject as a process of self / **Sue Golding** the politics of Foucault's poetics / **James Miller** from Socrates to Foucault / **Robert J.C. Young** on Foucault, race and colonialism / **John Marks** a new image of thought / **Wendy Wheeler** after grief / **Nick Couldry** on Rachel Whiteread's *House*.

26 *PSYCHOANALYSIS AND CULTURE* – **Malcolm Bowie** Memory and Desire in Civilisation and its Discontents / **Lesley Caldwell** Interview with Andre Green / **Dominique Scarfone** Conflictuality / **D.W. Winnicott** The Psychology of Madness / **Jim Hopkins** Wittgenstein and Interpretation / **Clare Pajaczowska** Art as a Symptom of Not Dying / **Alex Tarnopolsky** Loss and Mourning in *Rigoletto* / **Christopher Wintle** *Rigoletto*'s Bottle / **Special Section – Revisiting Psychoanalysis and Feminism**: Ann Scott, Juliet Mitchell, Margot Waddell, Joanna Ryan, Joan Raphael-Leff.

27 *PERFORMANCE MATTERS* – **Simon Frith** Popular Performance / **Lydia Goehr** The Perfect Musical Performance / **Nicholas Cook** Rock, Theory and Peformance / **Martin Stokes** Arabesk in Turkey / **Sally Banes** and **John F. Szwed** Dance Instruction Songs / **John Stokes** Frank Norman / **Gill Frith** Gender and Performance in Women's Fiction / **Karen Lury** Television Performance / **Les Back** Apache Indian and the Cultural Intermezzo.

28 *CONSERVATIVEMODERNITY* – **Harriet Guest** feminism and sensibility / **Geoff Eley** German exceptionalism before 1914 / **Janet Wolff** Mark Gertler / **Paul Gilroy** revolutionary conservatism / **Lynne Segal** feminism in psychoanalysis / **Bill Schwarz** British Conservatism / **John Kraniauskas** Eva Peron / **Peter Osborne** times (modern), modernity (conservative).

29 *TECHNOSCIENCE* – **Rosi Braidotti** cyberfeminism / **Andrew Barry** the European network / **Nell Tenhanf** machines for evolving / **Terri Kapsalis** Norplant: contraceptive technology and science fiction / **Simon Penny** the Darwin machine / **Tiziana Terranova** Digital Darwin / **Sue Owen** chaos theory and marxism / **Cheryl Sourkes** genes and genesis / **Janine Marchessault** the secret of life.

30 *CULTURAL MEMORY* – **Michael Rowlands** sacrifice and the nation / **Tony Kushner** memory of Belsen / **Anna Vidali** political identity / **Susan Taylor** classifications / **Imruh Bakari** Caribbean cinema / **Sylvie Lindeperg** memory to allegory / **Mamadou Diouf** terrorism as social identity / **Erica Burman** false memories / **Tricia Cusack** carnival and patriarchy.

31 *UNCIVIL SOCIETIES* – **Jeremy Gilbert** rave culture / **Drew Hemment** e is for ekstasis / **Richard Cavell** the race of space / **Ien Ang and Jon Stratton** the Singapore way / **Michael Humphrey** civil war / **Albert Paolini** the place of Africa / **Fiona Nicoll** facializing the nation / **Vicki Callahan** landscaping the eternal / **Lee Grieveson** Foucault on Lacan

32 *LEGAL FICTIONS* – **Josephine McDonagh** infanticide and the nation / **David Glover** legislating the immigrant body / **Ian Ward** writing constitutions / **Stella Swain** narrative and legality / **Ruth Robbins** Oscar Wild before the law / **Philip Leonard** degenerescent lections / **Joseph Valente** gender injustice in *The Crucible* / **Sally Munt** the lesbian outlaw / **Timothy Bewes** the concept of sleaze

33 FRONTLINE BACKYARDS – **Phil Cohen** who needs an island? / **Stuart Hall** aspiration and attitude ... reflections on black Britain in the nineties / **Bill Schwarz** segregation tomorrow / **Mary Chamberlain** 'I belong to whoever wants me' / **Les Back** inside out: racism, class and masculinity in the 'inner city' and the English suburbs / **David A Bailey** rhapsodizing black: Harlem in London, 1997.

34 *DREAMING IN THEORY* – **Rachel Bowlby** the other day: the interpretation of dreams / **Sara Ahmed** tanning the body: skin, colour and gender / **Nicholas Daly** the ferris wheel of identity / **Laura Chrisman** imperial space, imperial place / **Maureen Moynagh** Cunard's political lines: political tourism and its texts / **Benita Parry** Tono-Bungay: modernisation, modernity and imperialism, or the failed electrification of the empire / **Michael Pickering and Keith Negus** the value of value / **Simon Frith** a note on the 'value of value' / **Wendy Wheeler** in the middle of ordinary things / **Simon Wortham** surviving theory, 'as if I(t) were dead.